Landmarks in the Landscape

Historic Architecture in the National Parks of the West

Harvey H. Kaiser

CHRONICLE BOOKS

SAN FRANCISCO

LIBRARY OF CONGRESS CATALOGING-IN-PUBLICATION DATA:
Kaiser, Harvey H., 1936-
   Landmarks in the landscape : historic architecture in the
national parks of the West / Harvey H. Kaiser.
                    p.   cm.
   Includes bibliographical references and index.
   ISBN 0-8118-1854-3 (hc)
   1. Architecture—West (U.S.) 2. Historic buildings—
West (U.S.) 3. Architecture, Modern—19th century—West
(U.S.) 4. Architecture, Modern—20th century—West (U.S.)
5. National parks and reserves—West (U.S.) I. Title
   NA725.K35 1997
   720'.978—dc21   97-851
                                              CIP

Book and Cover design by Wynne Patterson
Edited by Merry Jayne Taylor
Cover photograph: Many Glacier Lodge at Glacier National Park

Printed in Hong Kong

Distributed in Canada by
Raincoast Books
8680 Cambie Street
Vancouver, B.C. V6P 6M9

10 9 8 7 6 5 4 3 2 1

Chronicle Books
85 Second Street
San Francisco, CA 94105

Web site: www.chronbooks.com

Contents

Acknowledgments

The National Endowment for the Arts supported research for this project with a generous grant. I wish to express my appreciation for their encouragement.

Laura Soullière Harrison has been a major contributor to this work. A National Park Service employee, she is the epitome of the dedicated public servant, deeply committed to historic resource preservation. Mrs. Harrison's manuscript "National Park Service Rustic Architecture" (written with William C. Tweed and Henry G. Law) was influential in the development of the concept for this project. Her book *Architecture in the Parks, National Historic Landmark Theme Study,* is a model of thoroughness for historic architecture researchers and writers. She is a skilled historian, observer, and writer, and I gratefully acknowledge her words and ideas as they appear in this book.

I owe a large debt of gratitude to the National Park Service (NPS) staff members whose published research on individual structures was a primary source of information. Their works, often the only reference for the cultural resources of a particular national park, monument, or historic site, were assembled and evaluated for selection of important structures. Only an easterner, ignorant of the vast distances and seasonal limitations of access, would undertake the challenge of this project. Every western national park with at least one structure on the National Register of Historic Places was visited, but not every building could be included in the study.

The reader with an interest in Rustic architecture is referred to two extraordinary NPS publications. *Park Structures and Facilities,* published in 1935, is a collection of reports on Rustic building types. The NPS expanded this to a three-volume publication in 1938, *Park and Recreation Structures,* by Albert H. Good. The role of the National Park Service in providing guidelines to state and regional park design groups is detailed in the pages of these books, which influenced the vast work of federal relief programs. Long out of print, the 1938 book has recently been reissued by Graybooks.

Several "companions" faithfully accompanied me on my travels, and I recommend them to anyone planning a visit to the western national parks. The Sierra Club's *Guides to the National Parks,* Sunset Books' *National Parks of the West,* and KC Publications' *Story Behind the Scenery* series are all helpful in itinerary preparation. They will enhance visitors' enjoyment before, during, and after park visits, as the photography and text are superb interpretive guides. I used them frequently and have made every effort to credit them when I have drawn upon their excellent research.

A comprehensive source of information for National Park Service historic buildings is the NPS List of Classified Structures. It was especially useful as a working index in the field. The researcher will find its descriptions helpful for their comprehensive documentation of buildings in the national park system. Another important resource is the collection of National Register Nomination Forms found at the parks, regional NPS offices, and NPS Headquarters in Washington. The Forms are sometimes the only thorough documentation for a structure and represent exhaustive research by NPS staff. In addition to Historic Resource Studies, which describe the history of development and important structures in individual parks, researchers may consult Historic Structure Reports. The information contained in these studies offers insights into the personalities and events that shaped the origin and evolution of the parks.

I'd like to say thank you to the National Park Service staff who assisted me, with apologies for any possible oversights. Their continued encouragement and dedication to preservation of natural and cultural resources and values of the national park system were important in sustaining my work. Members of the NPS at Washington Headquarters, the Denver Service Center, and the regional offices in Seattle, San Francisco, Denver, and Santa Fe were especially helpful. Park superintendents, historians, secretaries, and other staff members were patient, tolerant, and generous in sparing time from their busy schedules. And I greatly respect the many rangers who cultivate and freely share a wealth of information about their respective parks.

At the NPS Historic Architecture Division, in Washington, D.C., Hugh Miller, Randall Biallas, Karen Rehm, and Alicia Weber made available their exhaustive knowledge of the national park system's cultural resources. I owe the suggestion for the title of this book to Hugh Miller. Thomas DuRant, librarian at the NPS Harpers Ferry Center, was extremely helpful in identifying important material and assisted in obtaining photographs used in this book. He has an extraordinary facility for retrieving a specific image from the vast and uncatalogued NPS collection.

In Denver, several staff members offered observations on NPS Rocky Mountain Region historic structures and made suggestions for specialized research. Kate Stevenson wisely hinted at the length of time required to do justice to this ambitious project. Mary (Marcy) Shivers Culpin has continued her assistance by answering long-distance questions and supplying important documents Michael Schene helped place in perspective the history of cultural resources in the Rockies and the Pacific Northwest. Rodd L. Wheaton's papers, field experience in preservation, lists of buildings, and road directions were invaluable in familiarizing me with the rigors of stewardship in the vast and often isolated areas under NPS responsibility.

The Seattle office of the NPS Pacific Northwest Region is fortunate in having Stephanie Toothman, Chief, Division of Cultural Resources, who combines in her work erudition and a passion for preserving historic architecture. She patiently continued to encourage me and assisted in locating source material long after an interview early in the research stage.

At the NPS Southwest Regional Office – a marvelous adobe office building in Santa Fe – former regional historian Melody Webb provided a valuable transition for me from the traditional concept of Rustic as log and stone into the specialized Rustic forms of the Southwest. In addition, Dr. Webb shed light on NPS policies for preservation by explaining the distinctions between primary and secondary resources as outlined in park-enabling legislation. Her explanations helped clarify policy issues for allocating building preservation funds that were secondary to the natural resource priorities of a national park.

At Mount Rainier, former superintendent Neil Guse, along with Barry Siglin and Barry Kennedy, graciously guided me through the preservation history of one of the finest Rustic complexes ever built by the NPS. Crater Lake Superintendent Robert Benton offered assistance, and Ron Warfield, chief of interpretation, provided winter photos of Crater Lake Lodge. At Yosemite, former

superintendent Robert Binneweis and curator David Forgang patiently explained the park's history and the current pressures of visitors. At Yellowstone, Sonya Capek and Jim Peaco of the NPS provided valuable material, and TW Recreational Service's Steve Tedder offered the concessioner's perspective. Grand Teton's Bill Swift and Dick Bowman efficiently located an important photo included in the book. At Sequoia, Bill Tweed shared many insights about that park and his research on Rustic park architecture. Billy Garrett, formerly at the Grand Canyon North Rim, was an enthusiastic guide and interpreter of complex preservation issues. It was a pleasure meeting Harrison Goodall, who has done some of the most impressive preservation work for the National Park Service in the West.

The concessioner's role in preserving the grand hotels and other visitor facilities of landmark stature is long-standing. In all cases, this courteous and dedicated group of people extended hospitality to me and offered insights into the vexing problems of combining preservation with economic realities. Richard L. Kohnstamm, the savior of Timberline Lodge, generously provided a long and informative interview. His dedication to historic preservation and his ability at sustaining a viable economic enterprise that also serves as a museum of fine Pacific Northwest handicrafts are readily apparent in the lodge's welcoming ambience. Curator Linny Anderson has the enviable task of supervising restoration and preservation of the magnificent collection, working with the Friends of Timberline, the creative support group assembled for this landmark structure.

It is a pleasant coincidence when acquaintances appear in conjunction with a research project. Lester and Renee Schine Crown assisted in arranging my meeting officers and staff of TW Recreational Services in Chicago, including George Toney and Michael Kosiak. Their generosity, and that of Donald Schaefer, Jean Donaldson, and Steve Tedder in making facilities and staff available at Yellowstone, Zion, Bryce, and Grand Canyon National Parks, is gratefully acknowledged.

At Mount Rainier, Robert Seney, GSI manager, was representative of the concessioner's struggle with the cost of maintaining a rustic hotel complex while at the same time meeting NPS expectations. Allan Naille of Amfac

Resort Company proudly described his employer's sizable investment in the historic preservation of the Grand Canyon's El Tovar Hotel.

Phyllis Myers, of the Conservation Foundation, provided an important information source with her articles in *Architecture.* In person, she was extremely helpful in describing her research, and she directed me to the wonders of the NPS photo archives. Her passion for historic preservation and her encouragement to pursue the idea behind this book were an early inspiration.

Joyce Zaitlin's *Underwood* is a treasure, and the researcher who tracks it down is fortunate indeed. Published in 1989, her book is a polished work that I commend to anyone interested in Rustic architecture. I appreciate her advice and hope I have done justice to her analyses of the Gilbert Stanley Underwood buildings.

All researchers bow humbly to librarians who tirelessly seek out references for them–both within their domain and elsewhere. I was fortunate in my proximity to the Syracuse University and State University of New York College of Environmental Science and Forestry libraries and the assistance of their excellent staff.

I remain deeply indebted to David H. McAlpin for his encouragement, guidance, friendship, and good company that began many years ago and continued to his death in 1989. Dave was a conservationist long before it became fashionable. He was a patron of photography, among other arts, and profoundly influenced its acceptance in America's museums. To Dave, I owe my introduction to Ansel and Virginia Adams.

My visits at the Adamses' Carmel home in 1983 opened windows of awareness both to Yosemite and to the other sources of Ansel's extraordinary images of western national parks. Each time I see "Clearing Winter Storm, Yosemite Valley" (1944) or "Moonrise, Hernandez, New Mexico" (1941), I recall the sprightly octogenarian and his passion for protecting the environment. The interest of Dr. Michael and Jeanne Adams has been rewarding. Their hospitality in Fresno and Yosemite helped sustain a lengthy and ambitious project. I modestly hope that my debt of gratitude to them is finally repaid by the completion of this work.

I am grateful for my family's patience and forbearance during this project, particularly when I was away on research trips. My wife, Linda, was a never-ending source of encouragement, and when I did not need to work alone, she was a matchless traveling companion. My daughter Christina shared her interest in the writer's craft, and my sons, Sven-Erik and Robert, contributed valuable insights. Finally, I am grateful to Emily Miller and Caroline Herter of Chronicle Books, and Gary Chassman of Verve Editions for their support and encouragement in seeing the book published. Jane Taylor's editorial assistance and Wynne Patterson's design excellence are evident throughout the book. Their judgment and intelligent suggestions were instrumental in shaping the stucture of this book and providing it with its final form.

Despite the generous assistance and support I have received, I must acknowledge responsibility for any errors or omissions, and the ideas expressed in these pages.

Preface

Walking the streets of American cities, one is astounded by the accelerated pace of architectural preservation. High-rise skyscrapers, abandoned waterfront mills, shuttered movie houses, and once elegant Victorian houses are being restored and put to new uses. Communities and individuals are no longer automatically accepting the convenient route of demolition, but are more often choosing the challenging path of establishing designated historic districts to restore and maintain our cultural heritage. William Prescott's words are echoing across the land: "The surest test of a civilization of a people . . . is to be found in their architecture." And finding it we are.

The preservation movement in our nation has grown from the early champions of patriotic monuments into the current broad-based ground swell of public support. It is a mass rekindling of interest in our past as a foundation for the future. Solid economic reasoning accompanies this idealism. Inflation, energy costs, and favorable tax policies encourage rescuing the residual value of a structure and inspire rehabilitation. Interest in the richness of historic form, decoration, and detail is a reaction to our boredom with mass-produced architecture and the homogeneity of highway strips and suburbia.

A variation on this theme occurs with buildings in the natural setting. Away from cities, often sited for prominence and spectacular views or isolated for privacy, there are many rich examples of architecture worthy of preservation. These structures—mansions or humble homes, grand hotels or modest inns—provide strong ties to our past. Because they lack a populist movement for their preservation and are in conflict with the desires of those who would conserve a natural environment by eliminating all "intrusions," there is a real danger that they will be lost to future generations.

This book's concern is historic architecture in the natural setting. Its aim is to draw attention to those structures too distant from population centers to enjoy readily available voices of preservation support. It grew out of an earlier curiosity about rustic summer homes built in the Adirondack Mountains of upper New York State, structures facing the same risk through neglect or destruction. Unless a mechanism for preservation is put into place, the unique enabling legislation in the Adirondack Park will require destruction of the Great Camps as

they are acquired by the state. The problem of preservation in the Adirondacks is repeated in other locales; structures of historical significance, exceptional design, or those simply representative of an important moment in our nation's past are at risk of falling into neglect for lack of an active advocacy.

Properties in the public domain under the stewardship of government agencies present a special case for preservation. Although preservation must have legislative support, federal, state, and local public policy agendas have lacked strong leadership for implementation. Politics also sometimes comes into play. The National Park Service has limited funds available for preservation, occasionally supported by concessioners' investments, and agency administrators turn to Congress for special appropriations for a specific park or resource. The results are decaying properties because of inadequate funding and lost opportunities for acquisition of endangered land and buildings. We are in danger of losing part of our nation's cultural heritage.

For several reasons, this book concentrates on the vast resources and numerous historic buildings in the American West, particularly in the national parks. First, the settings presented extraordinary challenges to those who would build in harmony with the environment. Repeating out West the familiar eastern forms and traditions would have been difficult, with massive logistical problems. Fortunately, builders turned to indigenous designs and readily available materials, and they produced structures as varied as the terrain and climate. Homesteaders' cabins, early settlers' accommodations for tourists, luxury hotels built by railroaders, and NPS buildings were located in environmentally sensitive settings. They were constructed with forms, materials, and architecture compatible with their environment.

Second, the richness and diversity of the architecture provide a wealth of cultural resources. A majestic hotel next to Old Faithful geyser or deep in Yosemite Valley, a ranch along the Snake River in the shadow of the Tetons, a cabin in the Olympic Peninsula rain forest, an adobe visitor complex in the southwest Indian country, an NPS log administration building—these are fine examples of buildings worthy of preservation. Current threats from overuse, neglect, and in some cases abandonment are compelling reasons for the public to be aware of the dangers facing the structures I call "Landmarks of the Western Landscape."

Finally, the fundamental question of who is responsible for historic architecture in the public domain is sharply defined in the western national parks. The *natural* environment has a broad constituency of support in the Sierra Club, The Nature Conservancy, the Wilderness Society, and a host of other organizations. Several act as private overseer groups for the national parks but have little interest in historic preservation. The public's interests for preservation are delegated to federal bureaucracies with legislative mandate to protect natural *and* cultural resources. Implementation and interpretation of these laws are inconsistent and problematical, based on priorities and available funding. Private and quasi-public historic preservation organizations tend to concentrate their attention on urban structures or the few high-profile landmarks in the wilderness. As a result, many fine examples of Rustic architecture lack a voice of support.

The strained conflict between defenders of environmental conservation and advocates for historic architectural preservation is a further complication. Vigorous and often bitter debates are conducted over any proposal to retain or restore existing structures. The issue has become sharply defined: Should "intrusions" be allowed to remain or be removed to restore an "unspoiled" scenery? Sometimes the debate becomes pitched, like the one that raged for years over whether to remove, replace, or restore Crater Lake Lodge, which was recently resolved in favor of reconstruction.

The spectacular scenery of the national parks is as diverse as the buildings in them. The parks provide a setting where historic architecture in the public domain can promote an awareness of the issues and action for preservation. A founding principle of the NPS for the national parks was "to conserve the scenery and natural and historic objects and the wildlife therein . . . unimpaired for the enjoyment of future generations." Preserving historic places has always been as important to the NPS as setting aside places of unique natural beauty. The NPS has not lacked policies or administrative procedures for historic preservation. The struggle is more concerned with lack of staffing and funding.

The early roots of western national park Rustic architecture are found in the vacation camps of the lakes, forests, and mountains of the Adirondack region in northern New York State. Architects and railroaders adopted the style and created grand lodges in the West to attract travelers along the new transcontinental rail lines. Under the guiding hand of the founding director of the NPS, Stephen Mather, the basic principles of compatibility with the environment evolved into a true American design idiom, the NPS Rustic style. The use of native materials and indigenous forms took hold in the Rockies, on the Olympic Peninsula, and in Sierra forests; it also inspired the work in the Southwest, where Indian and Spanish Colonial motifs were emulated.

Historic architecture in western national parks is often a juxtaposition of high-quality national landmarks next to rather ordinary buildings. Terrain, climate, and available building materials vary, and so does the architecture. Clusters of buildings typically surround the familiar grand hotels because recreation and support complexes grew to serve large numbers of park visitors. NPS structures, whether administrative and residential complexes or remote ranger stations, include the finest of the NPS Rustic style, and the not so fine. Many buildings are isolated, accessible only after a long drive through stunning scenery or a hike into the backcountry. Sometimes, a building may be virtually invisible in its natural setting until one arrives at its doorstep.

Variety in form and materials comes into play upon close inspection. Regularity or smoothness of form is rare; asymmetrical plans were frequently used to adapt a building to the terrain. A play of light and shadow may have been achieved by strategic use of masses, voids, and rough-textured materials that mimic the surrounding landscape. The randomness of hand-set materials may be warmed by a patina created by years in the sun, and rough edges may have been softened by wind-driven rain, snow, or sand. The end result is an architecture that merges with its setting and offers a strong image – both of the whole and of its parts and pieces. Many of these structures make an impression that lingers in visitors' memories long after they depart.

Deciding which buildings to examine in this book was extremely difficult. Each park and the structures in it required time to study and observe, to contemplate and ponder. Those singled out were selected because of special qualities of site, construction, or use of materials. Admittedly, some choices are simply the author's preference and may not meet rigorous preservationist criteria. Special attention was given to photographing each historic structure. The memorable western landscape images by a succession of photographers, including Carleton E. Watkins, Timothy H. O'Sullivan, William Henry Jackson, and Ansel Adams, are an intimidating challenge to any photographer today. And modern equipment and film hardly seems to guarantee any improvement over older, bulky cameras and wet plates.

The book has been organized into three regions that share common architectural elements: terrain, indigenous materials, and local building traditions. A driving tour can cover each region in several weeks, but travelers are cautioned not to rush—savor these splendid structures. Be wary of surprise weather changes, and be respectful of the private residential areas that are off-limits to the general public except by invitation.

Landmarks
in the Landscape

△ *George Catlin,* BUFFALO CHASE, *1832. George Catlin often reflected on the effects of expanding civilization. He was convinced that "the further we become separated from that pristine wildness and beauty, the* more pleasure does the mind of enlightened man feel in recurring to those scenes." In this 1844 lithograph, Catlin honored the power and endurance of the animal and the courage of his Indian pursuer.

A Sense of Place

Speaking of old buildings, they are not just ours. They partly belong to those who built them and partly to all generations of mankind who are to follow us. . . . What other men gave their strength and wealth and life to accomplish . . . belongs to all their successors.

John Ruskin, THE SEVEN LAMPS OF ARCHITECTURE

At Yosemite Valley, visitors are overwhelmed by the grandeur of the granite-walled canyon, cascading waterfalls, and meandering Merced River, a reaction that precludes paying attention to anything that may have been built there. The eye slowly shifts from the pinnacles to plumes of water tumbling thousands of feet, to gray talus slopes with lush green meadows below. The visitor doubts that any construction could compete with nature's own dramatic architecture. Buildings fade into insignificance; as objects of convenience, they become invisible against the colors, textures, shapes, and forms of nature.

This experience is repeated in other western national parks – among the forests of sequoias, redwoods, and Douglas fir, the volcanic peaks of Mount Rainier and Crater Lake, the geysers and canyons at Yellowstone, the ochre, red, and gray stone of Grand Canyon's minarets, the serene Painted Desert, and the vibrantly colored mesa landscape of Utah and Arizona. Nestled within the majestic beauty of these natural areas are structures built with such a strong sense of design and purpose that they rise above the classification of mere buildings into the realm of architecture. The impact of sublime scenery understandably subordinates buildings to secondary importance. A few exceptions – Old Faithful Inn, Timberline Lodge, and the Painted Desert Inn – compete with their powerful natural settings for attention.

Many natural areas in the public domain contain cultural resources worthy of preservation – true landmarks in the landscape. The paradox of the American heritage is that preservation of splendid publicly owned acreage goes relatively unquestioned, while there is no such consensus for cultural resources in natural areas. The great western parks of the national park system, often referred to as the NPS "crown jewels," illustrate the need for enhanced awareness and enforcement of agency management guidelines to preserve the physical architecture as well as the physical settings.

Fortunately, some structures have been designated National Historic Landmarks. The Statue of Liberty, Independence Hall, Lincoln Memorial, and Fort McHenry are revered and appropriately protected. These are structures or monuments typically unanimously acclaimed as part of our national heritage, structures worthy of protection for present and future generations.

◁ *Thomas Moran,* LOWER FALLS OF THE YELLOWSTONE, *1893.*

As such, they exemplify the first formal preservation activity in the United States and are lodged in the popular consciousness.

Historian James Marston Fitch acknowledges that "until recently, most national preservation programs have been preponderantly upper-class and urbane in their emphasis."[1] The result of this inherent bias is the study and preservation of places associated with the powerful and famous: palaces, castles, cathedrals, and parliaments. Fitch posits that even in Western Europe and the United States, much historical experience has never been recorded. As a consequence, vernacular architecture – urban or rural – went unnoticed, and the contextual settings of the structures, sites, and monuments were ignored.

This preservation concept in the United States has been interpreted as an obsession with the past because people in this country are constantly appealing to their history as justification for their plans for the future.[2] In contrast to older societies that preserve a sense of the object, in this country it is a sense of place that is important – the idea of preserving hallowed ground even though little remains of the events that took place there.

Sense of place has been translated from a broad purpose of preservation into an activity to save architecturally significant buildings from destruction in urban contexts.[3] Even with an obeisance to environmental context, preservation of structures outside urban settings is relegated to an elitist, upper-class bias that results in an unbalanced view of the past. The social and economic revitalizing force of preservation to link the culture of the present to that of the past is through a juxtaposition of architecture. The "built" environment means an urban environment.

Where then does the free-standing structure in the natural setting, outside the urban environment, fit into a preservationist scheme? While citizens rally to save indi-vidual structures and sites in cities and villages, vital elements of the inheritance from our past are lost. The built environment signifies townscape, in contrast to landscape. Landmarks in the natural landscape are left out of the scheme–those structural treasures that remind us of the great human capacity to build what is humble and subservient to its setting.

Landmarks in natural settings comprise a diverse collection of structures in private and public hands: Biltmore in Piedmont, North Carolina, in contrast to the Pfeiffer Homestead in Grand Teton National Park; Olana on the Hudson and the Humes Cabin in Olympic National Park; Old Faithful Inn in Yellowstone and Sagamore Camp in the Adirondacks. Some have been rescued by private restoration or a devoted constituency, but others are left to decay. Along the north shore of Long Island, in the lower Mississippi Valley, and in the Hudson River Highlands, significant structures in magnificent settings sit dormant, slowly deteriorating as unwanted relics of the past. No longer economically viable, or dismissed by heirs as labor-intensive relics, weather and time will take their toll. The tragedy is a loss of sense of place. Also lost is a tremendous variety of architectural heritage.

Conservation and Enjoyment

Preservation of culturally important structures in the United States is relatively recent compared to the tradition of conserving natural areas. Reverence for wilderness areas emerged in the nineteenth century, but half a century later, private efforts to preserve historic buildings were only sporadic and occasional. Roderick Nash's seminal *Wilderness and the American Mind* portrays how attitudes toward the wild underwent change in the seventeenth and eighteenth centuries.[4] Fear slowly moderated toward appreciation. An early explorer, Thaddeus Harris, describes this new approach toward the Ameri-

▽ *William Henry Jackson photograph of artist Thomas Moran on Mammoth Hot Springs Terrace, July 21, 1871. Jackson and Moran accompanied the Hayden survey expedition to Yellowstone, where Jackson produced the first pictures of Yellowstone and Moran his* painting, THE GRAND CANYON OF THE YELLOWSTONE. *When Congress was considering legislation to enable Yellowstone National Park, each member was presented with a bound volume of Jackson's photographs, including this one.*

can landscape: "The sublime in nature captivates while it awes: and charms while it elevates and expands the soul."[5]

The return to nature, inspired in part by Thoreau and Emerson, the reaction to industrialism, and the principles of transcendentalism, became a restless force in our culture. Without the cathedrals, castles, and old cities of Europe, people in the United States began to take pride in the vast scenery of the West – the awesome canyons and wild mountains that far surpassed the more tranquil scenery of Europe.[6]

The movement to conserve parks for public use stressed the theme that a life lived in close contact with nature resulted in moral and sociological benefits. An important figure in this movement was Andrew Jackson Downing, a prolific writer and landscape architect. Frederick Law Olmsted followed in his tradition in the planning and creation of New York City's Central Park and promoted the principles of wilderness preservation in his Yosemite Valley report of 1865.

Landscape painters and photographers, who were influenced by Hudson River School artists Thomas Cole and Asher Brown Durand, provided the eastern establishment with visual proof of the western landscape's unique power and grandeur. Indeed, the artwork that captured the natural beauty of the American wilderness on canvas and photographic plates was critical in furthering the national concerns that led to that unique American institution, the national park.[7]

Foremost among the artists who portrayed the region were Albert Bierstadt and Thomas Moran. Their works helped establish Yosemite and Yellowstone national parks. Bierstadt's enormous, spectacular paintings of the Rocky Mountains were the first of a series of works to achieve cultural acclaim. Moran, a genuine explorer in the traditional sense, accompanied one of the four major geological surveys of the West from the 1860s into the early 1870s.[8]

Grand paintings were sometimes criticized as overly romantic or exaggerated, but the precision of albumen photography unquestionably conveyed realism that substantiated the claims of true grandeur in the West. Carleton E. Watkins' massive Yosemite folio, completed in 1868, depicts the majesty of the natural landscape. Timothy H. O'Sullivan and William Henry Jackson

accompanied survey teams exploring the West, and Yellowstone in particular, and recorded memorable images that became a potent force in directing attention to national wilderness as a source of national pride.[9]

The swing toward conservation came from a combination of this pride and anxiety; cultural nationalism inspired a confidence that the natural wonders of the United States rivaled and even surpassed European cultural achievements.[10] The valley and giant sequoias at Yosemite were turned over to the state of California for "public use, resort and recreation … inalienable for all time" out of anxiety that what had happened in places like Niagara Falls, a treasure confiscated for private gain, might be repeated there.[11]

The national park idea originated with the creation of Yellowstone National Park in 1872, "dedicated and set apart as a public park or pleasuring ground for the benefit and the enjoyment of the people." With the exception of Mackinac Island National Park (1875), Congress enacted no other permanent national parks for nearly two decades. (The hot springs at Hot Springs, Arkansas, was set aside in 1832 and was named a federal Reservation in 1870 and a national park in 1921. Mackinac Island National Park was created in 1875 and ceded to Michigan for use as a state park in 1895.)

When the national park idea revived, it was due to

▷ *William Henry Jackson (left) "photographing in high places," 1872, with his wife's 18-year-old cousin, Charley Campbell. When Jackson reached this ledge, he stopped to prepare wet plates in his "dark tent." The arduous task of trekking with mules across rugged terrain with 300 pounds of equipment seems daunting today. This exposure was made by the packer, Aleck; the water source for photographic processing was a trickling snow-bag. The Grand Tetons are in the background.*

PHOTOGRAPHING IN HIGH PLACES

a combination of cultural nationalism and changing attitudes toward natural preserves provoked by the 1890 report of the U.S. Bureau of the Census. As the nineteenth century drew to a close, indistinct boundaries distinguished settled from unsettled portions of the West. Convinced that cities discourage cultural greatness, Charles Eliot Norton, Frederick Law Olmsted, and other easterners supported the conservation of nature as the antithesis to urban stagnation.[12] Yosemite, Sequoia, and General Grant national parks received congressional designation in 1890 as people feared the destruction of California's "big trees." Scenic nationalism continued as the impetus for park designation through the creation of Mount Rainier (1899) and Crater Lake (1902) National Parks.

Conservation of natural resources was further promoted by the Federal Forest Reserve Act of 1891. The Bill gave the president unilateral authority to proclaim appropriate areas of the public domain "reservations," thereby making more attractive the idea of utilitarian conservation in the form of public parks. Four presidents (Harrison, Cleveland, McKinley, and Theodore Roosevelt) set aside a total of 175 million acres of Na-

tional Forest lands before the abolition of this executive authority in 1907. With each national park requiring a separate act of Congress, scenic preservationists stood at a disadvantage against the arguments of Gifford Pinchot: "The first duty of the human race is to control the earth it lives upon."[13] The vindication of Pinchot's viewpoint, with the founding of the U.S. Forest Service in 1905, was symbolic of the struggle for power within the conservation movement. Runte points out that "while esthetic advocates still struggled to consolidate their gains, resource managers enjoyed growing popularity and prestige."[14]

It was not until the fledgling National Park Service came into play under the strong guiding hand of Stephen Mather that the national park system began to develop the arguments to support funding for visitor improvements. Preserving natural settings simultaneously protected resources and attracted tourists. As tourism increased, due to railroad expansion, automobile ownership, and public investments in park access, the virtues of scenic preservation were supported by more revenue than could be achieved by exploiting park resources.

By 1900, the national park system was firmly in place,

◁ *William Henry Jackson recorded the 1871 Hayden Survey on the march in Yellowstone. Lieutenant Doane is in the lead, followed by Dr. Ferdinand Vandiveer Hayden. The wheeled object is an odometer, used to measure trail distances. Survey leaders employed photographers, including Watkins, O'Sullivan, and Jackson, to promote the survey parties as they competed for government funding. Indirectly, they helped to advance landscape photography, and the nation benefited through documentation of previously unrecorded scenic wonders.*

with Yosemite and Yellowstone and other scenic wonders of the West established for public use. In contrast, historic preservation of individual structures did not receive congressional attention until 1935, with passage of the Historic Sites and Building Act.

As Charles B. Hosmer, Jr., cites in *Presence of the Past,* architectural preservation was launched early in the nation's history.[15] The need to establish a national identity that would inspire architectural preservation manifested itself in the middle of the nineteenth century through the patriotic desire to commemorate historic sites. Private action, led by Pamela Cunningham, rescued Mount Vernon from being converted to a hotel in 1858. Noble efforts accomplished restoration for many buildings that became shrines, monuments, or museums: Andrew Jackson's Hermitage (1856); Carpenter Hall in Philadelphia (1856); George Washington's Headquarters in Morristown, New Jersey (1873); Valley Forge (1878); Abraham Lincoln's Homestead (1883); and the Governor's Palace in Santa Fe (1881).

The patriotic motive was lodged in the public's consciousness as the basis for the first formal preservation activity in the United States. Hosmer describes the rescue of Mount Vernon and Hermitage as an indigenous movement, a truly grassroots action by the general public. "Preservation work remained in the hands of private groups formed for that purpose" and took the place of state or federal action.[16] Ranging from West to East coasts, the Native Sons of the Golden West (1888), the Historical Society of New Mexico (1881), The Association for the Preservation of Virginia Antiquities (1888), the Daughters of the American Revolution (1890), and the Society of Colonial Dames (1890) were actively engaged in preservation efforts by the end of the nineteenth century.

The underlying themes of these early preservation efforts were associative: connections with important events or people, or an understanding of the nation's past. Buildings were highly esteemed where famous people had lived or landmark events had taken place, rather than for their intrinsic value or their relation to their surroundings. At the beginning of the twentieth century, an aesthetic argument—preservation for architecture's sake—was put forward by William Sumner Appleton. The Society for the Preservation of New England Antiquities, founded by Appleton in 1910, was organized with "its chief purpose to preserve for future generations structures … which are architecturally beautiful or unique, or have special significance. Such buildings once destroyed can never be replaced." The aesthetic motive vied with associative arguments as the inspiration for conservation.[17]

The federal government first became involved with preserving aspects of the American culture other than scenic values when it addressed concerns about archaeological ruins in the Southwest.[18] Disturbed over the looting of cliff dwellings and pueblo ruins, individuals and organizations urged congressional action. Photographs of the White House Ruins at Canyon de Chelly by Timothy H. O'Sullivan in 1873 helped generate public support for legislation.

When Mesa Verde National Park was founded, it boosted the precedent for historic preservation to the national level.[19] Shortly before establishing Mesa Verde, in 1906, Congress passed the Act for the Preservation of American Antiquities.[20] Under the leadership of Senator John Lacey of Iowa, the act empowered the president to proclaim as national monuments "historic landmarks, historic or prehistoric structures, and other objects of historic or scientific interest" on federal lands.

The early years of the National Park Service continued to focus on conserving natural wonders, with little interest in historic preservation. Meanwhile, private actions were led by John D. Rockefeller, Jr., at Colonial Williamsburg and Henry Ford at Greenfield Village. Through the efforts of Horace Albright, the NPS' second director, a reorganization of the NPS in 1933 led to its assuming responsibility for historic sites in Washington, D.C., adding 47 historical areas in 17 predominately eastern states to the national park system.

The Historic Sites and Building Act was passed in 1935 "to provide for the preservation of historic American sites, buildings, objects, and antiquities of national importance."[21] Thus, a national policy was declared and the NPS was to undertake a survey of nationally important historic sites. The act also authorized the NPS to preserve properties and archaeological sites of national historic value with the National Historic Landmark designation.

The growth in historic preservation interest and activities following World War II resulted in a congressional charter creating the National Trust for Historic Preservation. Intended to act as a national clearinghouse for preservation matters, the trust was established in 1949 to create an organization with the independence of a private corporation that would supplement the role of the NPS "to further the policy enunciated in the Act of August 21, 1935,… and to facilitate public participation in the preservation of sites, buildings, and objects of national significance or interest."[22]

By the mid-1960s, preservation activities were part of the mainstream national mood. The vast federal public works programs of urban renewal and highway construction led to increased public resentment and were generally viewed as an assault on the environment. In 1966, spurred by public outrage at indiscriminate destruction of distinguished old buildings by urban renewal and highway construction, Congress passed the National Historic Preservation Act.[23] This act provided the means for implementing what had been stated as national policy as early as 1906: *To foster conditions under which our modern society and historic resources can exist in productive harmony and fulfill social, economic, and other requirements of present and future generations … and give maximum encouragement to organizations and individuals undertaking preservation by private means.*

The provisions of the National Historic Preservation Act, as amended, dramatically accelerated preservation activity. A National Register of Historic Places based on the national Survey of Historic Sites and Buildings made up an inventory of significant historic districts, sites, structures, and objects of state, local, and national importance. After twenty-five years, more than 58,000 listings were on the National Register.

The National Historic Preservation Act also created the Advisory Council on Historic Preservation, a review agency made up of federal officials and private citizens to advise the president and Congress on historic preservation. An important function of the council is acting on their authority to comment on plans for federally funded or licensed projects likely to have an impact on structures on or eligible for the National Register.

The act provided special protection for federally managed historic structures, an important provision

▷ *Frederick Law Olmsted (1822–1903). Olmsted strongly influenced American attitudes toward landscape design and wilderness preservation because of his reputation as the foremost landscape architect of his time. His principles unwittingly set into motion the ongoing debate between conservation and preservation groups.*

concerning structures in the national parks. State and local involvement in preservation was fostered by regulations established for state historic preservation programs.

To stimulate preservation activities, the act authorized the Department of the Interior to distribute matching grants to aid states and the National Trust in carrying on preservation programs. Legislative support for preservation achieved enormous gains through tax incentives initiated in 1976 under the Tax Reform Act. Under this system, tax credits channeled more than $15 billion in private investment into some 23,300 preservation projects through 1992.

Utility versus Enjoyment

Historic preservation's evolution into the mainstream of American culture has followed a tenuous path over the past century. Architectural preservation through state and federal legislation has finally secured a position similar to the long-established conservation movement. Local, state, and national organizations, and a diverse press of both general and specialized interests, encourage a vigilant preservation stance. Mutual interests are reinforced, often creating a ground swell of support for the protection of cherished landmarks.

Preservationist fervor is aroused, for example, when mansions are rejected by heirs or found no longer viable for beneficiary institutions. Demolition to create subdivisions of smaller "estates" with the cachet of vanished grandeur is a typical saga outside metropolitan areas and formerly exclusive vacation areas. These threats generate support for preservation, in some cases producing creative compromises for adaptive reuse and, in others, the

inspiration for a revitalized district of residential and commercial properties.

Preservation and adaptive reuse, phrases now common in the architectural preservationists' vocabulary, had a different meaning in the earlier debates over utility versus enjoyment for public lands. Conservation, preservation, and utility had subtle distinctions that were not always clear. *Conserve* meant to save in a present state and protect against change or exploitation; *utility* meant exploitation and enjoyment resulting from the experience of unspoiled, natural scenery. In contrast, *preservation* meant to save and restore historic structures for future use, even if they intruded on the enjoyment of the natural setting. Conservation and use values for public lands echo the arguments begun by Frederick Law Olmsted in his 1865 Yosemite report, emphasizing that one of the features of conserving America's scenic wealth was to be its "accessibility to all citizens for use and enjoyment."[24]

Olmsted elaborated in that document, for the first time in the United States, the policy underlying the government's reserving for the public a particular and fine scenic area, and he gave it a general application.[25] In advising the California state officials who were managing the unspoiled expanses of Yosemite Valley and Mariposa Big Tree Grove, he defined what their objectives ought to include: *The preservation and maintenance as is exactly possible of the natural scenery ... within the narrowest limits consistent with the necessary accommodation of visitors [and] the prevention of all construction markedly inharmonious with the scenery or which would unnecessarily obscure, distort, or detract from the dignity of the scenery.* The emphasis was on preservation of fine scenery – aesthetics – rather than cultural resources.

With keen foresight, he made a prediction about Yosemite: "In a century the whole number of visitors will be counted in the millions." The ambiguity of the use and enjoyment philosophy left uncertain the methods to achieve Olmsted's goal of finding acceptable ways to encourage visitors while preserving the natural scene. In formulating the philosophic base for establishing state and national parks, Olmsted's democratic views began the debate as to what kinds of use and forms of enjoyment were appropriate for public lands. From this point of view stems the perpetually unresolved dispute over whether structures are intrusions or acceptable elements in their natural setting.

The two sides of the debate have often run parallel courses, sometimes converging as allies but more often clashing as adversaries. "Intrusive" and "harmony" are the polarities of the conflicting philosophies. Differences in opinion originate with the movement to preserve the natural setting in its original state. Thoreau advocated keeping a few wild places "for modesty and reverence's sake, or if only to suggest this earth has higher uses than we put her to."[26]

Even in the romantic era, when wilderness was largely extolled for the value of its sublime beauty, the other side of the debate often emerged. Emerson commented in 1844 that "the forests should become graceful parks, for use and delight."[27] But two decades later, the *New York Times* editorialized on the preservation of the Adirondack wilderness, simultaneously offering a place for progress and industry. Urging the state to acquire this land before it was "despoiled," the *Times* suggested that sawmills and foundries could exist outside the reserve. *While the hunting lodges of our citizens will adorn its more remote mountain sides and the wooded islands of its delightful lakes ... in spite of all the din and dust of furnaces and foundries, the Adirondacks ... will furnish seclusion for all time to come: and will admirably realize the true union which should always exist between utility and enjoyment.*[28]

One must invest in the mid-nineteenth-century tenet of romanticism and the passion of the transcendentalists to appreciate their struggle to quell the movement toward "conquest" of the "untamed" American continent. While a robust nation was achieving economic success and ascendancy as a world power, it was rapidly destroying its heritage of natural beauty. The role of Thoreau and Emerson and other champions of the wilderness was to proclaim the sanctity of wild country – its mystical ability to inspire and refresh the mind and spirit.

Actions taken to protect the Adirondack Preserve, created in 1885, echoed this philosophy. Although lumber barons were dissatisfied and argued for exploitation of timber resources, Article VII, Section 7, was eventually incorporated into New York State's Constitution. *The*

lands of the State, now owned or hereafter acquired, constituting the Forest Preserve as now fixed by law, shall be forever kept as wild forest lands. They shall not be leased, sold, or exchanged, or be taken by any corporation, public or private, nor shall the timber thereon be sold, removed, or destroyed.

This legislation and its implied restrictions prohibit *any* actions for historic preservation in the public landholdings of the Adirondack Park. The collection of buildings caught in the preservation dilemma includes hotels, estate complexes, and leisure homes built on a grand scale – the Great Camps.[29] To resolve this conflict, legislative and agency actions will have to seek creative compromises to bring together the dissimilar philosophies of conservation and preservation.

Country Houses

Newport, the Hudson River Valley, the South Georgia coast, the lower Mississippi plantations, and Tidewater, Virginia, contain many examples of mansions set on country estates that are drawing preservationist attention. Some are large, sprawling, eighteenth-century homes built in the baronial fashion on thousands of acres, with attendant support complexes. Others represent the late nineteenth-century fortunes amassed by owners of railroads, utilities, oil and mineral interests, banks, and real estate development companies. These private estates served their owner's social needs and fulfilled their romantic notions of status and privilege.

The Great Depression sounded the death knell for these great country estates, and after World War II, landowners increasingly abandoned their holdings, demolished buildings, and began to sell off land at a brisk pace. Preservation of these estates, or at least their remnants, came about as a result of various concerns. Private individuals, nonprofit corporations, and sometimes state agencies purchased and restored properties, turning them into museums or adapting them for other public use. William Vanderbilt's Biltmore and William Randolph Hearst's San Simeon annually receive millions of visitors curious to see the grandeur of these fabled estates, and the National Trust for Historic Preservation has amassed a varied collection of properties across the country for restoration and public use. Following the energetic action of Ann Pamela Cunningham at Mount Vernon, these properties perpetuate the tradition of private action to secure examples of our architectural heritage for the public.

The great estate houses were built on sites carefully chosen for private enjoyment and their special settings. The nineteenth century inspired a reverence for landscape, convenience, and grandeur that produced a unique architecture. Grand houses were designed to harmonize with the landscape or to be an eclectic expression of the builder's taste. Preservationists treasured the architecture that showed civility toward its setting. This was not always the case, for some structures were built that commercially exploited scenic wonders.

The enjoyment of America's natural heritage raised concerns early on about defacement by utilitarian structures and commercial greed. Alexis de Tocqueville in 1831 urged a friend to "hasten" to Niagara Falls if he wished "to see this place with its grandeur. If you delay," he warned, "your Niagara will have been spoiled for you. Already the forest round is being cleared…. I don't give the Americans ten years to establish a saw or flour mill at the base of the cataract."[30] Half a century later, Frederick Law Olmsted and a few close associates roused the nation in support of efforts to restore the cataract and its environs to their natural condition.[31]

The western national parks contain many examples of structures fortunate in their reconciliation of conservation and enjoyment. The railroads, which supported the founding of the parks, linked their success to the quality of the developments they opened for tourism. The NPS followed this concept of harmony by producing "some of the most well-known elements of Americans' shared architectural heritage, sometimes defining a national park as much as the canyon or geyser." The underlying ethic of design, use of materials, and selection of site embraced "a spectrum of attitudes about 'harmony.' Some structures are created in nature's image, reflecting or vying with the awesome imagery. Others seek a dynamic fusion with the setting, others obscurity."[32]

Within most of the western national parks there are settlers' cabins, mining buildings, and guest accommodations that predate the park. For the most part, they were built with little concern for conservation or "appropri-ate" development. Resort hotels built by the railroads and other developers, and the smaller facilities built later under the New Deal for outdoor recreation and park management, "brought forward regional responses to the shapes and scale of the Western landscape and the designs of the American Indians, and for the eclectic echoes of English cottage, shingle, Oriental, and prairie styles."[33]

Some of the landmarks in the national park landscapes have been recently nominated for designation on the National Register or as National Historic Landmarks. Old Faithful Inn has been on the National Register since 1973. These buildings represent the preservation dilemma that government agencies face with responsibility for landholdings that have been set aside for public enjoyment: Is architectural preservation compatible with the spirit of conservation? Should the mark of human beings on the landscape be treated as an intrusion or be accepted as one evolutionary aspect of the "civilizing" influence? What guidelines should instruct the temporary custodians of public lands or natural landscapes in decisions concerning historic structures? The historic architecture in western national parks suggests answers to these questions.

The Western Landscape

Infinite variety, and no part is ever duplicated.

John Wesley Powell,

THE EXPLORATION OF

THE COLORADO RIVER

AND ITS CANYONS

△ *Major John Wesley Powell (1834–1902), shown here in 1873 with Chief Taugu of the Paiutes, was a geologist, capable administrator, and visionary for development of the American West. The loss of an arm in the Civil War did not inhibit his exploration of the Colorado River, and he became known for his energetic dedication to science.*

▷ *The one-room Fruita Schoolhouse in Capitol Reef National Park, Utah, was completed in 1896 and remained open until 1941. The original flat roof was covered with bentonite clay; a peaked, shingled roof modification was added in 1914. Log chinking and a woodstove warded off the cold and damp.*

The physical splendor of western national parks has captivated and inspired writers, painters, and photographers for decades. John Muir and Ansel Adams, explorers with pen and camera, spanned a century with paeans to their exceptional beauty.

Muir was a pioneer spokesperson for the national parks, who trekked thousands of miles and publicized little-known wonders. His philosophy regarded wilderness as an object to be venerated – a restorative for modern man: *Thousands of tired, nerve-shaken, over-civilized people are beginning to find out that going to the mountains is going home; that wildness is a necessity; and that the mountain parks and reservations are useful not only as fountains of timber and irrigating rivers, but as fountains of life.*[1]

Carrying on the great traditions of early western photographers, capturing the drama and the setting as a poet with a lens, Ansel Adams brought a special interpretation to the mountains and valleys, deserts and rivers. His words reflect the sensitivity of his photography: *The dawn wind in the High Sierra is not just a passage of cool air through forest conifers, but within the labyrinth of human consciousness becomes a stirring of some world-magic of most delicate persuasion. The grand lift of the Tetons is more than mechanistic fold and faulting of the earth's crust; it becomes a primal gesture of the earth beneath a greater sky.*[2]

The Settings

The diversity of settings in the West entranced the earliest explorers and today beguiles the media-saturated twentieth-century traveler. Heading west by airplane, the modern view from 30,000 feet unfolds: The dun brown of the western grassy plains merges into the eastern slope of the Rockies as they rise to the Continental Divide—not one range of mountains but a cordillera of interlocking ranges that disappear south across the unmarked boundary of Mexico and north toward Alaska. Glaciers and rivers carve wonderlands of canyons through sandstone and granite, polished by winds for millennia. The serrated peaks of the Rockies give way to great whalelike shapes to the south, merging mesas into plateaus and sandy-hued deserts. Lines of red and ochre are etched into the strata, separated by valleys and can-

yons. The desert basins of the Great Salt Lake, Mojave, and Colorado are wrung dry of moisture by the Sierra and Cascade ranges. Shadowy green bands of spruce and fir and pine descend from the white-tipped crowns of the coastal ranges, marked by the river systems that flow out to San Francisco Bay, Puget Sound, and the Pacific, which stretches in a blue rim along the edge of the continent.

Travel from east to west as Major John Wesley Powell did in another era, on his way to change the popular view of the West. Cross the Great Plains into the Rockies, onto the "plateau province" across the Great Basin. To the south lies the desert, and beyond the Sierra Nevada, the ocean. The landscape is alternately gnarled, forested, and barren, crisscrossed by canyons, marked by soaring peaks and multicolored troughs. To Powell, writing during his explorations down the Colorado River in 1869, appreciation of this landscape required a special pace: "It can be seen only in parts from hour to hour and from day to day and from week to week and from month to month.... A year scarcely suffices to see it all. It has infinite variety, and no part is ever duplicated."[3]

From the ground, at Powell's pace, a different perspective of form, shape, color, and light presents itself. Compare Bierstadt's color-saturated landscapes with Adams' dramatic contrasts in black and white, O'Keeffe's subtle pastels, and Porter's fine-grained color photographs: Sense the special characteristics of light in the West. Each artist has seen their own image of the landscape. Out West, writers, artists, and photographers must use adjectives, colors, and lens stops unnecessary elsewhere. A whitewashed seventeenth-century mission

church wall, the weathered boards of a pioneer cabin, or some crenellated peaks reflected in a shimmering lake—everything takes on a unique vibrancy in western light.

John Muir, effusive in describing the special light, christened the Sierra the "Range of Light," with its rich, pearl-gray snows and forest belts of blue and dark purple. He rejoiced "in its glorious floods of light, the white beams of the morning streaming through its passes, the noonday radiance on the crystal rocks, the flush of the alpenglow, and the irised spray of countless waterfalls." Powell, adding to the forms, color, and changing light, described "sounds that span the diapason from tempest to tinkling raindrops, from cataract to bubbling fountain."[4]

When he launched the *Emma Dean* and three companion boats into the Green River on May 24, 1869, Major Powell began a voyage of original exploration. One hundred days later, he and five companions had descended the Colorado River through the Grand Canyon. It marked the beginning of a career recording the West for the U.S. Geological Survey and defending it against economic exploitation. In his *Exploration of the Colorado River and Its Canyons,* magnificently illustrated with Thomas Moran's paintings and John K. Hillers' photographs, Powell presented the thrilling and hazardous adventure, complemented with rich geological and ethnographic details.

Many have succeeded and, indeed, triumphed in capturing the beauty of the Grand Canyon and other western scenic wonders. A pedantic tome of a geographic-social-cultural-historical nature could be filled to overflowing with early photographs, mammoth can-

△ *Hayden geological survey party in the Jackson Hole–Yellowstone area, 1872. Dr. Hayden, seated on the left (facing camera), trained as a medical doctor and served as a surgeon in the Civil War. In 1865 he was appointed professor of geology at the University of Pennsylvania, where he taught until 1872; in 1867 he began a twelve-year series of explorations and scientific investigations in the western territories. On his left is another member of the survey team, S. F. Hanks.*

△ President Wilson signed the
act creating the National Park
Service on August 25, 1916.

vasses, and inspired words from travelers who moved
across the terrain at Powell's recommended sedate pace.
Powell was privileged to be among the earliest explorers
who saw the dramatic scenery in the western United
States, and he realized how difficult it would be to faithfully convey its beauty to others: "The wonders of the
Grand Canyon cannot be adequately represented in
symbols of speech, nor by speech itself. The resources
of the graphic art are taxed beyond their powers in
attempting to portray its features. Language and illustration must fail."[5]

The National Park Idea Becomes Reality

Quite by coincidence, the Langford expedition through
Yellowstone occurred in the same year (1871) as Powell's
second trip down the Colorado. Nathaniel Langford's
articles, illustrated by Jackson and Moran and published
in *Scribner's Monthly,* provided a pictorial record of
Yellowstone country. For forty years the West had been
romanticized and falsified on the American continent
and abroad by novelists, travelers, painters, reporters,
speculators, the railroad industry, and Mormon prosely-
tizers. Powell and Langford corrected these misconcep-
tions by fact and illustration. With vigorous agitation
led by U.S. Geologist Ferdinand Hayden and others,
Congress was pressed to set aside Yellowstone as a "national park." Four hundred copies of Langford's articles,
illustrated with Moran woodcuts, were distributed to
Congress; Jackson's photographs and Moran's watercolors from life suddenly galvanized congressional committees.[6] Yellowstone was proclaimed the first national park
by an act of Congress on March 1, 1872.

What began with Yellowstone, "to be preserved for
the enjoyment of present and future generations,"
evolved into a complex system of natural wonders and
buildings. Yale University historian Robin W. Winks,
former chair of the Secretary of the Interior's Advisory
Board on National Parks, Historic Sites, Buildings, and
Monuments, concluded: *The national symbols people
choose to preserve – the visible reminders of how a nation
came to be what it is – serve as useful keys to understanding
values.… Societies, after all, choose to protect the objects
and emblems of their collective pride; great scenic wonders,
natural preserves, and game parks do not survive by accident.*[7] "National Parks are the best idea we ever had,"
Wallace Stegner observed. "Absolutely American, absolutely democratic, they reflect us at our best rather
than our worst."[8]

In 1992, the national park system included 357 areas,
with only 50 formally designated as "national parks."
The variety of titles assigned to these places represents
the diversity of resources and more than a dash of the
American penchant for political ingenuity. Some explanation of the terminology may be helpful.[9]

National parks generally cover large geographic areas.
In theory, a park contains a variety of resources and en-
compasses sufficient land or water to ensure adequate
protection of those resources. Some confusion sets in
with making a distinction between parks and *national
monuments.* The Antiquities Act of 1906 authorized the
president to proclaim areas "monuments"; *parks* are established by an act of Congress. An Executive Order in
1933 transferred 63 national monuments and military
sites from the jurisdiction of the Forest Service and the

War Department to the National Park Service. This action was a major step in the development of today's national park system, which includes areas of historical as well as scenic and scientific importance. The NPS makes the distinction that a national monument preserves at least one nationally significant resource, is usually smaller than a national park, and frequently lacks a diversity of attractions.

National historic sites and *national historical parks* commemorate persons, events, or activities and preserve places important in the nation's history. *Parks* are usually bigger and more complex than *sites.* There are additional categories to protect militarily significant sites: *national military parks, national battlefield parks, national battlefield sites,* and *national battlefields.*

More recently, certain resources have been protected by the designation *national preserve, national lakeshore, national seashore, national river,* or *wild and scenic riverway. National parkways,* two sites for *national parks for the performing arts,* and *national recreation areas* address other special resources. *National memorials* may have different designations; for example, Lincoln's home in Springfield, Illinois, is a national historic *site,* but the Lincoln Memorial in Washington is a national *memorial.* Finally, there are national recreation areas both inside the park system and outside the system separately administered by the National Forest Service, U.S. Department of Agriculture. All of these areas are bound together by over a century of landscape preservation; the familiar NPS shield at each entrance station (excluding non-NPS recreation areas) and the distinctive signage lettering–tan on a brown background–guide visitors to extraordinary experiences and discoveries.

The Architects and Builders

The National Geographic Society and the Grosvenor family have long championed the beauty of the West in the pages of the *National Geographic Magazine.* Gilbert H. Grosvenor became captivated by the importance of conservation as a result of a trip to the High Sierra in 1915 in the company of Stephen Mather, and the April 1916 issue of the magazine was devoted to "The Land of the Best."

Grosvenor acknowledged that Europe offered splen-did castles and cathedrals, but he suggested that the American tourist could do better by crossing the United States rather than the Atlantic: "In that architecture which is voiced in the glorious temples of the sequoia grove and in the castles of the Grand Canyon … there is an appeal that the mere handiwork of man, splendid though it may be, can never rival."[10]

Seventy years later, Grosvenor's words are readily contested. Harmony with the landscape through constructions of timber, stone, and adobe present valid attractions, albeit distinct from Europe's "splendid architecture," and have become part of the heritage of the western national parks. This handiwork relates people to the natural setting and creates a distinct sense of place.

The spirit of Old Faithful Inn, Paradise Inn, and the Ahwahnee Hotel define Yellowstone, Mount Rainier, and Yosemite as much as their geysers, glaciers, and granite canyons. Indeed, these concessioner-built hotels *are* spectacular architecture. The parks contain many other buildings, distinct individually or collectively for their architectural qualities. Ranger stations and entrance gates, concessioner stores and service buildings, interpretive structures, and utility complexes are grouped in recognized historic districts throughout the parks. The buildings represent the energies and ingenuity of architects and landscape designers, park service employees, and anonymous artisans.

There are many sources of historic architecture in the western national parks. Native Americans built cliff dwellings and pueblo villages. Spaniards arrived in the mid-sixteenth century and echoed prehistoric traditions by building in the stuccoed adobe-and-timber style that still characterizes the Southwest. During the era of Lewis and Clark, Jim Bridger, and Jedidiah Smith, missionaries and settlers headed west to convert the Indian and the land, and remnants of their legacy can still be seen in churches, cabins, and forts.

The earliest architectural landmarks in the western landscape were there long before European explorers, missionaries, and traders arrived. No one knows precisely when people first drifted into the canyon country of the Colorado Plateau. Known by the Navajo name *Anasazi,* the Ancient Ones, they probably arrived during the third and fourth centuries B.C. Centered around the

▷ *Six-horse stagecoaches at Yellowstone's Lake Hotel, around 1900. The classical porticos were added to a simple frame building to impress park visitors.*

Four Corners area of Utah, Colorado, New Mexico, and Arizona, the Anasazi keyed their lives to the rhythm of an unkind climate. A civilization emerged, with the first New World cities of pit houses, pueblos, cliff dwellings, and cave dwellings.

The Anasazi hunted, they gathered, they made intricate baskets and artful pots, they farmed and practiced irrigation, prospering for over six centuries. They developed complex structures made of sandstone blocks, saplings, and grasses covered by a layer of mud plaster. Free-standing pueblos in Chaco Canyon and the cliff dwellings at Mesa Verde and Bandelier preserve remains of the culture that mysteriously collapsed and dispersed in the thirteenth century with no written records left behind to offer explanation. We can only speculate that changing climates, overuse of resources, disease, and famine led to the abandonment of these buildings that so exemplified harmony with their environment.

Centuries later, the Anasazi designs were reinterpreted for modern use. Settlers, as well as designers hired by the railroads and the National Park Service, improved on the materials but copied the original forms. Thanks to the guiding hand of architect Mary Jane Colter at Grand Canyon and archaeologist Jesse Nusbaum and his wife, Aileen, at Mesa Verde, the sandstone blocks, timber vigas, and mud mortar of the Anasazi again offer inspiration to today's visitor.

William Jackson Downing, a nurseryman and self-taught landscape designer, had a strong influence on architects' appreciation for building in harmony with the landscape. During a brief career centered in the Hudson River Valley, in the mid-1800s, his works and writing stressed the importance of site. He based his designs and philosophy on romantic views of nature, and he achieved a satisfactory compromise between homes in the country and city. Particularly fond of the English picturesque, his designs were quickly adopted as aesthet-

ically pleasing homes for the common people of the United States.[11] His two books, *Cottage Residences* (1842) and *The Architecture of Country Houses* (1850), became trendsetters in his lifetime, celebrated in both the United States and Europe.[12]

By the time Downing's *Architecture of Country Houses* was published, he was a widely known and highly respected spokesperson for American taste. His singular achievement was in creating and widely disseminating a new architectural sensibility and style in America. Paradoxically, he disdained the American frontier architecture style as symbolic of an uncivilized society and relied instead on established European styles, particularly English and Swiss traditions.

The national mood favored a return to nature, having been inspired by the mid-nineteenth-century transcendentalists; it provided a suitable climate for an early appreciation of Rustic work. Rustic summer houses and garden furniture were popular along the eastern seaboard from the 1830s to the 1860s. Summer resorts in coastal and, later, mountainous areas also adopted the style. Local artisans in Appalachia experimented with slender hardwoods and rhododendron, creating rustic garden furniture that later evolved into tables, cupboards, and decorative objects. Downing's philosophies, his picturesque designs for cottage residences, and the artisan twig-and-branch furniture inspired a style of architecture and decoration suited to the growing appreciation of the wilderness and the increased leisure activities of the post–Civil War period.

By the turn of the century, the American architectural movement and public taste were undergoing another shift. A strengthening of academic eclecticism provided revivals – Gothic, Romanesque, Tudor, and Jacobean – expressed at the international expositions in Chicago (1893), Buffalo (1901), New Orleans (1904), and San Francisco (1915). The romantic and arts-and-crafts move-

▷ *Old Faithful Inn and Geyser. The Rustic architecture is perfectly harmonious with the natural spectacle. A swimming pool, since removed, is visible at lower right.*

ments were rejected in favor of grandiose architectural pretensions. The picturesque Rustic style and its principles of integrating people and nature became a legacy practiced by a small handful of clients and architects.[13]

The Railroaders

The railroads had linked the eastern and western United States by the end of the nineteenth century, and the frontier was closed. The resort builders – railroaders seeking customers – wanted to create comfortable accommodations set amid unusual, beautiful scenery. They built fantasies of log and stone in settings where visitors would remember not only the mountains, geysers, and canyons but the special buildings as well. They wanted visitors to send postcards home, describing their vacations and recommending these remarkable experiences.

The transcontinental railroads brought a new and different stream of visitors to the parks. Seizing the opportunity to carry tourists on their railroad mainlines, the railroad builders played a seminal role in developing the parks by promoting park excursions and accommodations. The railroaders' standards were linked to the comforts and traditions of European travel. Success for their investments required quality development in the wilderness, and they selected talented architectural designers to create elegant hotels, administrative offices, and stations. Their standard of achievement went beyond profits and was matched with designs that competed with Old World attractions. A measure of convenience and luxury was deemed necessary to soften the long, arduous trip west. Several of the Rustic hotels that were to become synonymous with the parks appeared within a decade.

The changes in accommodations introduced by the railroaders can be seen in the Lake Hotel, built on the shore of Yellowstone Lake in 1890 by the Yellowstone Park Company, a subsidiary of the Northern Pacific Railroad. A portentous greeting for stagecoach parties was offered by the symmetrical facade with three projecting porches supported by Ionic columns. Without much supervision from the Department of the Interior, the design ignored the rustic, western setting. More typically, early park concessioners built what their contemporaries offered visitors in other remote settings: either log buildings or simple frame hotels.

Robert C. Reamer designed Old Faithful Inn (1903) and the New Canyon Hotel (1910) for the Yellowstone Park Company. Charles Whittlesey, architect for the Santa Fe Railroad's El Tovar (1905) at Grand Canyon's South Rim, created an eclectic design with Swiss Chalet and Norwegian Villa influence. The Fred Harvey Company hired Mary Jane Colter, in whom they gained a creative designer skilled at interpreting Native American, Pueblo, and Spanish Colonial styles.

Under the determined guidance of the Great Northern Railway's president, Louis W. Hill, several Rustic hotels and a chain of mountain chalets in harmony with the alpine setting at Glacier National Park were designed by Thomas D. McMahon and Samuel Bartlett. Hill's Swiss-style hotels and chalets (an "Alps in America" theme) opened between 1913 and 1915, promoting his railroad line and proudly proclaiming their rusticity. The soaring lobbies framed by massive timbers, the huge stone fireplaces, and the informal layouts with generous public spaces added to the ambience.

◁ *William West Durant at Camp Pine Knot, Raquette Lake, New York, 1884. The private vacation retreats that Durant built in the Adirondacks were designed for the very wealthy. The rustic creations were quickly heralded in travel guidebooks and attracted tourists. Railroaders, industrialists, and bankers appreciated how appropriate this architecture would be in the setting of the western landscape.*

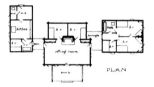

△ *Sketch of a "Log House in the Adirondacks" from William S. Wicks'* LOG CABINS: HOW TO BUILD AND FURNISH THEM *(1889). Wicks emphasized harmony between a building and its natural setting: "Indeed the structure should be the outgrowth of, and harmonize with the site, so that when your work is completed the structure shall be a new object added by the hand of man to perfect and beautify its surroundings."*

The inspiration for the Rustic architecture produced by the railroaders and their creative designers came from several sources. The primary source was the landscape, which offered materials long-used by indigenous peoples. The building forms and construction techniques adapted to the landscape were modified and refined by settlers bringing traditions from other places.

The railroaders and their designers could also draw on their exposure to the Rustic architecture in the Adirondack Mountains. The attractions of the region led Thomas C. Durant and his son, William West Durant, to develop a real estate and transportation venture in the 1870s. The younger Durant built progressively more adventurous enclaves of rustic buildings in remote forest and lake settings. Inspired by his European travels, he used local materials – logs and stone – and the skills of loggers and craftsmen to produce log structures with twig-and-branch embellishments and compatible furniture. Modest buildings evolved into ambitious complexes – massive lodges, guest cabins, staff housing, and support buildings – all later known as the Great Camps."[14]

Indigenous materials and vernacular forms, a desire to escape the monotony and crowds of eastern and midwestern cities, and the concept that natural settings could influence architecture took hold in the western national parks. Architects who could create a romantic image and sense of place found a welcome in the adventurous spirit of the railroaders. In the mountainous, forested Sierra and Rockies, logs and stone were used for private retreats and resort hotels; in the Southwest, native adobe and pine logs in Pueblo and Spanish Colonial styles were revived. Log hotels with soaring lobbies and a variety of Rustic spatial layouts greeted guests at Yellowstone, Glacier, and the Grand Canyon's North Rim.

National Park Service Rustic Architecture

After more than forty years of mixed administrative responsibility for the early western parks, the formation of the National Park Service in 1916 quickly produced a design ethic. Today, these parks contain a rich architectural legacy: The distinctive NPS Rustic-style buildings are set among the remnants of various legacies from earlier times and building initiatives.

Modern structures in the parks were built of readily available materials, using local construction techniques. Pioneer log cabins and rough frame shelters offered protection and functional use. Styles and interpretations reflected builders' needs and ingenuity. The new settlers followed the examples at hand with a keen eye to what fit well with the terrain and what other people had built before. Corner-notching skills were proven by the Humeses on the Olympic Peninsula and the Mormons

at Fruita schoolhouse at Capitol Reef. Hubbell Trading
Post was made of rubble stone and adobe, and the
Mormon Fort at Pipe Spring carried out eastern traditions of cut stone with Greek Revival details. Menors
Ferry Station on the Snake River at Grand Teton is a
rare example of an elegantly proportioned clapboard-siding structure, with the form and scale of a Greek temple.

Inholdings and leaseholds for private vacation retreats
were permitted as compromises when park acreage was
assembled, sometimes given to senators and representatives influential in park issues. Their existence was trou-
blesome to the NPS founders and is sometimes still trou-
blesome. In Secretary Lane's Policy Directive of 1918, the
private holdings were cited for purchase or donation
with first priority to "isolated tracts in important scenic
areas."[15] The great distances from major population centers and long treks by rail and horseback limited the interest in securing such property for private use. Those
few that remain in Glacier, Grand Teton, Kings Canyon,
and elsewhere occupy extraordinary sites that eventually
will be acquired as park lands through the purchase of
life leases. The abandoned ranches at Grand Teton, the
William Allen White complex at Rocky Mountain, and
the vacation houses on the shores of Lake McDonald at
Glacier and Lake Crescent on the Olympic Peninsula are
reminders of this vanishing privilege.

At the time the National Park Service was founded,
there were fourteen national parks. Settler holdings acquired at the time of a park's designation were incorporated into the new boundaries, providing examples of
early vernacular buildings, commercial structures, and

visitor accommodations. Some have been restored, but
many others have slowly decayed under the effects of
time, weather, neglect, and vandalism.

Before 1916, park administration was divided between
the Department of the Interior and the U.S. Army. At
Mount Rainier, Crater Lake, Glacier, and Mesa Verde,
simple log cabins, frame buildings, and tent platforms
satisfied park civilian administrative needs. A U.S. Army
military outpost produced a full complement of structures at Fort Yellowstone. In 1885, the War Department
authorized the army to protect Yellowstone against
poachers, vandalism, and illegal grazing; troops came
in 1886 and stayed for thirty years. Fort Yellowstone
became an important administrative complex with an
array of buildings similar to military installations at the
Presidio and West Point. Imposing stone or wood-frame
residences, stables, hospitals, and offices of neoclassical
and early midwestern Prairie styles were constructed
by an organization concerned primarily with park protection and administration. The army had no direct
interest in the landscape, and this was echoed in its
utilitarian architecture.[16]

The partnership between private sources and the
National Park Service for providing visitor accommodations began with the earliest parks. In fact, some private
facilities existed prior to park founding. It was assumed
that private groups and individuals would provide facilities and services for visitor enjoyment. Stephen Mather
strongly supported this policy of granting leases and permits on park lands for visitor accommodations. Fortunately, Mather retained control of the overall setting and

built up a staff of competent landscape engineers to carry out the building projects.

The first overnight lodging for travelers in the parks came about when local entrepreneurs organized tours. An elegant survivor of this era, now restored, is the Hotel Wawona at Yosemite, which opened its doors in 1879. The Vermont origins of the builders are recalled by clapboard siding, wide porches, and Victorian ginger-bread. The hotel has survived to today, but fire was a factor in the fate of many early wood-frame and log hotels remote from fire-fighting apparatus.

The concessioner-run tent camps were elegant com-plexes of striped canvas on wooden tent platforms. The Wylie Camping Company at Yellowstone and the Curry Company at Yosemite provided tent camps for stage-coach-touring park visitors. A few examples of this old-style camping still remain at Yosemite and Grand Teton.

Paradise Inn opened at Mount Rainier in 1917, the NPS' first year of operation. NPS director Stephen Mather had urged a group of Seattle and Tacoma busi-nessmen to build the massive, Rustic lodge, framed in Alaska red cedar. Assertive with their design philosophy, Mather and his assistant, Horace Albright, began to shape the future of visitor facilities by guiding conces-sioners and NPS facilities toward a distinct style that dur-ing the next twenty years became known as NPS Rustic.

The NPS launched a "See America First" campaign. They received support from the National Geographic Society, the American Civic Association, the General Federation of Women's Clubs, and had articles run in the *Saturday Evening Post*. Railroads and their subsidi-

aries were encouraged to accelerate travel promotion, expand existing hotels, and build new ones. Mather was strongly in favor of giving monopoly rights to conces-sioners for entire parks and encouraged the removal of "inappropriate" tourist accommodations.

A letter from Secretary of the Interior Frank K. Lane to Mather on May 13, 1918, stated a policy of providing for the Park Service's Rustic style: "In the construction of roads, trails, buildings, and other improvements, par-ticular attention must be devoted always to the harmo-nizing of these improvements in the landscape."[17]

The letter outlines the need for qualified staff "who either possess a knowledge of landscape architecture or have a proper appreciation of the aesthetic value of park lands." Lane instructed that "improvements will be car-ried out in accordance with a preconceived plan devel-oped with special reference to the preservation of the landscape" and suggested a variety of facilities for the traveler: "Low-priced camps operated by concessioners should be maintained, as well as comfortable and even luxurious hotels wherever the volume of travel warrants the establishment of these classes of accommodations."

Encouraged by Mather's enthusiasm, the NPS brought forth the first tentative Rustic work. Early utility build-ings of exposed frame construction, simple entrance-gate structures of log and stone, and administrative buildings were nonintrusive, although not of exceptional design. Gradually, refinements evolved. The Ranger's Club at Yosemite would be a model for later buildings. Modeled after a Swiss chalet, it was designed by Charles Sumner and personally funded by Mather. The building's steeply

▷ William W. Wylie was an enterprising school superinten- dent from Bozeman, Montana, who saw an opportunity to com- pete with established hotel and transportation companies for tourist trade. His "Wylie Way"

campsites, with gaily striped canvas tents on wooden plat- forms (here at Yellowstone's Upper Geyser Basin), offered informal, low-cost accommoda- tion. The appeal of the tent complexes gradually succumbed to the public's desire for com- fort—and indoor plumbing.

◁ Leidig's Hotel, built in 1869 near the foot of Glacier Point, is an example of the first tourist accommodations in Yosemite Valley. This was one of the pri- vate facilities that existed before Yosemite National Park was founded. At the time, Congress had denied appropriations for protecting and administering the early parks, and it was unthinkable that the federal government would operate visitor facilities. The hotel was torn down in 1888.

pitched roof, dormer windows, massive stone fireplace, and log elements exemplified Mather's feeling for the proper architecture in western mountain parks.

Architecture congenial with its setting soon began to infuse NPS designs. The creator of some of the park's finest concessions architecture, Gilbert Stanley Under- wood, was a thirty-three-year-old graduate of Harvard University's Master of Architecture program when he re- turned to Los Angeles in 1923 to establish an architec- tural practice.[18] It was his good fortune that two old friends, Paul P. Kiessig and Daniel P. Hull, held influen- tial positions in the NPS. Stephen Mather had created a professional staff to guide the service's building program in 1918 and, in 1920, Hull was appointed chief landscape engineer with Kiessig as his assistant. Hull promoted Mather's preferred style for nonintrusive structures, su- pervising design of administration buildings at Sequoia and Grand Canyon and a ranger station at Yellowstone Lake. Overburdened with the ambitious NPS building program, Hull turned to Underwood to design the Yosemite Administration Building and Post Office, and the buildings were completed in 1924.

The Union Pacific Railroad had plans to promote tourism in southern Utah. These included a motorcoach Loop Tour from Cedar City to Zion National Park, Bryce Canyon, Cedar Breaks National Monument, and the North Rim of the Grand Canyon. Competing with the Southern Pacific Railroad, the Union Pacific estab- lished the Utah Parks Company to implement their ambitious plans for tourist accommodations along the tour route. Underwood applied for the commission at Hull's suggestion and began work on hotels and other facilities in 1923.

Developing his Rustic style first at Zion National Park, Underwood produced buildings that are among the finest in the parks. Bryce Canyon Lodge, opened in 1924, combined local stone, logs, upper walls of shake siding, and a soaring roof with shingles laid in undulat- ing courses. Rustic log cabins added at Zion and Bryce were strongly reminiscent of Adirondack buildings in form, massing, and use of materials. The Adirondack Great Camps are echoed in the use of carefully selected peeled logs skillfully joined with corner notching, stone bases and fireplaces, casement sash, bent twigs, and sturdy log porches.

In the midst of Underwood's Utah Parks Company work, Mather was busy realizing his goal of building a modern hotel in Yosemite Valley. The newly created Yosemite Park and Curry Company selected an isolated forest site, far from the crowded valley, with a backdrop of the Royal Arches. Underwood was assigned the Ahwahnee Hotel commission.

Underwood's triumph, completed in 1927, incorpo- rated a modern steel and concrete frame sheathed in indigenous granite boulders. It was complemented by concrete formed and tinted to give the appearance of rough-cut redwood siding and beams. The multiwinged building has sweeping horizontal lines emphasized by low, hipped shingle roofs and is buttressed by massive piers and chimneys of cyclopean granite boulders. Rich Indian motifs and Art Deco forms abound in decorative patterns repeated on the floors and walls and woven into linen curtains.

Underwood's last major Rustic hotel in the national parks was Grand Canyon Lodge, built on the canyon's North Rim for the Utah Parks Company. The present

△ The proposed site of the Ahwahnee Hotel in Yosemite Valley, May 1926. From left to right, road engineers Taylor and Austin, NPS Director Stephen Mather, architect Gilbert Stanley Underwood, and Yosemite Park and Curry Company's Donald Tresidder. The Ahwahnee was to be a luxury hotel with 100 rooms, generous public spaces, and a 500-seat dining room. It represented the most ambitious NPS building project to date.

hotel, opened in 1932, replaced the original, which was destroyed by fire in 1928. The earlier design, also perched on the very rim of the canyon, was a dramatic contrast to the Ahwahnee Hotel. Rebuilt, its battered and buttressed stone walls rise up as a natural extension of the canyon. A low-pitched, shingled roof is stained dark green to match the surrounding forest. A U-shaped plan forms an entry courtyard that merges with a narrow lobby opening on different levels to a solarium and spacious dining room. The visitor is dazzled by light streaming through walls of plate glass, and the view stretches 85 miles to the south, past the canyon's South Rim to the peaks in the San Francisco range. Underwood complemented the lodge with log cabins similar to earlier designs at Zion and Bryce.

When the Ahwahnee Hotel and Grand Canyon Lodge were completed, they clearly demonstrated Underwood's versatility as a Rustic-style designer. Cleverly covering steel trusses with logs, and toning concrete to imitate redwood, Underwood was a master of natural materials and ingenious simulations. His informal plans, varied and asymmetrical building massing, deeply recessed openings, and massive stone pillars and fireplaces, all sheltered by shallow-pitched shingled roofs, produced a new architecture for the national parks: nonintrusive and harmonious.

Another talented designer employed by the NPS was Herbert Maier. Through the support of the Laura Spelman Rockefeller Memorial Foundation, Maier designed a series of museums that all reflected sensitive siting and inventive use of form and material. In 1926, he planned a museum for Yosemite with a lower floor of massive stone and concrete offset by an upper floor of peeled log framing and shingle cover. A versatile young architect, trained at the University of California (Berkeley), he designed the Pueblo-style Yavapai Point Museum at Grand Canyon in 1928.

Maier designed four museums at Yellowstone, which opened in 1929 and 1930. The modestly scaled one-story buildings (three of which remain today) were highly crafted examples of the Rustic style, using carefully selected boulders for lower walls, exposed log rafters, and wooden shingles. Maier showed versatility in the form and arrangement of interior spaces to serve administrative and visitor functions, while adhering to principles of unobtrusive massing. These burly buildings are a delight today for visitors who cluster at the indoor exhibits and on the outdoor patios. Eschewing routine adaptation of traditional log cabin models, Maier practiced the tenets of organic architecture: each building is precisely placed on its site, uses local materials, and displays unique massing and spatial planning that are skillfully subordinate to the natural surroundings.

In the Southwest, Mary Jane Colter's projects for the Fred Harvey Company explored Indian pueblo forms using local sandstone, timber *vigas* (peeled log beams), and earth-colored adobe. Her design dexterity is demon-

strated in a collection of buildings at the Grand Canyon, ranging from Hopi House to the medieval interiors of Hermit's Rest to the Kiva room and sand paintings at the Watchtower.

Superintendent Jesse Nusbaum and his wife, Aileen, began a construction program in 1921 at Mesa Verde based on ethnological research of Hopi pueblo construction. The buildings are particularly important as the first NPS structures built primarily on a cultural theme in a cultural park. In a letter to the NPS director, Nusbaum explained a design rationale that eventually produced fourteen red sandstone structures: *In working out the plans and elevations, we have drawn on the present architecture of the Hopi Indians for practically all details of construction.... This type of construction seems the most logical.... The materials for the most part are right on the ground and easily available. The type will not detract one iota from the ancient dwellings which abound in this Park, both in caves and on the Mesas, but will help preserve the Indian atmosphere which the ruins and environment create.*

The collection of structures at Mesa Verde provides a richly detailed example of local architecture as part of

the interpretive experience. Along with Pueblo forms, Spanish Colonial themes are interwoven with the use of log colonnades, bolster blocks, adze-finished woodwork, handmade furniture, and pierced-tin lighting fixtures. Other complexes in the Southwest – at Bandelier, Petrified Forest, and Casa Grande – continued this adaptation of Pueblo and Spanish Colonial themes.

The first three directors of the National Park Service – Stephen Mather (1916–29), Horace Albright (1929–33), and Arno Cammerer (1933–40) – established and guided the policies of Rustic park architecture with consistent dedication. They assured a diverse body of work by seeking suitable sites for construction, creating or appointing appropriate concessioner companies, selecting architects, and approving designs. Nonintrusive and compatible, the architecture these directors supported evolved gradually until work was curtailed during World War II.

The staffers appointed by Mather in 1918 grew as funding appropriations increased for building roads, administrative and service buildings, museums, and lodges. Under chief architect Thomas C. Vint, the San Fran-

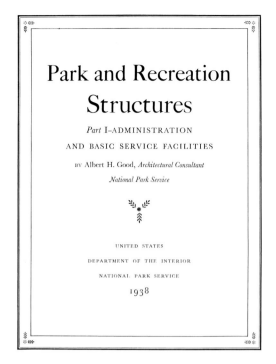

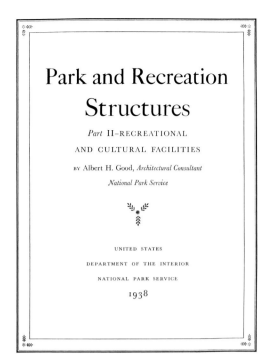

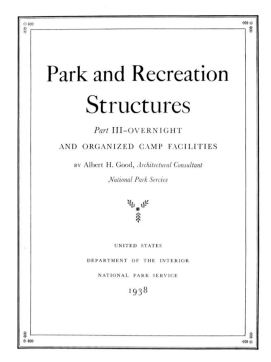

Park and Recreation
Structures

Part I–ADMINISTRATION
AND BASIC SERVICE FACILITIES

BY Albert H. Good, *Architectural Consultant*
National Park Service

UNITED STATES
DEPARTMENT OF THE INTERIOR
NATIONAL PARK SERVICE
1938

Park and Recreation
Structures

Part II–RECREATIONAL
AND CULTURAL FACILITIES

BY Albert H. Good, *Architectural Consultant*
National Park Service

UNITED STATES
DEPARTMENT OF THE INTERIOR
NATIONAL PARK SERVICE
1938

Park and Recreation
Structures

Part III–OVERNIGHT
AND ORGANIZED CAMP FACILITIES

BY Albert H. Good, *Architectural Consultant*
National Park Service

UNITED STATES
DEPARTMENT OF THE INTERIOR
NATIONAL PARK SERVICE
1938

△ *Title pages from the three-volume* PARK AND RECREATION STRUCTURES, *published in 1938. The philosophy that it presented—in text, photographs, and building details—served as a reference for park architectural projects across the country.*

cisco NPS field office became the headquarters for a period of dramatic park development. Vint sought as staff members people who had a sensitivity to the special needs of the parks. Trained architects and landscape architects were recruited to work alongside untrained but talented apprentices. Vint achieved high levels of cooperation among his staff by recognizing talent and assigning it to appropriate projects. Although working with smaller budgets than Underwood and Maier, Vint's associates were continually experimenting with new building forms, construction methods, and materials. The combination of sensitive leadership and talented, dedicated staff prospered in this era of labor-intensive projects.

The National Park Service proved a competent initiator of Rustic architecture under President Roosevelt's New Deal construction programs. With a confirmed design philosophy and trained professional cadre, Horace Albright capitalized on the opportunity by combining the president's emergency programs with the needs of the parks. The Projects Works Administration (PWA) and Civilian Conservation Corps (CCC) provided both funds and manpower for the NPS' greatest era of construction.

The work was directed by Albert Good from his Washington office and Herbert Maier, director of the Rocky Mountain District. Eventually, three million youths and three billion dollars flowed into the CCC. Many structures built under Good and Maier's supervision are now listed on or are determined eligible for the National Register of Historic Places. Entrance stations, road markers, benches, drinking fountains, and comfort stations all expressed the Rustic principles, as did the administration buildings, employee residences, community buildings, and lodges. Design interpretations were carefully selected for local site materials and regional influences. For administration buildings, the choice of logs

and massive boulders set against Mount Rainier was as apt as the adobe-and-stone buildings at Bandelier; the stone base, logs, and steeply pitched shingle roof at Crater Lake fit into the environment as agreeably as the Spanish Colonial design for the NPS Western Regional Office at Santa Fe.

In 1935, the NPS produced a guide for park architecture: *Park Structures and Facilities*. The original work proved so successful that an expanded edition appeared in 1938 as the three-volume *Park and Recreation Structures*. NPS director Arno B. Cammerer's introductory words applied Mather's guiding principles: *In any area in which the preservation of the beauty of Nature is a primary purpose, every modification of the natural landscape, whether it be construction of a road or erection of a shelter, is an intrusion. A basic objective of those who are entrusted with the development of such areas for the human uses for which they are established is, it seems to me, to hold these intrusions to a minimum and so to design them that, besides being attractive to look upon, they appear to belong to and be a part of their settings.*[19]

The Far West

Olympic National Park

Of all the national parks, the most diversified in character and climate is Olympic. Here you will find seacoast and mountain peak, rain forest and glacier, and an unbelievable abrupt change of weather pattern. The western side of the park has the wettest winter climate in the United States, with nearly twelve feet of precipitation annually. The eastern side is the driest part of the Pacific Coast outside of Southern California.

NATIONAL PARKS OF THE WEST

Olympic National Park occupies two sections of the Olympic Peninsula in the northwestern corner of Washington State. The land rises gently from the waters of the Pacific, the Strait of Juan de Fuca, and Puget Sound, then steepens abruptly into a tight, circular cluster of peaks. The summit of Mount Olympus rises to 7,965 feet. Below the jagged peaks and timberline, a network of thirteen rivers threads its way out to sea level. Rain forests, thick stands of conifers, deep-cut rivers, mountain streams pouring through alpine meadows, and lakes and shorelines provide an ecological haven worthy of its recent designation as a World Biosphere Park.

The park is divided into two parts, a 50-mile strip of shoreline and the inland block of forest, valley, meadow, and mountain. Roads radiate inland from the encircling U.S. Highway 101, following drainages to trailheads that access 600 miles of hiking trails. The wet, western area contains up-and-down country, full of peaks and ridges, where moisture-laden air from the Pacific Ocean becomes trapped; the dry, eastern side is marked by a series of peaks separated by short, steep river canyons.

Discovery and Settlement

The Olympic Peninsula, and especially its mountain core, has always been a remote, isolated place. Although less than 100 miles from Seattle, this wilderness for years defied settlement. Originally, Native American tribes populated the coast and peninsular lowlands.

Early reports of this region date back to late sixteenth-century explorers. Spanish and English mariners, including Captain James Cook, sailed these waters seeking a Northwest Passage to connect the Atlantic and Pacific oceans. Russian expeditions joined the British at the end of the eighteenth century in the pursuit of fur. At the same time, American expeditions were organized to explore the coast. The mysterious mountainous interior of the peninsula lured trappers and traders in the first half of the 1800s. After hearing reports from the Lewis and Clark expedition, the Hudson's Bay Company and U.S. ventures became interested in the area.

The first organized and publicized accounts of general public travel in the Olympic Range occurred in the late 1800s. Several parties crossed the peninsula, and their exploits were widely circulated in the regional and national

Overleaf: The ever-present pyramidal form of Mount Rainier as seen along the Road to Paradise.

▷ *Snowmelt-charged waters of the Elwha River.*

▷ Set at the edge of a meadow against a tree line, Humes Ranch Cabin is one of the few remaining homestead structures intact on the Olympic Peninsula. The oldest cabin in Olympic National Park, it is a solitary, one-story structure of log construction with a cedar-shake roof.

△ Humes Ranch Cabin. Original farming implements on the porch steps and log walls recall the Humes family homestead near the Elwha River.

△ Originally built in 1900 and restored in 1980, the Humes Ranch Cabin displays precisely cut dovetail corner joints and hemp chinking.

press. A resolve quickly emerged that the unspoiled mountains and wilderness should be preserved as a national park.

A checkered history of federal management began in 1897, when President McKinley established the Olympic Forest Reserve. After forty argumentative years, during which the region passed through various identities, it became established as Olympic National Park (1938). Administration shifted between the Department of Agriculture and the Department of the Interior. The park has fluctuated from its initial 615,000 acres down to a low of 300,000 acres in 1915 and back to its present 908,692 acres. Boundaries have been adjusted a half dozen times, with the coastal strip only added in 1953.

Struggles with lumbering interests account for most of the park's difficulties. Proponents for preserving the wilderness prevailed, arguing that creating a national park would yield long-term benefits to the entire country and outweigh the short-term benefits to the local economy. But the fight to save the forests became a pro-

tracted battle, moving in and out of congressional committees, engaging the president's cabinet, and even drawing President Franklin D. Roosevelt to Port Angeles, Washington, in 1937 in an attempt to settle the disputed issues. The park was legislated into existence in 1938, and attempts to alter its public domain protection status were rejected during the war years and again in later years when local congressional representatives renewed the issue.

Historic Structures

Discovering the historic structures in Olympic National Park may involve an automobile trip to a specific resort, a long drive to a remote trailhead, or the serendipitous discovery of a shelter, cabin, or chalet along a hiking trail. Because of natural deterioration and park administration actions, all the nineteenth-century structures in the park have vanished. The twentieth-century buildings, retaining their integrity in stunning settings, are precious cultural resources.

◁ *Michael's Cabin was rebuilt in the 1970s, preserving the original rectangular plan. The cabin has log walls and saddle-notched corner joints, a shake roof, and a porch that parallels the roof ridge. Gable ends are of split shakes, and the interior has exposed pole rafters and purlins with long roof shakes spanning the purlins.*

◁ *Michael's Cabin. Built in 1937, this fine example of a homesteader's cabin is a reminder of the self-sufficiency required in the remote Olympic Peninsula interior. The cabin is located about a mile north of the Humes Cabin, and a mile closer to the Whiskey Bend trailhead.*

The relatively few examples of historic structures that remain represent an interpretive resource for the history of Olympic National Park. Insights into the park's identity can be found at the Humes Cabin (1900), the Park Headquarters (1940), and the buildings that were put up either by early settlers, through recreation development, or by depression-era relief programs. Backcountry trails and shelters, private chalets, lakeside and hot springs resorts, housekeeping cabins, and auto campgrounds on lakes and streams—all had their day and left their mark. They provided a certain level of safety and comfort for people who wanted to venture cautiously into the wilderness places.[1]

When the Forest Service (USFS) developed trails, shelters, and chalets on the peninsula, it promoted the public's early interest and participation in the backcountry, which inspired the popular support essential to the creation of Olympic National Park. The frontcountry lake shore, coastal beach, hot springs resort, and campgrounds also attracted large numbers of visitors, who were exposed to a very different version of the wilderness experience. Under USFS and NPS supervision, work relief programs such as the Civilian Conservation Corps, dedicated to expanding and improving park facilities, strengthened the appeal of both the frontcountry and backcountry. The National Park Service summarized the dualism of the popular, more accessible portions of the park with the remote interior when it stated, "This increasingly popular sense of the need for wild and quiet places both supported and threatened the Olympic National Park resources it most highly respected."[2]

Olympic National Park historic structures show a remarkable consistency in materials and design. Whether this was conscious or accidental, private as well as public buildings were built on a scale and with materials appropriate for their surroundings. Dictated by the availability of local materials and labor, log or drop-channel siding, shingle or shake roofs, and small-pane wood-framed windows prevail. Locations respect rather than dominate sites. Widely differing objectives follow these themes,

▷ *Chris Morgenroth's home, built in 1905, was remodeled in 1937 by the NPS to serve as the Storm King Ranger Station. Presently unused and in need of repair, the cabin is one of the few buildings remaining in the park dating from the early days of federal administration. It retains much of its original design, materials, and workmanship— horizontal log walls with cross-notched corners on a post-and-pier foundation, double-hung sash windows on the lower floor, fixed sash in the two dormers, a generous porch on peeled-pole logs across the front of the cabin, and a cedar shake roof.*

▷ *Lake Quinault Lodge, outside the park boundary in the Olympic National Forest, was built in 1926. The shingle-clad lodge, with spacious ground-floor public rooms facing the lake, retains its 1920s ambience. Builders hauled materials 50 miles along dirt roads, worked 24 hours a day, and completed the lodge in 10 weeks. President Franklin D. Roosevelt, after a stay here in 1937, set in motion the process that established the national park and forest.*

from cabin to Forest Service shelter to private resort or chalet.

Although the NPS did not assume formal responsibility for the region until Olympic National Park was created in 1938, after that time it closely followed the widely disseminated NPS design guidelines laid out in *Park Structures and Facilities*. When the CCC, PWA, or WPA relief programs built new structures in the park, they followed NPS Rustic design principles both to minimize intrusions and "design them that, besides being attractive to look upon they appear to belong to and be a part of their settings."[3]

Humes Ranch Cabin

Will Humes, with a brother and a cousin, went to Washington State from New York seeking gold. Disappointed by their mining attempts, the Humes family nonetheless found the plentiful fish and game and good pasture land appealing. In 1900, Will and a third broth-er, Grant, built their log cabin. Will returned East in 1916, but Grant stayed on at the cabin until his death in 1934. Commenting on his reasons for remaining in that solitary, wet place, Grant wrote Will his observations from a 1928 visit to Seattle: "The life they lead has no attraction for me and I am glad to get back to the cool, green wood and the peace and quiet and beauty to be enjoyed there."

Grant's subsistence farming life was supplemented by guiding packing parties, including the first group ascent of Mount Olympus. Like their counterparts, the resourceful Adirondack guides, the Humes men developed a homestead that expanded into a complex of barns and sheds to lodge summer and fall packing parties. Gable roofed and rectangular in shape, the Humes Cabin is typical of early settler homestead residences. The builders turned to the streambeds and forests for their major building materials: stone for foundations, logs for the walls, and cedar-shake roofs. Window sash and dimensioned lumber might have come from the nearest lumber mill. Porches often were built across the cabin front to extend interior living space and provide shelter from the peninsula weather. Windows were used sparingly. Fireplaces were rare, and heat generally was provided by wood stoves with flue pipes extending through the roof. The gable roof has a welcoming hip-roofed porch supported by peeled poles. One can easily picture Grant Humes standing on the porch, a dog at his side, looking over a tarpaulin-covered collection of pack luggage as he prepared his guests for an adventurous trip along the mountain trails of the Elwha River.

◁ Olympic Hot Springs pool and cabins on Boulder Creek. Pack trains carried visitors to the natural hot springs — an 11-mile trip from Elwha.

△ Mrs. Janice Voorhies, the Low Divide Chalet manager's wife, on the porch of the log-framed main lodge in 1936. The complex was a 20-mile hike from road's end at North Fork and a part of the Olympic Chalet Company's chain of lodges and shelters in the interior wilderness of the park.

△ The Low Divide Chalet complex included a main lodge, built in late 1927, and a bathhouse added the following year. Five cabins were built nearby in 1929 and 1930. The Great Depression brought about the end of the Olympic Chalet Company, and the main lodge and cabins were destroyed by an avalanche in 1944.

Old Storm King Ranger Station

In the early 1890s, when Chris Morgenroth settled near the Bogachiel River close to the park's current western boundary, he was in the company of a dozen other homesteaders. When the Olympic Forest Reserve was created in 1897, the settlers' freedom to cut timber was restricted, and the lack of access roads ended many of their dreams. In 1905, Morgenroth joined the Forest Service, moved to a site near Barnes Point on Lake Crescent, and built a cabin.

The steeply pitched gable roof with two dormers, the generous window openings, and well-crafted construction suggest a greater sense of permanency than many other structures in the park. This was a residence for a family independent of the land. A slate stone fireplace, interior walls of knotty cedar, and tongue-and-groove flooring augmented the owner's comfortable lifestyle.

Resorts and Lodges

Beginning in the 1890s, vacationers spread across the peninsula and created a market for resort lodgings. The coastline, lake shorelines, hot springs, and remote valleys hosted the growing urban middle class seeking a wilderness experience. When the loop highway was completed, in 1931, older resorts expanded to accommodate the growing numbers of automobiles. Many early resorts were lost to fire, one to an avalanche, and at least two to levels of success that dictated near total replacement.

Although most of the early resort hotels bordering the shores of Lake Crescent are gone, two resort complexes dating from the lake's heyday in the Forest Reserve's first twenty years are still standing. Located at Barnes Point, Singer's Tavern (now the Lake Crescent Lodge) and Rosemary Inn both opened in 1915. Separated by only a few hundred yards of thick forest, the two resorts evoke the scale, setting, and landscaping of an earlier era.

Outside the park boundaries, on the south shore of Lake Quinault, the Quinault Lodge suggests the more elegant style of accommodations that was once available in the park. Located in the park interior, Sol Duc Hot Springs was a large resort for people drawn to the therapeutic waters. The original buildings were destroyed by fire four years after opening, and the modern replacement is of ordinary, functional design. Only one resort remains in the backcountry. A successful preservation story surrounds the Enchanted Valley Chalet, opened in 1931 and recently rebuilt by volunteers.

Lake Crescent Lodge

Twelve-mile-long Lake Crescent was one of the first sites in Olympic National Park to be developed as a resort area. About 20 miles west of Port Angeles, rough trails opened the lake in the early 1890s to travelers attracted by the scenery of surrounding 3,000-to-4,000-foot ridges and peaks. Plentiful lake trout, an impressive setting, and a chance to explore an edge of the rugged peninsula created a demand for tourist accommodations.

A rough log cabin hotel opened in 1891 and a steam launch, *The Lady of the Lake,* provided tours around the lake. A burgeoning resort area soon developed, with several hotels offering attractive lodgings, spacious and well-furnished public rooms, gardens, and recreation areas. Resorts like the Log Cabin Hotel, Fairholme, Marymere, Qui Si Sana, and the Lake Crescent Hotel were all built before World War II. All have since vanished, destroyed by fire or removed by the NPS.

Al Singer's lodge kept growing until 30 cottages complemented the main lodge. Modern motel accommodations were added in the 1950s. Guests arrived by ferry until 1922, when the first road around the lake's southern shore was completed. The Singers and later owners made improvements to the original buildings, eventually adding electricity and running water to the cabins. Today, the two-story shingled, wood-frame main lodge remains essentially unchanged. A wide verandah provides shelter for the entrance. The lobby and main public room's comfortable Arts-and-Crafts furniture, board-and-batten walls, bric-a-brac, and memorabilia on tables and walls provide a cozy greeting for travelers. A stone fireplace, with a mounted Roosevelt elk head above, warms the lodge on chilly days. Only five of the ten second-floor rooms sharing a common bath are open to the public, but they provide superb views of the lake, forests, and ridges.

Few lodges in the national park system have enjoyed the distinction of a president's visit. A party led by President Franklin D. Roosevelt, with cabinet officers, congressmen, Park Service officials, Washington State politi-

cal leaders, and prominent journalists, gathered at Lake Crescent Lodge in 1937 to reconcile differing opinions about whether or not a national park ought to be established. The Roosevelt charm, aided by a White House conference and a special message to Congress the following April, laid the groundwork for successful passage of the bill creating Olympic National Park.

Rosemary Inn

"Quaint" and "charming" describe the meadow setting of Rosemary Inn. The cabin names – Cara Mia, Dreamerie, Summerie, Dixie, Alabam, Honeysuckle, Silver Moon, and Red Wing – reflect Mrs. Rose Littleton's care and hospitality in creating this enclave, which she began in 1915. The fascination of Rosemary Inn lies in the timelessness of the sheltered setting and simple buildings, recalling the days of travel on unpaved roads through the peninsular rain forests.

Guests, arriving by ferry across Lake Crescent, were welcomed by a tall, rustic, peeled-pole gateway decorated with latticework and "Rosemary" in large, peeled-stick letters. Rows of canvas tents were arranged on either side of a meadow as lodgings. Over a period of five to fifteen years, cabins were built to replace the tents. Rose Littleton cultivated a large area along the meadow's edge, planting fruit trees, shrubs, and flower gardens.

Trellises were built and fountains were added to enhance the landscape design.

The visitor finds no coherent organization to the randomly sited cabins. Much of the delight in Rosemary Inn comes from the almost whimsical mixture of building forms, materials, and the sequence of charmingly named cabins. Two of the original buildings were of log construction; the others were wood framed. Remnants of the original groomed lawns and formal landscaping can be seen in the three stone-and-concrete fountains and an occasional exotic shrub. The best way to view the cabins is by strolling through the meadow toward the

◁ Rosemary Inn main lodge and cabins in the 1930s. The inn opened in 1914, but Mrs. Rose Littleton's building campaign continued into the 1930s. A local builder and craftsman, John Daum, constructed the complex that began with a small, wood-frame main lodge and grew to include the manager's residence, guest cabins, and an assortment of outbuildings.

▽ *The Rosemary Inn main lodge in the mid-1980s. In the late 1920s, additions were built onto both ends of the original building; gables and dormers have further altered the original rectangular plan. The lodge is shingled in alternating wide and narrow widths. Peeled poles support porch roofs, and rustic touches are carried into the interior with a massive stone fireplace, the lobby's wide-planked walls, floors, and ceiling, and a main stairway of peeled logs and branches.*

▷ *The rustic gateway to Rosemary Inn greeted guests at the lakeside as they arrived by ferry and launch. After an access road to Barnes Point was completed, the gateway was dismantled and rebuilt on the other side of the inn facing the road.*

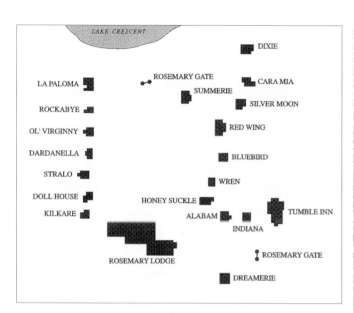

△ *Plan of Rosemary Inn in 1926, showing the main lodge, Tumble Inn, and the whimsically named cabins.*

shoreline. Mostly of wood-frame construction on post-and-pier foundations, there are no twins in the group. Each is unique in design, no larger than 15' x 20' in plan, L-shaped or rectangular, with extended porches and sheds. The eclectic whimsy of design continues with the sheathing materials, which include horizontal clapboards, vertical board-and-batten, wood shingles, cedar bark, and stucco. A bay window here, a diamond-shaped casement window there, porch roof brackets of peeled logs, jerkinhead roofs – unexpected building elements are at every turn. Each cabin is identified by a small signboard over the entrance. A three-sided shelter of peeled-log construction sits at the edge of the meadow by the shoreline.

Rosemary Inn was the setting for two historic moments in park history. During President Roosevelt's visit to nearby Lake Crescent Lodge, in 1937, the presidential party breakfasted at Rosemary Inn. Nine years later, it was the setting for the Olympic National Park dedication ceremony, led by Secretary of the Interior Julius A. Krug. In 1943, the National Park Service acquired the property to operate as a concession. Rosemary Inn was placed on the National Register of Historic Places in 1979. The complex is now used as housing for Lake Crescent Lodge employees.

A holiday postcard and a sampler of cabins at Rosemary's Lodge
"Silver Moon"
"Summerie"
"Cara Mia"
"Red Wing"
"Dreamerie"

▷ *Enchanted Valley Chalet.
The building was framed with
locally cut, full-length, squared
cedar logs, which end in diago-
nal-cut dovetail joints. Minor
rustic touches were added with
peeled-pole purlins and supporting braces for the overhanging
roof at the gable ends. Two
small shed roofs over the entrances are recent additions.
Bricks and mortar for the
chimney, disassembled window
frames and sash, and milled
lumber for interiors were
hauled to the site by pack horses.
After a water system was added,
in 1934, a bathtub was skidded
into the valley behind a pack
horse and installed on the second floor.*

Enchanted Valley Chalet

The Valley of a Thousand Waterfalls, the original name
of Enchanted Valley, catches the rare quality of the 100-
acre meadow surrounded by mountains and a 2,000-
foot wall of rock to the north. In wet seasons, waterfalls
cascade over the rocky precipices. The five Olson brothers of Hoquiam, Washington, had formed a hiking and
trail-guide service in the late 1920s and vied for the right
to develop the North Fork of the Quinault River. They
were turned down and searched elsewhere for a chalet
site. The Forest Service invited a proposal from them in
1929 for the Enchanted Valley location, 13 miles from
the trailhead at Graves Creek on the East Fork of the
Quinault River. The Olsons' application was approved,
and construction of the Enchanted Valley Chalet began
in 1931.[4]

The log building measures 28' x 40' and follows the
USFS guidelines for "architect's plans embodying a harmonious design either in Rustic, Swiss Chalet or other
suitable style." Interiors have tongue-and-groove flooring throughout, peeled-pole ceiling joists, and exposed
pole rafters in the attic. There are three rooms on the
first floor, including a kitchen, bedroom, and living
room; six sleeping rooms on the second floor; and a
large room in the attic. Walls are made of flattened log
faces, running vertically.

The chalet was a favorite stopping place for hikers
and horse caravans during the 1930s. On a 13-mile pack
trip through the Olympics, the fifth day brought the
party to Enchanted Valley. The prospect of a fireplace,
cooks, good food, beds, and a bath were as welcome as
the spectacular setting. After incorporation into the

park, the Olympic Recreation Company owners decided
to sell their holdings to the NPS, who kept it in operation until 1943, when it was manned by the Aircraft
Warning Service. By 1951, the NPS had finally consum-
mated the purchase, and the chalet was put back into
operation in 1953.

The final chapter in the history of Enchanted Valley
Chalet is a happy one. A hiking club from Hoquiam
(The Olympians) and the NPS worked to stabilize and
restore it after several years of decay and vandalism. With
volunteer labor and NPS guidance, the welcoming chalet
is once again available for travelers into Enchanted Valley. The chalet serves as a reminder of private commercial efforts to develop recreational opportunities in
Olympic's interior wilderness and plays an important
role in the park's interpretive history.

The Federal Influence: CCC,
Shelters, and Headquarters

Soon after the Forest Service took over management of
Olympic Forest Reserve, in 1905, plans were laid to open
the interior wilderness for recreation. Administration by
the NPS, which began in 1938, superseded forty years of
Forest Service management of the Olympic National
Forest. Overlapping the transition from one federal
agency to another, there was a brief period of enormous
activity (1933–42) when funds and labor were available
through relief programs – Civilian Conservation Corps
(CCC), Public Works Administration (PWA), and Works
Projects Administration (WPA).

A variety of structures – ranger stations, trail shelters,
and outbuildings – reflects the Forest Service's concern

◁ *The* CCC*-built Elwha Ranger Station's oil and gas house illustrated the U.S. Forest Service's idea of "acceptable plans." The clapboard-siding structure in the Bungalow style was embellished with squared-timber porch supports. The Forest Service and* CCC *pine tree was cut into the vertical boards on gable ends.*

with wilderness preservation through multiple resource management. The need to provide access to timber and a parallel need for fire prevention and control led to the development of a comprehensive trail system. The original system of trails, houses, and shelters conceived for USFS use also provided access to the interior of the Olympic Peninsula for a growing number of hikers and hunting and fishing enthusiasts.

By the mid-1930s, hundreds of miles of trails and numerous shelters had been constructed on the peninsula. Built of readily available logs and split-cedar shakes, the simple structures were based on Adirondack shelter design: open on one side with a peeled-pole log frame, a gable shake roof with two unequal pitches, split shake walls and roofs, and a dirt floor. The shelters were spaced along the trails at reasonable hiking distances and became part of the USFS promotion of recreational opportunities in the reserve.

Design and placement of the shelters adhered to principles of preserving the primitive wilderness: "Building should be in the way of such Forest Service improvements as are absolutely necessary.… Other buildings beyond such rough shelters as may be considered necessary should be kept out."[5] Of the fewer than twenty extant shelters, only a handful have not been altered by maintenance crews, who changed exteriors to board-and-batten siding and added raised wooden floors. The best examples are found along the Bogachiel River in the Hoh subdistrict. An inspired peeled-log structure in the NPS Rustic style is the Soleduck Falls Shelter (1939). NPS Rustic work is also illustrated by the CCC-built Elwha Shelter kitchen (1938). Ranger stations at Elwha (1932) and Altaire (1935) are simple designs in "Forest Service Rustic"—functional clapboard siding incorporating the pine-tree symbol of both the Forest Service and the CCC in the gable ends.

Elwha Ranger Station and Campgrounds

The Elwha Ranger Station and nearby campgrounds contain groupings of structures that illustrate the transition from Forest Service to CCC building in the park. The Ranger Station is an unremarkable complex of sixteen buildings from the early 1930s, although the wood-frame structures with clapboard, shake, or half-log siding

exteriors and casement windows did follow the Forest Service's dictates for aesthetically pleasing as well as substantial buildings compatible with their surroundings.[6]

These buildings might well be said to follow the Bungalow style, a common residential design of the 1930s, but are slightly embellished with heavy, squared-timber porch supports and brackets. The CCC touch is evident in the decorative pine-tree design cut into shutters, porch railings, and gable end boards. The Elwha Ranger Station complex serves as a reminder of the Forest Service's unobtrusive design style, and the buildings in this grouping remain substantially as they were over fifty years ago.

Elwha and Altaire campgrounds, one a mile north of the Ranger Station and the other a mile south, contain the two examples of CCC community kitchens that survive in the park.

△ *The Elwha community kitchen is a fine example of an* NPS *Rustic-style design. It was built in 1935 by the* CCC, *with oversized peeled-pole columns, an exposed-log purlin roof covered with shake shingles, and a central fireplace. Original* wooden railings have been removed, but the framing notches are still visible; otherwise, the original shelter is intact. The octagonal plan was used frequently by the NPS in community rustic structures.*

Soleduck Falls Shelter

Less than a mile from the Soleduck River trailhead, the CCC built one of three rustic log shelters in the park. This fine example of workmanship and design, and the only remaining CCC shelter, was completed in 1939. Workers from the Elwha CCC camp provided labor for the project, which was in a wooded setting on a high bank 30 feet from the Soleduck River.

Unlike the Forest Service's simple Adirondack-design shelters, covered with split shakes, the Soleduck shelter's more elaborate rustic form in logs shows the influence of the distinctive design, attention to detail, use of native building materials, quality of workmanship, and nonintrusive siting that are hallmarks of NPS Rustic design.

The sensitivity of the design and quality of the workmanship in this simple structure are highlighted by the subtlety of intersecting forms and the projecting log ends. The shelter's main log walls end in a horizontal wedge shape; roof purlins are pointed; and gable logs end in a lancet shape. The Soleduck Falls shelter is an excellent example of the craftsmanship practiced by the CCC prior to, and during, the formative years of Olympic National Park.

Park Headquarters

A high priority for the newly created Olympic National Park was the building of an administrative headquarters. A location was selected at Peabody Heights in Port Angeles, four miles from the park's main northern boundary, and with PWA funds allocated to the National Park Service, the first five buildings of the sixteen-building complex were completed in 1941.

Construction at the site under both the PWA and CCC proceeded slowly at first. Continuous rainfall delayed excavation work, and then there were delays in obtaining materials. A lack of qualified stone masons and the cost of skilled labor quickly put the project over budget. Additional funds were procured and the first two structures, the Administration Building and the Superintendent's Residence, were ready for occupancy by June 1940.

As is the case for several other Olympic National Park buildings, the Park Headquarters complex is of greater interest for its interpretive history than as an example of distinctive architecture. By 1940, the NPS Rustic design tradition was in eclipse. The "exaggerated rustic" was disappearing in favor of more contemporary trends. It was replaced with only minor concessions to immediate settings and most typically with unexceptional wood-frame houses incorporating rustic siding and stone-veneer walls. The NPS' design philosophy retained its principle of nonintrusive architecture, but modern functionalism with simpler, more efficient design replaced the older traditions.[7]

The historic architecture in this park is a modest collection of buildings, with occasional fine legacies of NPS design work. Buildings alongside trails or lakeshores are selective remnants of the park's history and are reminders of the exploration, commercial development, recreation, federal management, and relief programs that have taken place in it. As one discovers a cabin or trailside shelter, resort hotel or ranger station, the desire to classify a building by its role in interpretive history is lost in the simple act of discovery. After hours of hiking through the wilderness, the sighting of one of these structures is a poignant reminder that in this region weather dominates, and people and buildings are transient. John Muir may have had the Olympic Peninsula in mind when he wrote, "Come to the woods, for here is rest.... Of all the upness accessible to mortals, there is no upness compared to the mountains."[8]

Mount Rainier National Park

The Frozen Octopus: This mountain has a glacier system far exceeding in size and impressive beauty that of any other in the United States. From its snow-covered summit twenty-eight rivers of ice pour slowly down its sides. Seen upon the map, as if from an aeroplane, one thinks of it as an enormous frozen octopus stretching its icy tentacles down upon every side among the rich gardens of wild flowers and splendid forests of firs and cedars below.

NATIONAL PARKS PORTFOLIO

Seen from a hundred miles away, snow-capped Mount Rainier floats ethereally in the distance. The peak of the truncated volcanic cone in northwestern Washington State rises in dramatic isolation 8,000 feet higher than the surrounding foothills. John Muir, supporting the enactment of a national park from what was then forest reserve, described Mount Rainier: *Of all the fire-mountains, which, like beacons, once blazed along the Pacific Coast, Mount Rainier is the noblest in form.... Its massive dome rises out of its forests ... the loveliest flowers ... so closely planted and luxuriant that it seems as if Nature, glad to make an open space between woods so dense and ice so deep, were economizing the precious ground, and trying to see how many of her darlings he can get together in one mountain wreath.*[9]

Seen from above, alternating ridges of rock (called "cleavers") and ice radiate out from the peak to the lowlands. The dense snowpack forms a dozen major glaciers to the 7,000-foot level – the largest mass of easily accessible glaciers in the lower 48 states. Below the ice fields lie a succession of plant zones to be explored by road or trail. Subalpine meadows are brightened in spring by blossoms that advance behind the melting snow in a stunning array of blue, red, white, pink, and yellow. Dense forests of Alaska cedar, Douglas fir, western white pine, and western hemlock splay out along the ridges, girdling the peak in thick stands above the lushly shaded forest floor.

The mountain attracted its first formal exploratory expedition in August 1833. William Tolmie, a Hudson's Bay Company employee at nearby Fort Nisqually, organized an expedition to the mountain to collect plants and explore the countryside. Later ascents of the mountain were claimed in the 1850s, but the first well-documented summit climb was undertaken in 1870 by Hazard Stevens and Philemon Trump. Their guide was James Longmire.

Longmire was a pioneer in the Oregon Country in 1853. He farmed there and became a guide for explorers on the mountain. In 1883, Longmire opened a trail and built a cabin for hikers and climbers near the springs that now bear his name. John Muir records renting horses from Longmire and visiting the cabin in 1888. "Longmire Medical Springs" was advertised for travelers, and

Overleaf: Mount Rainier's 14,410-foot summit is a weather maker – on otherwise clear days, condensation in the upper airstream forms a cloud cover at the mountain's peak. The western slopes and peak trap an average precipitation of 110 inches a year from the moisture-laden winds that sweep in from the Pacific Ocean. Paradise holds the world record for annual snow accumulation: 1,122 inches in the winter of 1971–72 – over 93 feet – leaving a snowpack 30 feet deep. The shielded eastern slopes are desert, with an annual precipitation of only ten inches or less.

an enclave of cabins and tents evolved into a bustling community. The oldest extant historic structure in Mount Rainier National Park is the cabin built in 1888 by Elcaine Longmire, James' son.

Federal protection of Mount Rainier began in 1893 with the creation of the 35-square-mile Pacific Forest Reserve and expanded in 1897 to an enlarged and renamed Mount Rainier Forest Reserve. After a brief five-year period of lobbying by scientific and conservation groups, including the National Geographic Society, the act establishing Mount Rainier as the nation's fifth national park was signed by President McKinley in 1899. Creation of the park seems to have followed an uncontested assessment of it as worthless.[10] There was not much in the area to attract commercial interests, it was inaccessible, much of the area was bare rock, and there were no valuable minerals. John Ise described it as best fitted for "a national park and not much else."[11]

Today, many travelers visit Mount Rainier each year to hike, climb, fish, ride trails, and take in the glorious scenery. In addition, the park has a superb collection of historic structures. Inaccessibility discouraged settlement, and the early date of the park's founding limited inholding claims or commercial activity to a few visitor accommodations. The buildings at the four historic districts – Nisqually, Longmire, Paradise, and Sunrise – along with patrol cabins and bridges, present an appealing and consistent array of Rustic park architecture.

As one of the crown jewels in the national park system, Mount Rainier received significant attention in the form of funding allotments and design services coincidental with the emergence of the NPS Rustic style in the 1920s and 1930s. Earlier private commercial and federal buildings were of a rustic nature compatible with NPS philosophy. Park administration buildings, visitor service centers, residences, and maintenance facilities were all designed and constructed within the framework of the Rustic style; the level of detailing was directly proportional to the importance and visibility of the structure. This remarkably consistent theme was not disturbed until the Mission 66 influence, with the intrusive, contemporary-designed Visitor Center at Paradise. Fortunately, the NPS Master Plan for post–World War II expansion placed administration and residential structures

⊲ Camp Muir Shelter, high among Mount Rainier's glaciers at 10,188 feet, serves as a base for the summit climb. The NPS built the stone shelter in 1921 where the naturalist's camp had been based for his 1888 climb to the peak.

outside the park at the Nisqually Entrance. Although Mission 66 was the well-intentioned fiftieth anniversary program designed to improve visitor services, it resulted in some regrettable architectural legacies for the national parks.

Nisqually Entrance

A two-hour drive from Seattle to Ashford leads to a sequence of four historic districts beginning at the Nisqually Entrance gate. A massive log archway spanning the road is the visitor's first contact with Rustic architecture. To the right of the entranceway is the finely crafted Oscar Brown cabin. Early access to Mount Rainier National Park was along a wagon trail from the Nisqually Entrance to Longmire Springs. A road built by the Department of the Interior increased demand for opening the park to automobiles, which occurred in 1907. Entry fees and access by permit justified the funding of this, the park's first government building.

⊲ The monumentally proportioned Nisqually entrance gate resulted from a visit to the park in 1910 by Secretary of the Interior Bollinger, who requested the construction of a rustic gateway. Four cedar-log columns almost 4 feet in diameter and three log beams spanning the roadway were erected in 1911 to create a pergola with a clearance of 18½ feet. The structure was completed in time for President Taft's visit to the park that fall. The massive coped logs stood until they deteriorated and were replaced in 1973. The replacement was identical to the original, including the traditional log sign with the park's name.

Named for the first permanent ranger assigned to the park – Oscar Brown, in 1906 – the cabin was completed in 1908 and served as park headquarters until 1915. The interior has plank floors and exposed log walls and ceiling joists. The upper floor, which served as a bedroom, was accessible by ladder. In 1980 the interiors were completely remodeled, additions removed, and the balcony railing was added. The building is presently used as a private residence and is off-limits to the public.

Just beyond Oscar Brown's cabin is the entrance checking station. Of historical note as one of the earliest projects from the NPS Landscape Engineering Division, this log-framed building was completed in 1926 to handle increased park traffic and provide additional ranger quarters. The original design was L-shaped, a plan with carefully proportioned log walls, columns, projecting purlins and joists, and a shake roof with a pole-capped ridge. *Park and Recreation Structures* critically assessed the design: "A splendid log structure deserving of the impressive background it enjoys. Only the trivial chimneys fail to register to the high standards all other details maintain."[12]

The building's original fine detailing and form has been altered over the years. Interior remodeling, extensions to the porte-cochère, and the addition of an entrance door canopy by the CCC in 1936–37 were well-intentioned maintenance work, functional changes to accommodate traffic and higher vehicles. Unfortunately, the work included removal of a bay from the porte-cochère and the addition of an extension without projecting beam ends, thereby creating an imbalance to the keen eye.

△ *The delicate gable fan of thin logs carried on a gracefully arched log beam is a unique decorative element in the 1908 Oscar Brown cabin. The 16' x 22' log frame, with projecting saddle-notched corners and steeply pitched cedar shingle roof, is a forerunner of the NPS Rustic style.*

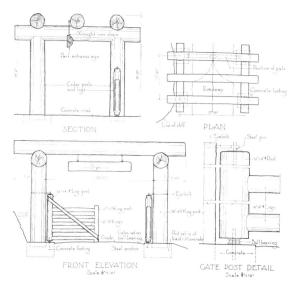

△ *Original plans called for massive cedar logs to form the rustic Nisqually entrance gate.*

△ *The Tacoma and Eastern Railroad's guest clubhouse built in 1911 now serves as the Hiker's Center. Form and massing are residential in scale, and Douglas fir logs are used throughout for framing and exterior walls. Logs with plaster-chinked joints and corner saddle notching form the exterior walls. Gable ends are covered by vertical logs at half the diameter of the wall logs and finished with rounded bottoms that create a scalloped shadow on the wall. The shallow-pitched cedar shingle roof, extended over the front entrance as a porch, provides a welcoming atmosphere for backcountry hikers.*

△ *Longmire cabin, the oldest structure in the park, was built in 1888 by Elcaine Longmire near mineral springs discovered by his father, James Longmire. The original one-story rectangular cabin was replaced by the CCC in 1934.*

Longmire

The road from Nisqually to Paradise offers views of thick forests, rushing streams, and flower borders. One is tempted to bypass the cluster of buildings at Longmire, six miles from the entrance, to reach the Visitor Center at Paradise. What may appear to be a random collection of buildings, made of logs and shingles painted brown, is actually a group of NPS and concessioner structures significant in the interpretive history of Mount Rainier National Park.

The horse "trains" run by the Longmires on the road they built between Ashford and the mineral springs reached a favorite destination at the wildflower-carpeted meadow and natural springs. A health spa resort with a 30-room hotel, cabins, tents, and bathhouses over the springs attracted visitors and played an important role in developing the land as a national park.

The open meadow on the north side of the road offers a pleasant walk along the Trail of Shadows, bordered by towering Douglas fir and western hemlock, past the remnants of James Longmire's early mineral spring development. Soda Springs, Iron Mike Springs, and Elcaine Longmire's cabin are evidence of what was a bustling community at the turn of the century.

Activity at the park intensified when the Tacoma and Eastern Railroad built their National Park Inn. The three-story hotel, which could sleep 60 guests, was completed in 1906, but fire destroyed it twenty years later. In 1911, the railroad expanded its facilities by erecting a clubhouse for guests. Now used as the Longmire Hiker's Center, the building is a well-conceived and well-constructed example of the early Rustic design common at Rainier. Interior log columns rise to the exposed log purlin roof framing and act as the center posts

▷ *The original 1924 log suspension bridge across the Nisqually River shows a graceful combination of art and engineering somewhat lost in the 1951 reconstruction built of timber members with bolted connections.*

▷ *Timber suspension bridge with a 180-foot span on the site of a 1924 bridge. This reconstruction replaced the original log towers with milled timbers, but the appearance remains essentially the same, with the illusion of Rustic towers and trusses. There is a brutish elegance to the skeletal collection of short timber pieces connected by exposed boltheads. From a distance, the wire cables are barely visible against the mass of timbers and the forested shores. The alternating-width roadway planks (11 to 18 inches) both slow the driver and create the illusion of a forest from shore to shore.*

for log trusses supporting the roof. The coped-log interior framing is a fine example of Rustic architecture.

A competitor to James Longmire and the railroad, the Rainier National Park Company entered the area in 1916 with the construction of a hotel. In 1920, the company moved the hotel next to the original National Park Inn on the south side of Longmire Plaza, and it became known as the National Park Inn Annex. After the inn was destroyed by fire in 1926, the Annex was remodeled and assumed the name National Park Inn. The modest appearance of the building – only two-and-a-half stories high with seventeen guest rooms – is explained by its varied history. Never conceived as a dramatic attraction, the unpretentious exterior design and plain interiors were intended simply to provide adequate lodging in a superb setting. Its location, at the start of the 93-mile Wonderland Trail encircling Mount Rainier, and its

place of honor as the surviving hotel, add to its interest. The inn has recently been renovated.

As visitor activity increased, the park's administration center was shifted from Nisqually to Longmire. Two early administration buildings are now used as the Library (1910) and the Museum and Visitor Center (1916). Both buildings are log framed, rectangular, and sheltered by steeply pitched cedar shake roofs. The Library originally served as a community kitchen and the Museum was the park's first administration building.

In 1924, an automobile campground was opened across the Nisqually River from Longmire Springs and the administrative area. A light, narrow suspension bridge was replaced with a dramatic log, timber, and plank bridge capable of carrying automobile traffic to and from the campground. It was built in 1951. The present bridge spans 180 feet from center to center of the towers. Wire-rope cables connected to steel-rod suspenders carry a timber Howe stiffening truss and the 15-foot-wide plank decking.

A competent and energetic Landscape Engineering Division was developed in the NPS San Francisco office and had a strong impact on Longmire. Under the direction of chief architect Thomas C. Vint, a group of talented young men sought out design elements that would make the park buildings compatible with principles of unobtrusive construction in natural settings. Designers and on-site construction supervisors carefully studied the natural materials of the surrounding landscape – their scale, color, massing, and texture – and incorporated what they could into their designs. The staff's field experience and mature design skills produced a group of coordinated structures at Longmire that harmonized with the rugged slopes of Mount Rainier. The NPS buildings simultaneously acknowledged and emphasized the beauty of the surrounding landscape, using simple sheltering forms and native materials in proper scale.

The general development plan, prepared in 1927, gave a sense of order to the half-dozen government and concessioner buildings south of Longmire Plaza and created a park headquarters with visitor facilities, administrative offices, ranger residences, and maintenance buildings. Three buildings that demonstrate the outstanding talents and efforts of the NPS staff are the

▽ *Longmire Community Build-ing. Exterior columns are half-logs that provide appropriate scale and proportion to exterior elevations. The 24' x 60' main hall has a porch with a shed roof sheltering the entrance. A two-story residence is attached to the rear. Foundation walls* made of glacial boulders support paired log columns with infill walls of thick slab log veneer on the interior and exterior. The main hall front elevation is divided into four bays with paired casement windows in groups of twos and threes with transoms above. A steeply pitched cedar shingle roof is *carried on exposed-log scissor trusses, log rafters and purlins, and cedar tongue-and-groove boards. A decorative log ridge beam originally ran the entire length of the roof.*

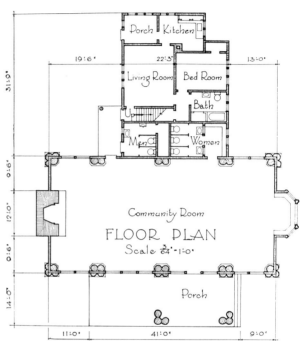

Community Building, Administration Building, and Service Station.

The first of these was the Longmire Community Building, completed in 1927. Sited between the suspension bridge and the campgrounds, the two-story, T-plan, timber-framed structure serves as the social and cultural center for Longmire. The exterior building form is dominated by the steep roof and rhythms of paired-log columns scaled smaller than the surrounding towering trees. The interior of the main hall is a revelation of timber columns and trusses, log slab siding, wooden floor and ceiling – all immersed in light from the ribbons of casement and dormer windows. The exterior paired-log column theme is repeated inside in the structural supports for the trusses. Wrought-iron chandeliers and wall sconces add to the character. One gable end wall contains a massive stone fireplace and chimney. Stones in the lower portion are coursed and roughly squared; those above, including the central niche into the chimney, are glacial boulders. The main hall's opposite end contains a small stage set into a projecting window bay.

The designers' dexterity in manipulating natural materials for both decorative and structural use is illustrated by the paired-log column motif. The porch supports,

clusters of three full logs, can be read as a pair from front or side. Log columns on the exterior walls are really half logs, reflecting the framing concept and rhythms. Interior pairs of freestanding logs are whole logs used as truss framing supports. Rather than using the notched corner log technique of a conventional cabin, the designers created a more formal expression by placing pairs of columns at the corners and using the paired columns to define the bays in the front elevation. The careful workmanship in the coping of exterior and interior logs makes the Community Building a prime example of the Rustic style.

◁ *Longmire Community Build-ing, where a freestanding frame of paired cedar logs supports roof trusses inside the log walls. It is an elegant display of log coping skills used to join columns and truss chords.*

▷ Longmire Administration Building, where it was important to the NPS designers to present a rugged yet slightly formal image. The building was carefully sited at the end of the road in an open area against a background of tall firs, cedars, and spruce. A well-proportioned structure, it has strong visual ties to the site,

△ The Longmire Administration Building shows a highly refined composition of rustic elements executed with superb field skills and craftsmanship. Rounded glacial boulders flow upward from the ground in a careful plan of graduated sizes, achieving visual stability. The stones, although available on-site, were difficult to put in place and were selected for size and surface variety. They help tie the building to the ground and mask its essentially rectilinear foundation lines.

▷ Floor plans of the Administration Building show the services required to support the park in 1928. Although the interior room configuration has undergone slight changes, the original plan and surfaces remain intact. A large glacial boulder fireplace is in the lobby; walls are of log slab siding; windows and doors are framed out of massive logs; wrought-iron chandeliers embellish the room and add to its character.

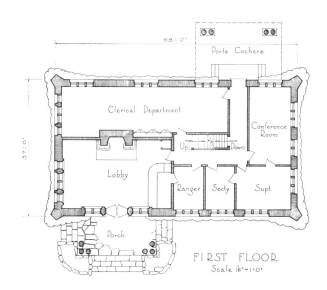

FIRST FLOOR
Scale 16" = 1'-0"

SECOND FLOOR

▷ *The Longmire administration complex was completed in 1929 with construction of the Rustic gas station. Whole log columns mounted on an island of glacial boulders and beams frame the overhanging porch and shelter the gas pumps while providing a one-lane drive-through. Walls of glacial boulders run up to window sills sheathed with log half-rounds. Log corner posts match the overhang support columns. Windows on the first floor are multipane casement, and a single, square casement is placed in the gable of the front elevation. The eave at the gable has brackets with whittled log ends. The steeply pitched roof is covered with thick cedar-shake shingles.*

Despite these fine touches, *Park and Recreation Structures* described the Community Building as "a park structure of importance that, after pointing the way for many later buildings, has been surpassed in achievement of the subtleties of design and execution that make for true park structural character."[13] Singled out for criticism were the thin roof shingles, the character of the masonry chimneys, and the "almost mechanical stiffness" of the projecting log purlin rafters with sawn rather than whittled ends. Nevertheless, the building represents an architectural achievement that has been widely popular with NPS employees and visitors.

The most architecturally important NPS structure at Longmire is the Administration Building, completed in 1928. Borrowing design features from the 1924 Yosemite Administration Building, the materials used, such as heavy masonry on the first floor and the timber-framed second story, give this structure its special relationship to the Mount Rainier area. Here, the architects and on-site construction supervisors carefully studied local materials and sensitively incorporated oversize boulders and logs into the building construction to match elements of the surrounding landscape.

The upper story was veneered with horizontal logs, and the gable ends have contrasting vertical logs. Corners, visually strengthened by three massive vertical logs, draw the masonry of the lower story together with projecting rafters, eaves, and brackets of 12-inch logs with whittled ends. The corner logs continue the visual pattern established in the entrance porch. The rhythm of casement windows grouped in threes capped with log lintels is identical on both floors. The battered glacial boulders (tapered from bottom to top) on the lower wall emphasize the deeply recessed windows. Thick cedar shakes extend this theme of solid construction, as does the log ridgepole capping the roof. A boulder masonry chimney and a porch framed with logs complete the structure's exterior.

The Longmire Administration Building illustrates the maturing NPS philosophy of nonintrusive architecture in a glacial forest setting. Lower walls, veneered with native stone, rise irregularly out of the earth. The massive logs used in the porch, upper story, and visible roof structure are proportional to the surrounding conifer forest. Plantings along the foundation walls establish yet another connection between the building and the forest. The Administration Building continued to function as the park headquarters until 1968, when the Mission 66 facility constructed outside the park at Tahoma was completed. Today, the building serves as a ranger station and a center for park maintenance operations.

The third building of importance at Longmire is the Service Station, completed in 1929. Sited next to the National Park Inn on the approach road to the Administration Building, the Service Station is so well designed and nestled back into the trees that it is barely noticeable. Even its function does not seem incongruous within the forest setting. The NPS design staff managed to introduce local materials and ordinary features into the design for a building type that was basically simple but difficult to execute.

Paradise

The road to Paradise climbs 2,600 feet in 13 miles of gentle grades and switchbacks from Longmire to Paradise Valley. Along the route, the road crosses Christine Falls Bridge. The 56-foot span is one of the finest examples of a necessarily functional design that blends with the natural setting. Another example along the route is the Narada Falls Bridge, now only used for access to the Narada utility area.

As the traveler approaches Paradise, the cloud-wreathed peak of Mount Rainier is an ever-expanding presence as the forest thins and alpine meadows with wildflowers come into view. The Cascade Range is arrayed to the south; snow-capped Mount Adams and Mount Hood and the truncated cone of Mount Saint Helens are visible on the horizon. The Visitor Center, a strikingly modern shallow-domed structure, hovers over the snowfields. A remnant of the Mission 66 architectural misadventures, it is a sharp contrast to the shake-covered walls and steeply pitched roofs of the Paradise Inn complex and other NPS buildings.[14]

Paradise Inn

The area known as Paradise resulted from a forest fire in 1885 that burned a thickly vegetated area on the western slope of Mount Rainier and left a stand of dead Alaska

△ *Mission 66 Visitor Center, diminished in scale in comparison to Mount Rainier.*

▷ *Auto stages in the 1920s leaving Paradise Inn for the four- and five-hour trip to Tacoma and Seattle. Tops were removable for viewing the scenery.*

▷ *The Paradise Inn complex on a summer's day, free of winter's 30-foot snowpack. To allow the building some flexibility under heavy snow loads, the architects augmented the structural system with a series of adjustable cables so the building could respond to varying stresses.*

cedars. Eventually, the dead limbs broke off and the charred bark wore away. Years of exposure weathered the cedars to a shimmering silver color, and the stand became known as the silver forest. It remained untouched for thirty-one years, when NPS director Stephen Mather encouraged a group of Seattle and Tacoma businessmen to form a concession company for Mount Rainier and build a hotel in the silver forest area. He firmly believed in the dual mandate of the fledgling Park Service – preservation and use – and he felt that regulated concession companies in national parks would provide better control over the fragile natural resources. Paradise had been a popular Mount Rainier camping area for climbers and hikers since the nineteenth century, but the landscape was littered with a haphazard collection of tents and cottages. A better solution had to be found through NPS and private cooperation.

Alert to the threat of outside developers, the local businessmen formed the Rainier National Park Company (RNPC) and financed construction of Paradise Inn in 1916. A site was selected – apparently an informal affair when the company's founders met at the end of the Paradise automobile road one spring day and hiked up to Paradise Valley, where they could see the summit of Mount Rainier, the Tatoosh Range, and the rest of the valley. They decided then and there that the location was perfect for their new hotel and winter sports resort.

The RNPC selected the Tacoma architectural firm of Heath, Gove, and Bell to design the hotel as the development's central feature. They also planned a large group of "bungalow" tents, a ski lift, and a guide house for the company's mountaineering service. Construction began during the summer of 1916, and the inn opened on July 1, 1917.

Following the pattern established by concessioners in other crown jewel national parks, the RNPC set out to create a unique image for itself through its architecture. The company turned to the silver forest and harvested the well-seasoned timbers. The aged wood, with its silver patina, had obvious potential for unusual architectural effects. Reminiscent of Old Faithful Inn, the two-and-a-half-story inn has three steeply pitched roofs to shed the severe Cascade winter snows that annually average over 700 inches. The huge gable roofs over the main lobby section, the dining room wing, and the annex are more than two-thirds the height of the structure. This dominating architectural form makes the inn – in its isolated setting – seem particularly protective and sheltering. Dormers pierce the main roofs of the lobby and dining room sections, allowing light to penetrate into the deep interiors.

A second-story mezzanine (added in 1925) was wrapped around the upper portion – a place where visitors could sit at small writing tables to send letters or postcards home or just relax, people-watching and looking down on the scene below.

The fourteen lobby bays each had french doors facing

△△ *The 50' x 112' lobby, the largest public space at Paradise Inn, is a masterpiece of Rustic framing and spatial architecture. The lobby is a delightful place for skiers, hikers, climbers, and*

other visitors. Fireplaces with huge stone chimneys, 50 and 60 feet high, warm each end of the lobby. Designers solved the problem of supporting the steeply pitched roof with a display of fine log-working skills used to

assemble a pleasing rhythm of posts, beams, and trusses. The multilevel space is furnished with stout furniture and decorated with lanterns and Native American rugs.

◁ *Log framing, log chandeliers, and stone fireplace in the Paradise Inn dining room.*

△ *German woodcrafter Hans Fraehnke skillfully executed the lobby grandfather clock and other rustic pieces. The carefully carved quoins, spiky cornerposts, and a capping of a broken pediment give the clock a sense of alpine grandeur.*

△ *Paradise Inn Annex.*

north-northwest. The doors could be opened on warm days to let in the brisk alpine air and were easily boarded up for winter. Japanese lanterns, common in resort hotels like Glacier Park and El Tovar, originally lit the lobby; they were replaced with parchment-colored shades painted with pictures of local fauna.

An important decorative element in the lobby is the handcrafted Alaska cedar furniture. During the winter of 1916–17, Hans Fraehnke, a creative German woodcrafter, lived at Paradise Inn. To help pass the time during the long winter, he crafted a piano, a grandfather clock, and probably the woodwork around the registration desk. His work possesses a Gothicism reminiscent of the Bavarian Alps. The piano, played by President Harry S. Truman during a visit, has heavy cornerposts of peeled logs with pointed, whittled ends.

Four years after its construction, the RNPC decided to expand the inn. The magical warmth of the inn drew many visitors, but the bungalow tents proved to be less popular. In response to visitor demand, and with the approval of the National Park Service, the company constructed the Annex in 1920. The inn itself was generally T-shaped, and the Annex ran parallel to the larger wing of the main building, with a multistory enclosed bridge connecting the Annex to the inn. Subsequent changes included the addition of a mezzanine level in the lobby; construction of a new, larger kitchen wing; an enclosed porch off the rear of the lobby converted into a gift shop; and a porch added onto the south end.

A Mission 66 prospectus evaluated Paradise Inn and, seeing the need for extensive maintenance work, recommended replacing it with a visitor center. Many Washingtonians considered the inn such an important landmark that they refused to see it torn down. The inn was spared and the concessioner began major renovations in 1980 to improve its safety and structural stability. Work has included replacing the whole-log exterior buttresses with half logs that encase structural steel members.

The Rainier National Park Company constructed a guide service building around 1920. Clever handling of the architectural form and materials was necessary to maintain compatibility with the nearby inn. Small in plan (32' x 74'), it has a gambrel roof with dormers and exterior surfaces of Alaska cedar shakes that effectively lower the scale of the tall, narrow building. White pine log trim around the windows suggests a log frame, although the structure is timber framed. Rainier Mountaineering, which leads climbs and provides training for rescue work, occupies the ground floor.

Paradise Inn, part of one of the earliest ski resorts in the country, still retains its original alpine character. Through the doors of the hostelry have passed movie stars, political dignitaries, and athletes participating in the 1936 Winter Olympic trials. Tyrone Power, Cecile B. DeMille, Sonja Henie, Harry S. Truman, the Crown Prince of Norway, and Shirley Temple warmed themselves by the hearth or sat quietly on the mezzanine level

▷ The Paradise Guide House, built around 1920 by the Rainier National Park Company, is the park's only structure with a gambrel roof. Its distinctive design, on a first-story base of rubble masonry walls, responds well to extremely heavy snowfalls.

▷ The Ranger Station at Paradise, with exteriors of stone, silvery gray shingles, and shakes. The timber-framed, steeply pitched roof on the Ranger Station was designed to blend with the nearby Guide House and is braced by counterbalance cabling that anchors the building and supports it against massive snowpack pressure.

enjoying the space and the activity below. Today this architectural gem of the Pacific Northwest attracts thousands of people every year. They come to relax after a rigorous day's hiking or mountaineering, or just to enjoy the spectacular scenery.

NPS Buildings at Paradise

The NPS contributions to the Paradise Valley area include the Ranger Station, the ski-tow building, and the comfort station. Stephen Mather personally approved the plans for the Ranger Station, which was completed in 1922. Even though the use of stone was rejected by the concessioners as too labor intensive, the NPS saw it as appropriate to Mount Rainier. Design experimentation is evident in the use of half logs at entrance doors and window surrounds and exposed first-floor log ceiling joists compared to milled lumber joists at the eaves. In later buildings, the NPS introduced log roof framing to express a combination of structural and decorative elements.

The ski tow is a reminder of the years beginning in 1912 when Paradise Valley was among the most popular ski areas in the Pacific Northwest. One of the early visitors, Miss Olive Rand, traveled on two long slabs of wood turned up at the ends and fastened to her feet with hoops, and explained that they were "skis." The NPS prohibited ski tow facilities, but a portable lift was installed by the CCC in 1937. The timber-framed, steeply pitched roof on the 12' x 14' lift structure was designed to blend with the Ranger Station and Guide House.

The modest-sized comfort station, built in 1928, has an interesting design background. Rather than emphasize the facility and follow the pattern of steeply pitched roofs to shed the snow, the NPS chose a shallow-sloped roof on rubble masonry walls to carry the heavy snow loads. The 6-inch-thick reinforced concrete slab was to be slate covered, but building costs were reduced by substituting a tar and gravel roof.

Sunrise

Planning for the third and last major development of government and concession facilities in the park began in the late 1920s, when state highway construction authorities promised to open an approach from eastern

▷ *An ambitious, privately financed development plan for Yakima Park ran out of money in the early years of the Great Depression and was not completed. Sunrise Lodge is 57' x 137' and lacks a well-defined entrance because it was only the first phase of the unfinished hotel project. Early photographs show a U-shaped foundation extending out from the south side. The barn framing is infilled, with walls sheathed in cedar shakes.*

▷ *Sunrise Lodge and the complex of over 200 guest cabins (since removed) in 1940.*

Washington. The NPS was determined to avoid haphazard development that would endanger the fragile subalpine environment. Plans for Sunrise Village, to be built at Yakima Park, were prepared by the NPS Branch of Plans and Design in San Francisco under the supervision of Ernest A. Davidson. The NPS started work on an administrative-residential complex in 1930, while the RNPC began construction of a large hotel.

The RNPC's ambitious plans for Sunrise Lodge proceeded with construction of the first wing of the hotel in the spring of 1931, following a design modified by NPS architects to make it more compatible with the overall concept. Containing a dining room, kitchen, and employee facilities, Sunrise Lodge opened in mid-July 1931, with foundations in place for the second wing. Before beginning to build the lodging portion of the hotel, the concessioner laid out a tightly packed grid of 215 small guest cabins. As a result of financial difficulties in the early depression years, the company never started the

lodging portion and they sold off the cabins to farmers in eastern Washington for migrant worker housing. The RNPC sold its holdings to the NPS in 1952.

The basement area in Sunrise Lodge now serves as a Ranger Station, the first floor functions as a cafeteria as it did when it originally opened, and the upper floors are an employee dormitory. In contrast to the lodge, the small log-and-stone concessioner-built Service Station is an excellent example of Rustic architecture. The low-silhouette battered stone walls, log framing and trim, and gabled shake roof compliment the subalpine setting.

In 1929, when the master plan for Yakima Park was prepared under Davidson's direction, the NPS was reaching the peak of its Rustic design strengths. The challenge here was to design buildings for administrative offices and visitor services in a completely undeveloped subalpine area at an elevation of 6,400 feet. The fragile ecosystem had to be taken into account, in addition to developing a design theme that would celebrate the magnificent views of Mount Rainier. A compact plan evolved that minimized both the impact of construction on the site and future unrestricted use of the site by visitors. Reviewing the project, Davidson showed great concern for the environmental impact: *It is true that, purely from a landscape viewpoint, the whole development might be classified as a failure since the area is far less attractive than it was before the development took place. On the other hand, the project may be considered one of the great successes, since the general result obtained is far superior to those other developments with which comparison may be made, and which, "just grew," like Topsy.*[15]

In sorting out design concepts for the project, David-

▷ Whittled-end log stockade fencing ties the Yakima Park complex together. The NPS designers promoted a distinct style here, calling for carefully studied details in corner notching; irregular wall log end projections; overhanging second floor; extending roof purlins; and chamfered log ends at the window jambs.

▷ Sixty years of Mount Rainier winters have weathered the red-hued cedar logs of the Visitor Center at Yakima Park.

▷ The Visitor Center is a masterpiece of log construction designed to provide a large, open interior (42' x 88'). Lodgepole pine log walls are drift-pin connected and saddle notched to the roof plates at the corners. The interior open space required a long span of logs capable of supporting heavy snow loads. The ingenious solution rests Pratt log trusses across the room's width on log columns freestanding from the log walls. A pair of interior ridge beams carries log purlins and an exposed wooden roof deck. Log knee braces provide additional support, and the trusswork is reinforced by tie rods. Carefully notched and coped, the supporting roof structure placed inside the log walls creates a dramatically rugged interior.

△ A surprise July snowstorm swirls around the Stockade group at Yakima Park. The site is exposed to severe winter snows and winds, and is dependably accessible only four months of the year.

FIRST FLOOR PLAN

SECOND FLOOR PLAN

son turned to local sources of historical interest. A frontier blockhouse-and-stockade theme was developed from resource material at the Historical Museum of Tacoma. The building designs were completed by architect A. Paul Brown in February 1930.

The master plan provided for a complete development at Yakima Park, including administrative offices, living quarters, campgrounds, trails, utility systems, and parking areas. In the headquarters area, plans called for a large Community Building (or Visitor Center) flanked by two square blockhouses. A vertical stockade fence would enclose a utility yard behind the Community Building. Plans were drawn so that construction could take place in three phases, but funding problems extended the project so that it was not completed until 1952. Initially, funds allowed for construction of only the South Blockhouse. In 1939, Public Works Administration funding was allocated for the construction of the second (North) Blockhouse and Visitor Center. Again, capital was exhausted, and these two structures were not completed until 1943. The Visitor Center acquired its stone-and-timber fireplace in 1952. The North Blockhouse is similar to the South Blockhouse, except for its more regular battered stonework.

The centerpiece of the complex is the Visitor Center; originally known as the "campers' shelter," it later became a museum. Seen from a distance, the three buildings blend together into the protective image of a frontier stockade. The three unattached blockhouses enclose a courtyard defined by the forms, textures, and tones of the surrounding walls. There is uniformity between rich textures and the reddish weathering of the building, which contrasts with the random whittled log-end projections. The buildings are visually unified by their stone foundations to window sill height, the carefully composed placement and proportions of window openings, and the consistent roof height.

Clerestory windows bring in light through the east and west walls; a large picture window on the south wall looks out on Mount Rainier. On sunny days, crowds cluster at the window to watch climbers on the mountain's northeast slope. A coursed, oversize stone fireplace at the room's north end is framed with log columns and beams.

The usually understated NPS *Park and Recreation Structures* deemed the Stockade group a design success: *Even without the magnificent backdrop of Mount Rainier this log building [the South Blockhouse] would be an outstanding contribution to park architecture. Obviously, but not too self-consciously, inspired by the early blockhouse here is a building representative of a logical and legitimate adaptation of a traditional form. The log work is neither too precise nor too laboriously rustic.*

Part of the success of Sunrise is due to its setting, for the simple forms, resting on a grassy slope surrounded by subalpine vegetation with the imposing presence of snow-covered Mount Rainier in the background, give the complex a wild, frontier appearance.

The buildings at Mount Rainier National Park represent public and private efforts to promote, develop, manage, and protect the park's natural and recreational resources. In their natural settings, the collection of Rustic structures is one of the most intact and extensive examples of a cultural landscape. The Nisqually Entrance gate; the Rustic structures at Longmire, Paradise, and Sunrise; the bridges and patrol cabins – together they exemplify the national park experience.

Fort Vancouver National Historic Site

No events of great drama occurred here. No battles were fought, no armed or diplomatic confrontations, no international treaties were signed in the chief factor's residence. Instead, Fort Vancouver represented, and still represents, long-term stability between two peoples and two governments.

FORT VANCOUVER, National Park Handbook

Surrounded by twentieth-century sights and sounds, Fort Vancouver National Historic Site is the reconstruction of a Hudson's Bay Company trading post. It recalls a time when the stockade and bastion with its orchards and gardens, on the north bank of the Columbia River, marked the place where top-hatted factors and clerks once mingled with voyageurs and Indians at the frontier settlement. For thirty-five years, a brief passage in the history of the Pacific Northwest, this remote trading post was the focus of a political and economic struggle for dominance in the region.

The fort was established by the Hudson's Bay Company in 1825. Despite its military appearance, employees and settlers feared little from attack. The enclosing stockade walls were for normal security purposes, primarily to deter thieves. The cannons were never fired in anger, only to salute approaching ships.

Fort Vancouver offers a step back in time; ignore the intrusive interstate highway bridge from Portland across the Columbia River, the high-powered transmission lines, and the light aircraft from an adjacent airport, and let this recreated British outpost bring to life the era of Northwest trappers and traders. The NPS has meticulously crafted a journey for visitors that begins with an interpretive center and leads back into history. Inside the 15-foot-tall Douglas fir pickets surrounding a grassy rectangle (734' x 318'), period-furnished structures and reenactments by people in costumes of the time instill the visitor with a sense of the fort's history.[16]

Struggle for an Empire

The American Northwest in the late 1700s and early 1800s was a vast expanse of land that stretched from Russian Alaska south to Spanish California and from the Pacific Ocean east to the Rocky Mountains. It was rich fur trapping and trading country, and Americans, British, Spanish, and Russians vied for control of the Pacific Coast and Columbia River watershed.

Successive discoveries brought the region under conflicting claims. For example, both British and American expeditions claimed to have "discovered" the mouth of the Columbia River in 1789. Fur traders and other commercial interests valued the Columbia River as a means of reaching the continent's interior. The river system

▷ *Fort Vancouver in its full glory, with ships arriving, crops in the fields, the British flag serenely flapping in the breeze, and the bastion towering over the stockade walls. Painted by an unknown artist in 1845.*

drains much of the Northwest and provided access through a water highway to some of the richest fur trapping country in North America.

The Louisiana Purchase (1803) secured a claim on the Oregon Country for the United States, and Lewis and Clark's expedition reports spelled out the rich resources of the region. During the War of 1812, conflicting British and American claims boiled over into the Pacific Northwest, and the British seized the town of Astoria on the south bank at the mouth of the Columbia River. The United States argued for possession of territory south of the 49th parallel; the British insisted that the border should follow the Columbia River from where it crosses the 49th parallel to the ocean. A Convention of Joint Occupancy in 1818 provided both nations with equal trade and settlement rights for the next decade, when the situation would again be reviewed.

Astoria (renamed Fort George), on the Columbia estuary, provided temporary headquarters for the British North West Company and its 1821 successor, the Hudson's Bay Company. They abandoned the fort in favor of a new, north-bank location 100 miles farther inland—one that would both strengthen British claims between the Columbia River and the 49th parallel and act as a political and economic center for the Hudson's Bay Company.

This north-bank site was located just above the Willamette River. An important feature of the location was that oceangoing vessels of up to 200 tons could ascend without lightering. The site for Fort Vancouver was on a bluff of open land three miles wide and a mile deep. The river floodplain and rich soil above it could support orchards and gardens. The bluff was long and broad, offering good protection against surprise attack via either water or land. Hauling supplies from the water's edge was a minor inconvenience compared to the secure defensive position. With merchandise transferred from Fort George upriver to the new fort, construction progressed slowly.

When the Convention of Joint Occupancy was renewed in 1828, it increased the need to reinforce the position of the British and the Hudson's Bay Company. Pressured by the company, Great Britain had refused to accept a United States proposal of the 49th parallel as the boundary. The Americans, equally stubborn, refused to accept the Columbia River as the boundary. A decision was reached to expand Fort Vancouver as the Hudson's Bay Company's principal supply depot and administrative center on the west coast of North America. Additional warehouses, offices, staff quarters, farm buildings, and fields were called for, so the original fort on top of the bluff was abandoned for a new complex nearer the river and its docks, about a half mile to the west and a quarter mile from the riverbank.

Work at a new site began in 1829. A stockade enclosed a dozen buildings – dwellings, warehouses, and workshops – ranged around an interior court. Indians went there to trade, trappers and traders took their furs and departed with goods for the Indians, clerks bustled in and out of the warehouses, and visiting sailors idled between trips.

The "Oregon Fever" that swept the United States in the 1840s changed the political future of the Northwest. Prior to 1840, the only permanent settlers from the East in the region were primarily missionaries serving the Indians or trappers. But in 1841, farmers, attracted by the fertile Willamette Valley, began to trickle into the area. By 1843, the Great Migration had begun, and wagon trains and herds of livestock were heading for Oregon Territory. Each year the number of migrants increased, and by 1846, when a wagon road was completed over the Cascade Mountains, the non-Indian population in Oregon was close to 6,000.

A provisional government was established in 1843 by

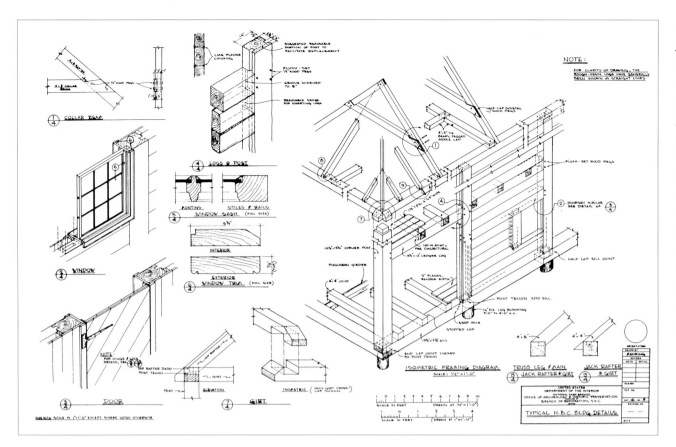

◁ *French Canadian post-on-sill framing details typically used by the Hudson's Bay Company. Sills 16" x 16" were hewn from logs and laid on the ground or placed on log posts set in the ground. Grooved uprights at intervals of about 6 feet were then mortised into the sills. Walls between the uprights were squared logs, either adzed or sawn with a tenon in each end, and laid upon the sills with the tenons in the grooves of uprights. Large horizontal log headers mortised and tenoned to the uprights ran around the tops of the walls.*

the settlers, who declared possession of the region. Accepting the authority of the provisional government brought an end to Fort Vancouver's importance to the Hudson's Bay Company.

In June 1846, the United States and Great Britain signed a treaty establishing the 49th parallel as the boundary between the crest of the Rockies and the Strait of Juan de Fuca. The Hudson's Bay Company sold its holdings south of the 49th parallel, in 1848 the Oregon Territory was established by Congress, and in May 1849 a U.S. military installation, Columbia Barracks, was founded on the bluff overlooking Fort Vancouver's stockade walls.

The remains of the abandoned fort, surrounded by the military reservation, burned to the ground in 1866. Settlement of the Hudson's Bay Company claims in 1869 included the surrender of the post to the United States. Within a few years, the 1,200 acres of Fort Vancouver were covered by Columbia Barracks and cropland. Construction of drainage ditches and occasional artillery practice obliterated the last traces of the old buildings and stockade foundations.

Preservation and Reconstruction

An act of Congress on June 19, 1948, authorized Fort Vancouver National Monument. Archaeological work and research followed, and on June 30, 1961, Fort Vancouver National Monument was redesignated as Fort Vancouver National Historic Site. Work proceeded on reconstruction of the original stockade, and by 1966 the north and east walls were completed. Construction on the remainder of the stockade and bastion resumed in

1972, and reconstructions began on buildings within the stockade. Archaeological activity still continues as foundations are uncovered and artifacts retrieved.

By the time reconstruction had begun, in 1966, all above-ground traces of the original fort complex had vanished. Archaeological excavation and meticulous research into the fort's recorded history revealed the location and features of the former stockade and buildings. Letters and journals from the fort's earliest visitors provided descriptions, plans, and sketches of the buildings as they evolved over thirty-five years. Invaluable information was gleaned from photographs taken during the fort's closing years. For some of the buildings, only informed guesses guided decisions about building design, interior layouts, and furnishings.

Framing methods used throughout the reconstruction were in the company's typical French-Canadian post-on-sill style. Additional headroom for a second story, loft, or attic was gained by extending the walls for several feet above the ceiling timber level. Floors and ceiling joists were made of squared timbers notched into sills and header beams. The roofs were formed by rafters and braces dovetailed and pegged for additional strength. Windows and door frames were formed by uprights tenoned into sills, headers, or horizontal logs. Ceiling beams were mortised into timbers of the course immediately above the window and door headers.

A walk down the rolling surface of the bluff, from the interpretive center past the orchard and garden outside the stockade, provides a gradual transition into the atmosphere of the mid-nineteenth century. Entry through the massive wooden gates on the north leads visitors

△ *Hinged shutters covered eight 3-pound guns mounted on sea carriages and armed for service. The guns were never fired in anger but stood ready to salute arriving ships.*

△ *The three-story octagonal bastion at the northwest corner of the stockade was built in the winter of 1844–45 at the height of fears of an American attack on the fort. Ironically, many Americans interpreted this action as aggressive rather than defensive.*

△ *The first two stories of the post-on-sill framed bastion were 20 feet square and about 20 feet high. Horizontal rifle loopholes were cut in the 12-inch-thick log walls. The top floor was octagonal and extended over the base, giving defenders a clear view of the land and a perfect platform from which to protect the fort.*

onto the grassy plain of the parallelogram-shaped enclosure. The 15-foot-high stockade walls running 734 feet in one direction and 318 feet across the ends deceive the eye; the scope here is that of five football fields placed side by side.

Stockade and Bastion

The protective walls of Douglas fir logs that enclose Fort Vancouver stand today as they did to receive the westward migration to the Oregon Territory in 1845. Douglas fir was an obvious choice because of its availability. Despite its resistance to rot, in the wet climate replacements were needed every four or five years.

Logs of appropriate length were cut off square at the bottom and charred for extra protection. Fifteen feet was a typical height for the pointed or wedge-shaped logs, each 5 to 10 inches in diameter. The logs were placed at a slight tilt toward the interior and were strengthened by horizontal girths of logs mortised and pegged into the posts 2 to 4 feet above the ground and below the tops of the pickets.

Chief Factor's Residence

The large, white house inside Fort Vancouver's stockade walls served as the official residence provided by the Hudson's Bay Company for its chief factor, John Mc-Loughlin.[17] As the center of business, social, and political activity for much of the Oregon Country, the house was intended to impress the Indians and settlers with the power and majesty of the London-based company. Construction began in 1829 and took seven years to complete. A succession of travelers described the masterful building and elegant furnishings.

The floor plan in the reconstruction is the result of archaeological research, examination of archives, and reflection upon Dr. McLoughlin's physique and character. He was a large man, and his home would naturally reflect his stature. To the left of the entrance hall is the chief factor's apartment—a sitting room, two bedrooms, and his office; to the right is the apartment of the assistant chief factor, James Douglas, comprising a sitting room and three bedrooms.

The values of England and its rigid class structure were perpetuated in the activities of the chief factor's

▷ *The kitchen for the chief factor's residence was strictly utilitarian. It was connected to the house by a covered passageway.*

△ *When the original chief factor's residence was completed in 1837 after seven years' construction, it was reputed to be the grandest house north of San Francisco and west of St. Joseph, Missouri. The white clapboard walls and sweeping paired stairways greatly impressed visitors. The building measures approximately 80' x 40', is one story high, and contains ten rooms. The main floor, about five feet above ground, left room for a wine cellar below. Curved iron arbors and veranda uprights supported grapevines, which acted as awnings against the sun. A pair of mounted cannon ceremonially guard the entrance.*

▷ *The 20' x 30' mess hall, or common dining room, was the social center for Fort Vancouver. It was large enough to seat up to thirty persons and host social events. Holidays were celebrated here with furnishings, dinner service, and decorations uncommon in the Northwest at the time; some were purchased by Dr. McLoughlin during a visit to London in the winter of 1838–39.*

△ *The kitchen attached to the residence has been meticulously reconstructed using archaeological excavations and historical records. It contains a food preparation area, laundry room, and pantry. Several rooms above provided servant living quarters.*

house. Dinners were limited strictly to the company's commissioned officers. Guests to the post were well received, but officers' wives were not welcome. Apprentice clerks were the lowest on the social ladder, only occasionally attending dances at the house. When church services were held in the mess hall, anyone could attend, but this was the only time when common laborers could enter the house.

Some of the comforts of home were brought by ship from England and carried overland across Canada by company traders. Excavations have yielded shards of export china, earthenware, and other artifacts that provided valuable clues as to what the original furnishings in the house were. A visitor in 1841 described the "elegant Queen's ware" and the "glittering glasses and decanters" that graced the table in the mess hall. The restoration relied heavily upon such written records. Journals and letters that made reference to the Big House have helped restorers know that the original house had pine-boarded walls and ceilings and a Carron stove from Scotland. A copy of von Humboldt's *Personal Narrative of Travels to South America* is on the chief factor's desk because a visitor in 1833 wrote about borrowing it from Dr. McLoughlin.

Kitchen

The kitchen, a building of post-on-sill framing, was directly to the north of the chief factor's house and connected to it by a covered passageway. The kitchen was the scene for the preparation of the main meal of the day, served at midday, for the fifteen or twenty commis-

△ *The main meal of the day was prepared in the kitchen at midday and consisted of seven or eight courses, all served formally. The cook, a manservant, was aided by a number of male assistants. An open hearth at the level of the earth-packed, white plaster-covered floor was supplemented by a small brick oven.*

The prepared food was transferred to serving dishes in the pantry at the foot of the stairs leading to the passageway and carried hot to the mess hall as soon as each course was finished. The dinnerware, cutlery, and glasses were also stored here.

△ *The washhouse, reconstructed on the site of the 1845 original. The simple post-on-sill frame building probably served as a washing place for clothes, persons, or both.*

sioned officers. The meals were overwhelming, as described by an 1837 visitor: *Our first course was soup, next boiled salmon, then roasted ducks, then such a roast turkey as I never saw or ate. It was a monster, it was like cutting slices of pork, then wheat pancakes, after that bread and butter and cheese all of their own make, and excellent too.*

A staff of women worked in the laundry room, where they cleaned and pressed the clothing of the chief factor, his family, and the commissioned officers and clerks. A stove heated water and indoor drying was used, following rules of the fort that forbade hanging the laundry out to dry in the yard.

▽ *The post-on-sill framing in the bakery is typical of the Hudson's Bay Company standard use of squared timber posts and sills on log skirting. The framing and wood-planked floor were raised about a foot off the ground on log posts. Split-log skirting around the grade sill prevented skunks from getting under the floorboards.*

◁ *Detail of the post-on-sill framing in the corner posts at the smithy, and dovetailed plates carrying the roof trusses.*

◁ *The Fort's smithy is unusually low for a Fort Vancouver building. The eave line is eight feet high, and the ridge of the gabled roof is not much higher than the stockade.*

△ The Indian Trade Shop and Dispensary had the unusual distinction of being located inside the stockade's walls. Fixed windows above the heavily planked doors provide light for the trade shop, with double-hung windows used in the dispensary. The original fur room windows were protected by horizontal bars on the inside. As elsewhere, the post doors and the door and window trim are painted Spanish brown, and window frames white. A loft above the trading store was used for storing furs, and here the floors are tongue-and-groove planking two to three inches thick.

Bakery

The gabled, one-and-a-half-story bakery, about 25' x 40', contained two large brick ovens, with a sleeping loft above for the bakers.

Several bakers toiled long hours to bake bread for the 200 to 300 people at the fort, in addition to the sea biscuit (hardtack) for crews of company vessels, traders, and for other forts on the Northwest coast. Dough was mixed in large wooden bins and worked or shaped on long wooden tables. Fires were built directly in the ovens, and after two or three hours the coals were raked out and dough was put in to bake on the hot bricks.

The bakers were relatively well paid for the standards of the day, but an annual salary of £25 plus room and board did not prevent the baker from Outfit 1848 from leaving; the official report read: "Gone to California, Wages to 1 March 1849."

Blacksmith Shop

The blacksmith shop served as the principal smithy for the post. Approximately 45' x 27' and post-on-sill framed, the structure was built directly on the ground and had a hard-packed dirt floor.

The four forges of the blacksmith shop produced a variety of items for trade, and ironwork for building and ship repairs. Beaver traps, nails, hardware, parts for gun repair, and the axes coveted by Indians, up to fifty a day, came from the shop's anvils. England sent iron and steel, but fuel to fire the forge was a vexing problem. Coal from England was preferred by the chief factor, but the company's officers resented shipping expensive and bulky coal instead of valuable trading goods. Local coal was of poor quality, and after failed attempts by a Russian from Sitka to make charcoal from timber, the company relented and importation of coal resumed.

Indian Trade Shop and Dispensary

In keeping with the general Hudson's Bay Company practice, the Indian Trade Shop at Fort Vancouver was under the immediate charge of the post's surgeon, at least when one was in residence. The building housed not only the fur trading operations but also the dispensary, doctor's office, and doctor's residence, and served as the dispensing point for the servants' and laborers' rations.

The building is 80' x 30', equally divided between the trade shop and dispensary. Post-on-sill framing reaches twelve feet to the eaves and ridge roof. Walls are lined with planking, and the ceilings are planked above the dispensary. In the trade store, ceiling beams and loft planking are exposed.

The well-stocked shelves and the goods hanging from the ceiling in the reconstruction represent a typical inventory of trade items available from Outfit 1845. Caps, hats, clocks, crinolines, powder horns, blankets, kettles, beaver traps, beads, muskets, and other items were all available for sale or trade to Indians, settlers, or fort personnel. In 1845 almost 1,200 beaver pelts passed across the shop counter, as well as skins from otter, muskrat, mink, fox, wolves, and others – including two grizzly bears.

A recent visitor commented that the best time to see Fort Vancouver is "on a foggy weekend morning when the sights and sounds of this century are muted and all you can see are the tall fir timbers of the stockade and the outline of its buildings inside." Then modern intrusions are erased and the scene returns to the timeless quality of the stockade, the river plain, and the Columbia River flowing westward to the Pacific.

Timberline Lodge

Mount Hood National Forest

It's not all that much in retrospect. A few hundred thousand dollars. Credit with local contractors was extended way beyond what was reasonable. They knew I was trying to build something, and not take something out of it.

Richard L. Kohnstamm,

on negotiating his first lease with the Forest Service for

the derelict Timberline Lodge, in 1955

Timberline Lodge is a winter resort, a living museum of crafts, and a major achievement of breathtaking design and construction. Sixty miles east of Portland, Oregon, it sits just above the timberline on the south slope of Mount Hood. It is a dramatic, hexagonal-shaped stone and timber structure, with steeply pitched roofs and flanking wings—a dazzling piece of architecture. The volcanic peaks of Mounts Jefferson, Washington, and the Three Sisters are visible a hundred miles to the south.

The design is described as "Cascadian"—a grand American version of the European chateau and alpine chalet. The building echoes Mount Hood's majestic silhouette, presenting a form and massing designed to meet the demands of heavy snow and fierce winds. The silvery gray weathered stone and wood exterior, close in tone to the surrounding natural colors, give the lodge a special dignity. The massive basalt boulders at the ground-floor level meet the steeply sloping, shake roof that extends nearly to the ground in places, to protect against heavy snowfalls and spring runoffs.

Designated a depression-era Works Progress Administration project in 1935, the lodge was conceived for Forest Service ownership and private lease management. The Forest Service called upon Gilbert Stanley Underwood to act as consulting architect. Underwood's reputation as a designer for NPS projects in Yosemite and for the Union Pacific Railroad in southern Utah brought the project an experienced design hand. Underwood was then working for the federal government in Washington, and his representative, Stanley Stonaker, worked on the project from a Los Angeles office. Underwood's preliminary sketches were acknowledged as basic to the lodge's eventual form, including his concept of a large hexagonal core, with guest wings extending outward at angles. Limited funds made it impossible for the Forest Service to hire Underwood as a private architect, so the final drawings for the lodge were prepared by Forest Service staff, and Underwood was consulted by the decorators about the decor.[18]

When President Franklin Delano Roosevelt dedicated Timberline Lodge on September 28, 1937, work had been under way since June 1936. Building and furnishing the lodge in fifteen months were impressive undertakings. A

△ *The Cascadian design of Timberline Lodge silhouetted against Mount Hood. Linn Forrest, a Forest Service architect who worked on this project, described the concept: "The shape of the central lounge was inspired by the character and outline of the mountain peak.... It was our hope not to detract from the great natural beauty of the area. The entire exterior was made to blend with the mountain side." (From Muriel Adams' "Timberline Treasures," Oregonian, Northwest Magazine, May 21, 1967, p. 5.)*

△ Gilbert Stanley Underwood, acting as consulting architect when Timberline Lodge was designed, skillfully merged massive building volumes with the landscape by using steeply pitched roofs and random forms.

△ The hexagonal central unit with its dramatic, peaked head house is flanked by two wings of unequal length. A lofty main lounge built of massive stone and hand-adzed timbers extends to a wing with 59 guest rooms to the west, and lounges and a dining room to the east. President Franklin D. Roosevelt stood on the bunting-draped main porch on September 28, 1937, for the dedication of Timberline Lodge.

▷ *The conference wing, added in 1975, harmonizes with the original construction because of the stone base, shingled upper walls, and sweeping roofs.*

▷ *The graceful "Timberline Lodge arch" is repeated throughout the lodge in doorways and in furniture design, including the hand-carved Douglas fir backs of the dining room chairs.*

road was built to connect the site with a worker's camp seven miles away at Summit Meadows. Workers, paid 90 cents an hour, were housed there in tents and trucked daily, summer and winter, to the work site. A contract with the Lorenz Brothers of Portland required that 90 percent of the work crew be WPA employees, and crews were switched every two weeks to employ as many people as possible.

Timberline Lodge is a significant expression of the Great Depression, having been built by hundreds of WPA workers, with regional design themes and materials used wherever possible. All work was done by hand, utilizing traditional building and craft techniques. Tools were simple, allowing the integrity of the basic material to stand in balance and harmony with its function.

An inspired team effort was necessary to unite the unskilled crew. Speed was essential because survival of the WPA was uncertain. Despite the fast-paced construction schedule and harsh weather, there were no major accidents. Men worked as a matter of pride. Recorded reminiscences of contributors to the project are emotional, articulating their dedication to something special.

Construction pushed ahead through a severe winter, with hardly a day's loss of work. Snowplows routinely opened the access road, and small stoves were set up to warm the stonemasons' hands. Interior finish work continued into a second winter, and the lodge was opened to the public in February 1938. The WPA records $695,730 for construction costs; with roads and grounds added, the total was over $1,000,000.

The building materials were all local. Giant Douglas fir and pine were turned into rafters and columns, and native oak, pine, and cedar were used for flooring and paneling. More than 400 tons of stone were quarried nearby and used for exterior stairways, buttresses, and chimneys. Thirty-man teams split cedar into 36-inch shakes for the exterior.

Wherever possible, recycled materials were used. Utility poles were carved into newel posts and medallions, decorated with figures of wild rams, opposum, eagles, pelicans, owls, and bear cubs. Scraps from earlier WPA sewing projects found new life in appliquéd bedspreads and curtains. Old railroad tracks were transformed into massive andirons, hinges for doors and gates, window grilles, and a weathervane to crown the head house. Even uniforms and blankets from the Civilian Conservation Corps were cut into strips and hooked into rugs.

With its stone and timber designed for heavy use by hikers and skiers, the ground-level entrance under the main porch has a grottolike feeling. Large fireplaces in the base of the central chimney form a focal point. A major design element, framing the main entrance and repeated throughout the lodge, is curved timber posts and lintel arches. The design of the main lounge shows restraint in furnishings and decoration, allowing the drama of the large space to dominate the room's character.

The original guest rooms on the first and second floors varied in size and theme. Although twenty-three different design schemes were employed, they repeated

▷ *Roof shakes are one and one-quarter inches thick and placed in three thicknesses at the eaves for protection against storms. Typical board-and-batten construction places battens one foot apart, but to conform with the large scale of Timberline, the battens here are placed two feet apart. The perceived length of the wing is reduced by the use of shingles on part of the east wing balanced by clapboard siding over most of the west wing. Double-hung windows, dormers, and alternating vertical rhythms add to the overall character.*

▷ *A massive six-sided chimney supports a web of hand-hewn timber trusses holding up the planked inner roof of the head house. The hexagonal theme is carried throughout the construction and repeated in furnishings. Six great timber columns, each three and one-half feet in diameter, support the balconies and roof; they were shaped into hexagonals with broad-axe and foot-adze. The carver, Henry Steiner, agreed to shape them for $25 each if the logs were turned at his request as he worked.*

△ *Main lounge fireplace, built of 400 tons of rock. Stonemasons worked through the winter of 1936 to complete it, using large* cut stones brought from a quarry between Government Camp and the lodge.

◁ *The dining room entrance gate is richly embellished with wrought-iron craftwork. The design includes rows of animal heads, Indian patterns of semicircles and stair-step zigzags, and a door handle shaped like a rattlesnake.*

◁▽ *Main entrance to Timberline Lodge, framed by carved timbers embellished with carved rams heads and an incised thunderbird in the lintel.*

only two or three times, each carried out in fabrics and rugs, carvings on the furniture, and botanical watercolors. Each room contained hand-crafted beds, dressing tables, loveseats and chairs, and parchment-and-iron floor and table lamps.

Decorative details inside and outside the lodge seem to have been used at the designers' whimsy. Buffalo and bear heads carved on log ends stare from under the eaves, and rams' heads flank the main entrance. A thunderbird wood-carved relief on the lintel over the entrance door was inspired by a design one of the architects happened upon in his daughter's "Campfire Girls' Handbook."

Wrought ironwork adorns the main entrance door and exterior window grilles. The same deft handiwork is carried throughout the interiors, as seen in the andirons wrought from recycled railroad track, the door hardware, ashtrays, and furniture, and the elegant gates that

frame the dining room entrance. Overall coordination of furnishings and decorations was supervised by Margery Hoffman Smith, a Portland decorator. The project was conceived as an exercise in the Arts-and-Crafts style: to teach basic handicraft skills and produce attractive everyday objects of "honest" design. Trial designs by Mrs. Smith and two crafts supervisors, O. B. Dawson and Ray Neufer, were first crafted and then recorded on scale drawings for reproduction in workshops. Located at the construction work site and in Portland, the WPA workers produced wooden and wrought-iron furniture; handwoven fabric for upholstery, draperies and bedspreads; hand-stitched appliquéd draperies; hooked rugs; wrought-iron gates; and door hardware and straps. A high level of performance was required; anything of shoddy quality was rejected or remade.

Mrs. Smith convinced the Federal Arts Project to commission original works of art for Timberline Lodge. Oil paintings, watercolors, wood reliefs, mosaics, and newel-post carving throughout the lodge were created by artists paid $90 a month. The Timberline collection includes eleven oil canvasses and 144 watercolors of mountain plants. The Blue Ox Bar, an afterthought, is decorated with three glass mosaic scenes that depict the Paul Bunyan legend. Enriching the lodge, the artwork achieves one of the project's main goals: to serve as a living museum for the people of Oregon.

The lodge was built in perilous times. After it opened, it was available year-round until 1942 and then was

▷ *Geometric arrow designs form window grilles on two windows set on both sides of the front door.*

△ *Wrought-iron window grilles across hexagonal openings on either side of the main stairway leading to the front door. Design is an abstraction of a human shape.*

△ *A 750-pound wrought-iron weathervane reaches high over the head house. It almost fell when installed during a snowstorm.*

△ *Colorful, carved Indian head on the entrance door to the ski lounge. "Beadwork" below the face incorporates initials of some of the people instrumental in the lodge's design.*

△ *The 5' x 10' hand-adzed ponderosa planked entrance door weighs 1,000 pounds and is supported by hand-forged strap hinges. Functional elements designed by WPA staff include the narrow iron borders decorated* *with bolts, long strap hinges, handle, and door knocker, which is an animal head on a sunburst medallion.*

◁ *Old utility poles bought in Portland for $2.10 apiece were transformed into posts decorated with carved representations of Pacific Northwest birds and animals, and geometric and Native American designs.*

△ *Desk, chair, and lamp in mezzanine alcove. The space is framed by a Timberline Lodge arch.*

▷ *Glass mosaic mural in the Blue Ox Bar, one of many original works of art commissioned for Timberline Lodge.*

closed through the war years. Sadly, the lodge was subject to abuse and theft from the start. The laxity of Forest Service supervision, coupled with poor management, led to its being closed in February 1955 for unpaid electric bills.

A weekend skier, Richard L. Kohnstamm, fell in love with the lodge despite its appearance. He arranged a lease with the Forest Service and set out to restore Timberline to its former brilliance. Years of hard work followed, involving repairs to the heating and water systems and careful restoration of the interiors and furnishings. In 1975, a group called Friends of Timberline organized as a nonprofit foundation to assist in the repairs.

A dedicated management company and the Friends assure a successful future for the lodge. In Kohnstamm's words: "I take care of the plumbing and the Friends take care of the artwork." The Forest Service has recognized this successful partnership by awarding Kohnstamm's

company an operating lease to the year 2022. In 1981, the Forest Service built a lodge nearby for day skiers. Sensitive to Timberline Lodge's design and placement, it helps ease the burden of heavy usage sustained by the older structure.

By pooling the funds of the operating company, the Friends of Timberline, and the Forest Service, the life of this great lodge will be extended. Franklin D. Roosevelt's prediction "a place for generations of Americans to come … a new adjunct to the national prosperity" is well on its way to being fulfilled.

Crater Lake National Park

The eye beholds twenty miles of unbroken cliffs ranging from five hundred to two thousand feet in height, encircling a deep sheet of placid water in which the mirrored walls vie with the originals in brilliancy and greatly enhance the depth of the prospect.

Gilbert H. Grosvenor, NATIONAL GEOGRAPHIC MAGAZINE

A long drive through the Oregon portion of the Cascade Range offers spectacular views of many volcanic peaks – Mounts Baker, Rainier, Adams, Saint Helens, Hood, and Shasta. At the south end of the range, a truncated cone – the remains of Mount Mazama – holds a 1,932-foot-deep caldera filled with the waters as magnificent and intensely blue as the Oregon sky on a clear day.

Surrounding the lake is a rim of steep, jagged cliffs rising as high as 2,000 feet. The uptilt of the volcanic cone and the rim conceals the lake until the visitor reaches the edge of the cliffs. Even under sunny summer skies, traces of winter's heavy snows fill crevices down to the lake's surface. The extraordinary vivid blue of Crater Lake results from the water's purity; it contains almost no organic matter and few dissolved minerals.

Crater Lake has astonished visitors since gold prospectors first stumbled onto the site in 1852. Over the years, it remained unexploited until William Gladstone Steel arrived from Portland in 1885. As a Kansas schoolboy, Steel had read about the discovery of Crater Lake and became obsessed with the idea of seeing it in person. When he finally visited the lake and saw it was even lovelier than he imagined, he vowed to make it a national park. After seventeen years of devoted struggle, during which much of his fortune was dissipated, Steel succeeded. President Theodore Roosevelt signed the enabling legislation in 1902, and Crater Lake became the nation's sixth national park.

Early travelers had to endure a long journey to gaze over the rim at the fabulous, blue waters. The long distances from supply centers and heavy winter snowfall inhibited tourist development. Building was difficult in the severe climate, which seemed to be divided into two seasons: a short but beautiful three-month summer and a long, snowy winter. The yearly snowfall at Crater Lake averages 50 feet, and a record snowpack was measured in April 1983 at 23 feet.

Two collections of buildings are noteworthy at Crater Lake.[19] At the rim, Steel's vision evolved into a hotel overlooking the lake, Crater Lake Lodge. Nearby, the NPS began some of its earliest Rustic-style designs. As originally executed, the park's administrative center, a mile from the Rim Village at Munson Valley, contained the handsomest group of Rustic structures in the entire national park system.

▷ *Intensely blue Crater Lake, cradled by encircling cliffs. Blues range from indigo to turquoise depending on the light, weather, and season.*

△ *Winter snowpack often sweeps over and covers the main lodge roof. The first superintendent's home and office at the rim were destroyed by heavy* *snows in the winter of 1908–09. Caution became the watchword for the future, as stronger timber-frame buildings with steeper roofs were constructed.*

▷ *William Gladstone Steel, in 1929, describing to three Boy Scouts how he lowered the boats for the first survey of the lake. The boat* CLEETWOOD *is snubbed to the only tree remaining from the four originally on the site when Steel was there in the 1880s. Pictured, left to right, are Jack Edgemond, Steel, Don Kelley, and Drew Chick.*

Crater Lake Lodge

Despite the prime location and a sound original design concept, the lodge was disappointing in many respects. Compared to other national park concessioner-built lodges that might well have been obtrusive blights on choice landscapes, such as Timberline Lodge at Mount Hood or Grand Canyon Lodge at the North Rim, Crater Lake Lodge lacks those special features that could have made it truly fitting – dramatic forms, for example, or appropriate exterior materials, or special treatments for window and door openings. The original plans un-

derestimated the heavy snow loads at Crater Lake's 7,100-foot elevation, which often measure up to 60 feet a season. Construction techniques and materials better suited to lower elevations were used and in general, the workmanship was quite ordinary. Guests were not enthralled by the dreary double-loaded guest-room corridors and unappealing rooms. Inadequate mechanical and electrical systems plagued hotel operations from the start, and the insufficiency of fire exits and safety precautions was a gross oversight.

By the 1960s, safety deficiencies, material deterioration, and structural dilapidation had far outpaced concessioner's improvements. The NPS purchased the building, and after a decade, no one could deny that Crater Lake Lodge had clearly become a substandard hotel.[20]

The NPS alternately called for the removal and rehabilitation of Crater Lake Lodge. Much of the debate centered on its condition, the cost of its restoration, and the environmental impact a reconstruction would create. In many ways, the lodge epitomizes the dilemma between the NPS and the scenic conservationists as they debated the merits of historic structures set within prime natural resources. The Oregon historic preservation community nominated the lodge to the National Regis-

▷ *Crater Lake Lodge perched on the rim of the caldera. The first meal served at the lodge was Crater Lake trout, spawned from the dozen trout carried to the lake in pails by William Gladstone Steel years earlier.*

▷ *Massing of major building elements sweeping inward define the main entrance at Crater Lake Lodge. Compared to Underwood's work, the potential drama of the site and richness of form have been underplayed.*

▷ *The four-story lodge comes close to meeting the original prospectus: a first-story stone base has shingled upper walls and a shingled roof pierced with rows of dormers, and a large public room extends into the dining room and dominates the first floor. Crater Lake Lodge has been surrounded by controversy since it first opened, and various groups have debated the merits of restoring versus demolishing the lodge. The incomplete lodge received its first guests in June 1915. In 1924 an 85-room, four-story addition was opened, accentuating the building's commanding presence on the crater rim. By 1929 the lodge had 105 guest rooms, but only 20 had private baths. Between 1929 and 1932 an 80-foot-long verandah and an entry porch were added, and during the 1930s, 15 more rooms were fitted with bathrooms.*

△ *The ground floor is supported by stone walls on a shallow foundation, and there are three floors above, clad in cedar shakes. Reconstruction work required removal and replacement of 700 linear feet of stone wall in six-foot sections. The stone walls were anchored to newly poured concrete foundations.*

◁ *An alcove in the main lobby, with modest rustic touches.*

◁ A curiousity at Rim Village is the series of slender log poles, 25 to 30 feet high, stuck into the ground and bracketed to some buildings; they are there to mark the location of buildings underneath the winter snow-pack. When bulldozers clear snow in May and June, they have to be careful not to drive over buildings, for they run the risk of collapsing a roof and tumbling into a building.

△ The Visitor Center at Crater Lake was intended to be compatible with the lodge. This early design (1920) does not show the classic NPS Rustic features that evolved later – extended roof overhangs and deeply recessed window and door openings. The building is an L-shaped structure with walls made of local stone, horizontal lap siding in gable ends, and steeply pitched shake roofs. Gable detailing – a plank barge board flush with the roof edge and siding – suggests a veneered frame structure.

ter of Historic Places, and interest in the historic building, which had been a favorite honeymoon destination for seventy years, resulted in a 1988 NPS position favoring preservation rather than removal.

On the advice of structural engineers, the lodge was closed in 1989, and an accelerated plan for rehabilitation began, targeted for completion in 1994. Some parts of the building have been completely removed and replaced, and other areas have been gutted and rebuilt. The challenge of dealing with unusual circumstances has inspired some creative solutions; almost $12 million will have been spent on the renovation. Guest rooms will be enlarged, lowering the total number from 105 to 72 rooms. Some interesting new guest rooms were created by making use of attic spaces as the upper levels for two-story suites. Work is planned to follow historic standards whenever possible. When completed, the extensive structural rebuilding, replacement of mechanical and electrical systems, installation of new finishes and elevators, and additional exits and safety devices will make the lodge a safe and attractive accommodation.

The decision to maintain a lodge at the rim of Crater Lake will remain controversial. However, the efforts made by the NPS to retain the building's historic exterior and restore its interiors to a 1920s eclectic Rustic style should be applauded in light of the safety and comfort provided for guests at this historic cultural resource.

Park Service Buildings

Several buildings at the Rim Village demonstrate the evolving NPS Rustic style. The buildings are not a planned "village." They were constructed over a ten-year period, and stand somewhat isolated from each other. Some unity is achieved through the limited selection of building materials—stone, wood siding stained dark brown to contrast with white window frames, and steeply pitched shake roofs. An effort to achieve harmony with the site is evident in the use of local materials and the choice of designs suited to the harsh environment.

Two other structures at the Rim Village are the Sinnott Memorial Overlook and a comfort station. The memorial is naturally tiered into the edge of the lake rim. Built in 1930, it is constructed of uncoursed local boulders faced on a reinforced concrete foundation with

▷ *An example of advanced NPS Rustic design is expressed in the Rim Village comfort station. Massive, uncoursed boulders are capped by a steep, shake-shingled roof. Superb skills integrated the stone and infill plank-siding walls, which were a precursor of the Administration Center at Munson Valley.*

△ *The cafeteria and gift shop, showing an adaptation of the steeply pitched jerkinhead roof used at the lodge. Advanced Rustic detail concepts are seen in the squared timber rafters and purlins projecting beyond the*

roof. Some stone is used at gable ends. Roof pitches are so steep that an A-frame roof structure is formed at one wing by rafters that extend to the ground.

a log-framed roof. A stone parapet wall that extends out from the exterior walls guards the open observation platform. A museum is located along the interior walls.

Munson Valley Administration Center

The road from the Annie Springs Entrance passes Munson Valley a mile from the Rim Road. This was the site selected for one of the most comprehensive Rustic architectural programs ever undertaken by the National Park Service. Landscape architect Merel Sager was assigned the task of laying out the administrative, residential, and maintenance facilities and establishing design guidelines. The administrative core included an administration building and a ranger dormitory forming two sides of a plaza. The rustic character of the buildings was carried throughout a sequence of small stone-and-timber cottages that become progressively larger and culminated in the large Superintendent's Residence on a hill. The residential and maintenance areas were tucked out of view in the valley and trees.

Sager set out to achieve high-quality Rustic design in all the planned structures. Following the contours of the land, buildings are sited at the edge of the meadow and forest, and profiles were kept horizontal and low. Sager was especially conscious of the dramatic setting and overscaled many architectural features. In response to the local climate and geology, he chose massive stone masonry and steeply pitched roofs as the central theme. Native materials and natural colors were used, and severely straight lines were deliberately avoided to suggest the craftsmanship that was required.

Sager continued his experiments with stone walls of unprecedented size, which had begun with the Sinnott Memorial and comfort station at the Rim Village. In order to achieve the desired rustic effect for the one-and-a-half-story buildings in Munson Valley, a unique construction method was devised. First, a heavy wooden formwork was framed for the concrete and stone foundation walls outlining the interior surface of the exterior walls. The forms were braced by the wooden framing of the second floor and roof. Massive boulders, two to three feet in diameter and some as large as five feet

◁ *The Munson Valley Administration Center at Crater Lake.*
PARK AND RECREATION STRUCTURES *describes the buildings in this complex: "Unifying, well-defined structural traits persist. Steep roof pitch, dictated by the heavy snowfalls in the altitude here, and masonry employing boulders of impressive size, combined with rough-sawn or vertical boards and battens, are chief among the factors common to all."*

▷ *The Administration Building is a fine example of how a structure can be merged with the landscape. The design makes allowance for the building site, as well as form and materials and how they must respond to the local climate and geology.*

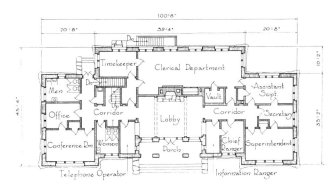

FIRST FLOOR PLAN

SECOND FLOOR PLAN

△ *Floor plans for the Administration Building show how the building's massing was modified to create more interesting exterior forms by recessing the central portion.*

FLOOR PLAN

FIRST FLOOR PLAN

▽ *The superindendent's house, and other staff housing at Crater Lake, carried exterior themes to the interior, where the buildings were finished with fine woodwork detailing, Mission-style furniture, and wrought-iron light fixtures.*

△ *The superintendent's residence (top) and ranger dormitory called for a compact floor plan and minimum building envelope because of the unique construction method employed in the Munson Valley administration buildings. Rapid construction was achieved in the short building season by removing formwork erected for the stone walls as soon as mortar cured and upper walls could be supported.*

▷ *The staff houses at Crater Lake as described in* PARK AND RECREATION STRUCTURES *"typify the ideal provision of living accommodations to meet the needs of the park." Massive local boulders, steeply pitched roofs, and deeply recessed window openings were repeated throughout all buildings. Similarly shaped boulders were carefully graduated in size from foundation to plates for the battered exterior walls.*

△ *The employees' dormitory and mess hall repeat common themes.*

across, were forced into place as work progressed on the upper wood framing. A space of several inches was left between the masonry and formwork and was later filled with concrete. As the masonry walls reached the eaves, and after the concrete was sufficiently cured, the formwork was removed and the weight of the second floor was transferred to the masonry walls.[21]

The battered stonework retains a strong visual tie to the steeply pitched gable roofs. The intersecting roofs and gable and shed dormers were covered with wooden shakes placed in a staggered, hit-or-miss pattern to give a textured appearance. Gable ends are finished with vertical board-and-batten siding. The eave detailing on the projecting gable ends adds a finely finished touch to the building; barge boards are pierced purlins, giving the buildings a tightly constructed feeling.[22]

The administration and residential building interiors were finished with wall planking, wrought-iron light fixtures, and stone fireplaces. Some of the period furnishings are still in place. A maintenance complex includes a mess hall, warehouse, and several support buildings, all executed with similar design and construction features.

Sager succeeded in conceiving a superb complex admirably suited to location and climate. The geology of the area is reflected in the stone "bases." The stone and concrete lower walls are perfect for the wet, cold climate, where rot and the pressure of deep snows easily destroy less substantial buildings. The thick stone walls provide insulation as well as protection. Verticality was emphasized to emulate the steep terrain and coniferous forest. Ingenious construction methods were employed to cope with the short construction season at Crater Lake. By using a combination of wooden formwork and upper-floor framing, the entire exteriors of several buildings were completed in one summer.

Fifty years of severe winters have taken their toll on the Crater Lake administration complex. Shake roofs have recently been replaced with metal roofs that more readily shed snow. Occupancy of the buildings in winter made necessary the addition of an A-frame shelter over the Administration Building entrance. But the complex remains an architectural jewel, endowed with a special identity from the past and continuing to serve a vital role in the present.

Oregon Caves National Monument

The new Chateau, unquestionably responsible for the major part of the business increase at Oregon Caves, is deserving of more than casual examination for several reasons: native materials were used in all places possible, which employment has resulted in a building in harmony with its surroundings.

THE SPECTATOR, October 13, 1934

The Chateau at Oregon Caves National Monument is one of the least-known lodges in the national park system. Although relatively unrecognized, the Chateau is a tour-de-force of organic architecture, well worth a visit. Constructed in 1934, a six-story lodge built into a gorge creates a strong architectural presence in a rich forest setting among tumbling waterfalls and moss-covered marble ledges.[23]

Oregon Caves National Monument

The Oregon Caves are carved out of limestone formations in the Siskiyou Mountains in southwestern Oregon. Off the well-beaten path, the caves are reached by an 18-mile mountain highway from the road between Crescent City, California, and Grants Pass, Oregon.

In 1874, an Oregonian named Elijah Davidson came upon the caves while deer hunting. During the 1890s, local business interests tried to exploit the area's resort potential, but the remote location of the caves limited the number of hardy visitors who made their way into the Siskiyou wilderness. A visit in 1907 by Joaquin Miller – the "Poet of the Sierra" – marked the beginning of a concerted effort to promote the caves' protection and preservation. By 1909, lobbying had become so intense that the site was designated a National Monument by President Taft under the jurisdiction of the U.S. Forest Service, Department of Agriculture.

Disgruntled local businessmen pushed their congressional delegation to have the area changed to a national park. They hoped that a redesignation would ease the federal regulations that made it difficult to build a resort and access road in a Forest Service area. Changes in 1915 to the Forest Service regulations on leased lands for hotel and recreation sites renewed local interest in developing Oregon Caves. In 1923, a group of businessmen from Grants Pass formed the Oregon Caves Company to manage the concession at the monument. The company planned to offer food services, overnight lodging, and cave tours, and they began by building the Chalet, a handful of cottages, and some tent-houses. By 1929, the company announced plans to construct the Chateau.

▷ *Architect Gust Liam skillfully sited the six-story Chateau to span the gorge and blend agreeably into the site. Main gable roofs are steeply pitched and are pierced by shed-roof dormers further broken by gabled-roof dormers. The exterior of the Chateau was covered in shaggy cedar-bark shiplap siding, so the building matched the texture of the surrounding conifer forest. In spite of its formidable mass, the building does not appear to intrude on its setting.*

The Chateau

To obtain a suitable design for the Chateau, the Oregon Caves Company contracted with a Grants Pass architect and builder, Gust Liam. Construction on the Chateau began in 1932 and was completed in 1934 at a cost of $50,000. The challenge for Liam was enormous. The steep sides of the gorge had to accommodate a road and parking area, limiting the available building space.

Rather than perching the Chateau on the mountainside, Liam chose to have it span the small gorge. The cave's stream discharged through the gorge, and the steady waters were used to architectural advantage. Liam allowed a small portion of the stream to pass through the dining room, channeled through a culvert in the Chateau's basement. He physically brought the outside in and reinforced this interplay with enormous picture windows. Visitors could sit in the dining room enjoying a tasty meal while looking out into the thick, green forest, a small stream rippling past their feet.

Most of the construction materials are of local origin. The principal timbers of Douglas fir were cut a short distance away and trimmed at a mill on the Caves Highway. The cedar bark for the vertical siding came from a nearby railroad-tie cutting operation. Marble for the double fireplace in the lobby was blasted out of bedrock on the site.

Liam scaled down the perceived mass of the building by constructing the largest portion down inside the gorge.[24] From the "ground" level, where the drive curves around the building, the visitor senses a two-story building—something smaller in scale than trees in the forest, something that fits with the terrain and primal atmosphere of the development. The full six-story height can be seen only from a distance, across the gorge.

The Chateau has a wood-frame superstructure on a concrete foundation that rests on natural bedrock. The lowest two floors house mechanical equipment and storage areas. The dining room, coffee shop, and kitchen areas are on the third floor – the same level as the lower trout pool grotto at the immediate head of the gorge. The fourth floor is at road level and contains the entrance lobby and some guest rooms. The two upper floors have additional guest rooms and the manager's living quarters.

The large lobby on the fourth floor, accessible from the parking lot, contains a double fireplace. The subtle, pale gray wood in the room has a history. During construction, workers beat sacks of cement against the wooden posts to loosen up the contents. Tiny particles of cement became imbedded in the wood. As the building neared completion, the crew stained wood not initially tinted by the cement to match it.

Construction on the Chateau had already been under way for a year when the National Monument came under jurisdiction of the NPS in 1933. As the federal agency responsible for approving all of the construction in the National Monument, the NPS brought its group of experts to the project—the people responsible for developing the Rustic design ethic. Additional funding under the CCC employed hundreds of young men to build the rock walls and reflecting pools around the Chateau and cave entrances.

The development at Oregon Caves was typical of work in other national parks and monuments during the 1930s. The concessioner worked closely with the Plans and Design branch of the NPS, headed by landscape architect Thomas C. Vint. Architectural drawings were presented to the NPS technical staff for approval and, possibly, suggestions on how the building could better fit into its environment. Simultaneously, NPS landscape

▷ *Chateau lobby. Douglas fir log columns, felled from surrounding hillsides, support the timber framing in the lobby lounge and dining rooms.*

◁ *Architectural details of the structural framing. The 18" x 24" exposed wooden beams are supported by 30-inchthick log columns. Wood decoration applied at the joints simulates wood joinery and is nonstructural.*

△ *The two-story main entrance to the Chateau. Shaggy bark siding, long shingles, and steeply pitched roofs and dormers are compatible with earlier buildings on the site.*

△ *A handsome, rustic staircase of oak, madrone, pine, and fir leads downstairs from the lobby to the dining room and upstairs to guest rooms. Oak treads, three inches thick, rest on a pair of massive log stringers. The darker wood of the peeled madrone balusters and the lighter wood of the handrails and newel posts are smooth-finished but retain softened gnarls and knots. Natural light from the large windows overlooking the trout pool emphasizes the stairwell and creates a pleasing contrast with the darker lobby.*

architects prepared landscape plans to enhance the site. At Oregon Caves, they laid out the stone walls and located sites for reflecting pools. The concessioners and NPS designers successfully achieved a development in harmony with the site: The hotel, residences, and parking areas fit comfortably into the surrounding landscape.

The CCC followed the landscape architect's designs. They built stone retaining walls, two trout pools and a waterfall, a campfire circle, and various walkways. The on-site landscape architect chose rubble boulders at the site, singling out the ones he wanted according to texture, color, and weathering. The resulting stone walls have a natural-looking, aged appearance that make the walls blend in with the weathered bedrock exposed around the site. This thoughtful approach to site design further enhanced the rustic feeling around the Chateau.

Laura Soullière Harrison describes how little the

building has changed over time: *Today's visitor is still enchanted by the rustic sense of place that the builder and the landscape architects created. Entering the area is very much like travelling back into the 1930s. Trout still swim in the small pools. Even the smell of the aging fiberboard contributes to that undeniably nostalgic feeling. The Chateau is more weathered but the furnishings are entirely original. More important than these subjective responses to the spaces is the strong architectural presence of the Chateau with its steep roofs and shaggy exterior. The builders' intent to create a structure in harmony with the surrounding landscape, and the landscape architects' enhancement of the setting, remain artistic pieces of the past.*[25]

Yosemite National Park

But to get all this into words is a hopeless task. The leanest sketch of each feature would need a whole chapter. Nor would any amount of space, however industriously scribbled, be of much avail. To defraud town toilers, parks in magazine articles are like pictures of bread to the hungry. I can write only hints to incite good wanderers to come to the feast.

John Muir, OUR NATIONAL PARKS

Yosemite National Park's 1,200 square miles contain glacial valleys, waterfalls of extraordinary height, giant sequoias, alpine meadows, Sierra peaks, lakes, and streams. The dramatic valley, with 3,000-foot granite walls, was not officially explored until 1849. Within a few years, tourists began to seek it out. Horace Greeley visited the valley in 1859 and pronounced it "the most unique and majestic of nature's marvels." *The Boston Evening Transcript* published eight articles by Thomas Starr King in 1860 and 1861 that aroused a great deal of interest. Soon, hotels were opened, toll roads built, and a stage line started. By 1864, the press of tourism, overdevelopment, and overgrazing threatened the valley's beauty.

President Lincoln issued an historic proclamation in 1864 ceding the valley and the Mariposa Grove of Big Trees to California "to be held for public use, resort, and recreation, inalienable for all time." Frederick Law Olmsted, then a commissioner of the state grant, wrote a landmark report in 1865, "The Yosemite Valley and the Mariposa Big Tree Grove," recommending public use and enjoyment in accordance with the philosophy of the grant. Olmsted's report formulated the philosophic base for the creation of state and national parks.[26] A national park was created around the original grant in 1890, and the state lands were returned to the federal government in 1906.

Yosemite's complex terrain and climate presented a tantalizing challenge to painters, photographers, and writers. Albert Bierstadt's ambitious canvases, Carleton Watkins' early photographs, and John Muir's energetic prose inspired the decision to officially preserve the valley and trees. Ansel Adams devoted a lifetime to recording memorable images of the eloquent light, the dramatic forms of massive granite, and the passage of the seasons in the valley and the Sierra.

John Muir described the Sierra as a "Range of Light." But it was Olmsted who first captured this special quality of Yosemite and the Sierra: *After midsummer a light, transparent haze generally pervades the atmosphere, giving an indescribable softness and exquisite dreamy charm to the scenery, like that of Indian summer of the east. Clouds gathering at this season upon the snowy peaks forty miles on either side of the chasm to a height of over twelve thousand feet, sometimes roll down over the cliffs in the afternoon*

▷ El Capitan towers almost 4,000 feet above the floor of Yosemite Valley. The sheer granite cliffs attract rock climbers from around the world.

△ Yosemite Valley and Bridal-veil Fall with Half Dome wreathed in clouds.

and, under the influence of the rays of the setting sun, form the gorgeous and magnificent thunder heads.[27]

The experience of Yosemite for most travelers is bound to the valley, the place that historically accounts for the very existence of Yosemite as a national park. A deep gorge, 7 miles long, 1 mile wide, and 3,000 feet deep, is as breathtaking today as it was when sighted by miners pursuing a wounded bear over a century and a half ago. But beyond the valley, to the north and south, are less-traveled routes of equally dramatic scenery. The Tioga Road, to the north, crosses east and west through Tuolumne Meadows and the high country; leading south out of the valley, the Wawona Road passes Discovery Point, the historic Wawona Hotel, and carries on to the Mariposa Grove of giant sequoias.

Yosemite Valley Chapel

This New England–style, 250-seat chapel was built under the sponsorship of the California State Sunday School Association in the summer of 1879. Designed by Charles Geddes, a San Francisco architect, it originally stood near the base of Four-Mile Trail, a mile or so down the valley from the present site. The chapel was re-modeled in 1901 and moved. The building was acquired by the NPS in 1927 and completely restored in 1982.

The chapel is the only building left at the site of the old village. Stephen Mather's personal interest in Yosemite Valley led to one of his first actions as director of the NPS, the relocation of the old commercial village to a new site on the north side of the Merced River, warmed by the winter sun. Mather accepted a new village plan in 1923. Gradually, the old buildings were re-moved, some to the new village or to the Pioneer Village at Wawona. All remnants of the old village were finally demolished in 1950.

There were good reasons for relocating the old village, beyond its unsightly and disorganized character. In December 1937, an overnight rain of almost twelve inches put the valley under water. Rescuers had to wade into the chapel to save the organ, pew cushions, and hymnals.

LeConte Memorial Lodge

The unusual granite LeConte Memorial Lodge was built in 1903 by the Sierra Club to serve as a library and club information center. Their founding president, John Muir, found his inspirations here, and the Sierra Club's dedication to wilderness preservation is rooted in the Yosemite region. Mountaineering expeditions originated at the lodge, and lectures by Muir inspired members to

◁ Galen Clark, the first guardian of the Yosemite Grant, which included the Mariposa Big Tree Grove, photographed by Carleton Watkins in 1858 next to the Grizzly Giant. Clark built a cabin where the Grove Museum now stands.

defend the valley and influence conservation policies relating to public lands. When an early member of the club, Joseph LeConte, died at Yosemite in 1901, his friends decided to establish a living memorial in his name.

The original location of the lodge was on a gentle rise of ground against a background of trees and the granite walls of Glacier Point. The owner of nearby Camp Curry needed space for additional guest accommodations and prevailed upon the club to move the lodge a short distance to the west. The roof was dismantled, most of the original stonework was saved, and the lodge was rebuilt according to the original plans. It reopened in the summer of 1919. Beginning in 1920, a young San Franciscan named Ansel Adams worked for the next four years as its summer custodian.

The lodge's style and execution are unique in the national park system. They derived from the emerging appreciation of the California rustic landscape as expressed by a group of San Francisco Bay Area architects. One of the leaders of this group, Bernard Maybeck, searched for innovative ways to relate structures to their site through building massing and using natural materials. Maybeck greatly influenced the work of his brother-in-law, John White, the architect of LeConte Memorial Lodge. Both

believed that a building's site and the choice of construction materials had a strong influence on the building's design. Architectural interest was provided by form and exposed structural framing on the interior; ornamentation or decorative detail were not necessary.

The roof is the lodge's dominant architectural feature, on both the exterior and interior. An unusual hammer-beam structure, it rests on engaged stone piers built into the walls and supports exposed scissor trusses above the interior spaces. The steep pitches and shapes of the roofs, and the parapet walls, emphasize the verticality of the structure. On the interior, this impression is reinforced by the exposed roof structure and a chimney that extends from the fireplace to the roof.

Rangers' Club

When Stephen Mather decided to relocate Yosemite Village to the valley's north side, the Rangers' Club and garage were the first major structures built there. Mather saw the need for a special structure to house the newly organized ranger force, and he decided to personally finance construction. His aim was to persuade Congress to build clubhouses in other parks, but the idea never took hold.

Mather retained a distinguished San Francisco archi-

△ *Bridalveil Fall drops 620 feet from a hanging valley. Gilbert Grosvenor, patriotic promoter of the national parks, in 1916 described his feelings for the region: "No words can adequately describe the majesty and friendliness of the giant redwood trees of the Sequoia and Yosemite national parks, the stately granite domes and sharp pinnacles, the roaring white cascades, the deep dark canyons.... The High Sierra so surpass the Alps that again no comparison can be made."*

tect, Charles Sumner Kaiser, to design the complex ("Kaiser" was dropped when World War I broke out). Sumner's concept would set a precedent for the kind of architecture that Mather wanted in the parks: rustic in character, made of natural materials to harmonize with the environment, with form and design that alluded to frontier and alpine traditions.

The interior of the Rangers' Club was arranged with common spaces on the first floor and bedrooms on the second floor. The first floor retains much of its original Arts-and-Crafts warmth – stout wooden furnishings, built-in bookcases with the added touch of jigsawn fir trees in the woodwork, and wagon wheel chandeliers fringed with giant sequoia cones. In the living and dining rooms, chamfered columns support corbelled capitals, and exposed beams with chevron designs carry hand-hewn joists that contrast with a light-colored stain on the diagonal-patterned wood ceiling. Dark, wooden wainscot paneling contrasts with light plaster finish above and is used throughout the building. The ornamental designs of forest, alpine, and Native American cultural elements add rusticity to the space. A note on behalf of the occupants: This is a private residence, and visitors are reminded to respect their privacy.

To the east of the Rangers' Club is the garage-wood-shed. It is L-shaped and similar to the clubhouse, with

steeply pitched gable roofs, shingle siding, and board-and-batten gable ends.

Administration Building, Post Office, and Museum
Mather's goal to relocate Yosemite Village took form following the completion of the Rangers' Club. During 1923, the NPS landscape staff at Yosemite submitted a master plan for an administration building, a post office, a museum, several concessioner studios and stores, and a hotel located on the north side of the Merced River. Although uses have changed and the buildings have been modified over the years, several retain the original qualities Mather sought.

The designer first chosen for the Administration Building and the Post Office was Gilbert Stanley Underwood.[28] Even though Underwood was to play an important role in designing future NPS and concessioner buildings, his Yosemite designs were rejected by the Washington-based Fine Arts Commission as inappropriate and too complex. Mather then turned to Los Angeles architect Myron Hunt. Hunt's concept for the new administration center buildings consisted of two-story structures with a horizontal emphasis that would blend with the granite cliffs behind the village.

Director Mather presided over the dedication of the new Administration Building and the laying of the Post

▷ *Yosemite Valley Chapel dates from 1879 and is a historical remembrance of pioneer settlement in the valley. The original structure consisted of a single room, 26' x 50', with a stone foundation, board-and-batten walls painted dark brown with light trim, a shingled roof, bell tower, and steeple. The interior and original furnishings included pews, an altar, coal-oil lamp fixtures, and exposed stud walls and rafters. The organ was donated in memory of Florence Hutchings, the first child of European descent born in Yosemite.*

△ *The Rangers' Club in Yosemite Valley illustrates Stephen Mather's personal commitment to an architectural aesthetic appropriate for the national parks. Built in the summer of 1920, it has a distinctive U shape and steeply pitched shake roofs. Massive peeled logs*

extending from the ground to the eaves along the exterior walls, and trim that projects above bay windows, accent verticality. The board-and-batten walls are shingled and stained dark brown and, together with the massive granite chimney and multilight windows and doors, afford the building a warm, domestic scale.

△ *Administration buildings at Yosemite implemented Mather's plan for a new Yosemite Valley Village. The three buildings have first-floor bases with battered stone veneers that give the appearance of structural masonry, and projecting shingled*

upper stories trimmed with logs. A regular rhythm of window openings recessed into the lower walls conveys the massive nature of the battered stone-wall bases; upper-story windows are spaced and sized to preserve a large, shingled plane. Shallow-pitched, shingled gable roofs reinforce the long, low lines.

△ *LeConte Memorial Lodge, with unique Tudor influences, was built in 1903, then moved and rebuilt in 1919. The verticality of the lodge, emphasized by an exaggerated pyramidal main roof and weathered granite walls, reflects the steep pitches of the granite cliffs surrounding Yosemite Valley. Symmetrically Y-shaped in plan, the building is dominated by the massive wood-shingled roof and gabled rough-cut granite end walls. Entrance steps lead to a hexagonal porch defined by the lodge's granite walls and low parapet walls that extend from the gable ends.*

Office and Museum cornerstones in November 1924. The Post Office, completed a year later, echoed the Administration Building's stone base and shingled upper-story concept with minor variations: four large, multilight windows and three wide entrance bays on the south side, a porte-cochère on the north side, and omission of log brackets and rafter ends.

In the early 1920s, the concept of national park museums was in the formative stages. The American Association of Museums was interested in the development of interpretive facilities and hired architect Herbert Maier to prepare a design proposal for Yosemite. The Laura Spelman Rockefeller Foundation responded with a sizable grant ($75,000), and construction began in 1925.

Maier followed the concepts of the other administration area buildings by designing a long, low two-story building with a stone base and shingled upper story. He successfully subordinated the design to the setting and wrote, "To attempt attitudinal impressiveness here in a building would have meant entering into competition with the cliffs; and for such competition the architect has no stomach. The horizontal key, on the other hand, makes the museum blend easily into the flat ground."[29] With further support from the Rockefeller Foundation, Maier went on to design other museums at Grand Canyon and Yellowstone, each with its own special interpretation of the setting.

The museum building, now only partially used for exhibit purposes, represents the early emphasis placed on interpretation of Yosemite's natural history. The Yosemite Museum Association, founded in 1920, was one of the first organizations in the national parks to support research and interpretive activities. Later it

▷ The site chosen for the Ah-wahnee Hotel is a deep, grassy meadow (the local Indian word for "meadow" is Ahwahnee) at the base of the Royal Arches. Located at the east end of the valley, it is surrounded by a for-est of black oak and Douglas fir, which provides seclusion from nearby development.

became the Yosemite Association, and the museum served as its center for collection and preservation of cul-tural artifacts, emphasizing Native American prehistory and history in the Yosemite region. Now known as the Valley District Building, exhibit functions were restored in 1976 with an Indian Cultural Center, and an art gallery opened in 1988.

▷ The Ansel Adams Gallery in the 1980s. Major alterations in 1969 changed the building's exterior, but retained its origi-nal character.

Pohono and the Ansel Adams Gallery

When the old village was relocated, the move included studios that has been owned by photographers and artists, some of whom had catered to Yosemite visitors since its earliest years. Two of those established around the turn of the century were given sites in the new vil-lage in 1925. Julius Boysen's Pohono Indian Studio has recently been restored to its original condition, and the massive peeled-log framed structure with shingle infill panels is now used as an arts activity center.

The other studio relocated from the old village is a complex of several buildings now operated as the Ansel Adams Gallery. Artist Harry Cassie Best opened a studio in the old village in 1902, which was destroyed by heavy snow loads in 1921 and rebuilt two years later. Plans for the new Best's Studio were incorporated into the relo-cated village, and construction was completed in 1926. The main building shows Rustic features – battered stone piers, simple post-and-beam construction, and shallow-pitched roofs. The studio was blended into its setting by using granite in the foundations, fire-place, and the massive columns that embrace the dark-stained structure.

Harry Cassie Best established a reputation as a painter of Western landscapes, and from his studio he sold his paintings, along with arts and crafts, curios, and pho-tographs. At the time of his death, in 1936, ownership and management of the studio passed to his daughter, Virginia, and her husband, Ansel Adams.

Adams first visited Yosemite as a teenager, returned during the summers, and became caretaker of LeConte Memorial Lodge when he was twenty. While working there, he studied the many moods and climates of the valley and the Sierra high country. Adams' extraordinary photographs carried on the legacy of Carleton Watkins and William Henry Jackson. In 1972, Best's Studio was renamed the Ansel Adams Gallery.

The Best complex included a studio, an attached residence, a darkroom, two employee residences, and a garage. The darkroom became the base for the world-famous Ansel Adams photography workshops begun in 1940.

The Ahwahnee Hotel

Stephen Mather was chagrined to hear that Lady Astor refused to stay in the park because of the crude lodgings. He vowed that Yosemite Valley would have a first-class hotel and forced a merger of competing Yosemite con-cessioners, thus forming the Yosemite Park and Curry Company. Investing $200,000, he demanded construc-tion of a new, fireproof luxury hotel capable of year-round operation. Gilbert Stanley Underwood was the recommended architect.

The owners planned a large hotel with 100 bedrooms and a dining room for 1,000, but required that it be un-obtrusive and take advantage of the magnificent views. Horace Albright commented: *We felt by offering a quiet, restful, spacious hotel that many well-to-do, influential peo-ple who had ceased coming to Yosemite, owing to the crowds, could be led to return to us again and that further-more the Ahwahnee would give us a suitable unit in which to promote all-year business, offering the most luxurious comfort at all seasons of the year.*[30]

The fireproof design required a structural steel frame encased in concrete. What appears as rough-cut siding is really board-formed concrete stained the color of red-wood. The exposed stone received similar care in detail-

▷ *The Ahwahnee Hotel was built on a grand scale, set against the Royal Arches. Gilbert Stanley Underwood knew that his building could not compete with the setting. He devised an asymmetrical plan with three wings, each three stories high, radiating out from a six-story central tower. The plan afforded good views of the dramatic scenery from every window.*

◁ Emphasized by green slate hip roofs and bands of windows, the horizontal sweep of the balconies and terraces at Ahwahnee provides visual interest on the exterior and varied spatial experiences on the interior. Massive granite boulder piers and chimneys match the cliff walls and soar vertically throughout the complex. Broadened at their bases, the piers cast the first-floor window openings into deep shadow.

▷ The stately Grand Lounge. Above the 77' x 51' floor space, exposed concrete beams and joists arranged in a coffered pattern are painted to resemble timbers and decorated with bands of angular Indian patterns. Akin to a cathedral floor plan, the 24-foot-high "nave" is graced by floor-to-ceiling window openings with 5' x 6' stained-glass panels at the top. Intimate seating arrangements with easy chairs, soft couches, and low wooden tables with oversized ceramic lamps make the space inviting. Patterned drapes and Oriental and Indian rugs on the polished oak floor add warmth. Enormous fireplaces made of cut sandstone face each other across the room. Above one hangs a Kilim rug, above the other a De-Stijl mural.

▽ Schematic floor plan of the Ahwahnee Hotel.

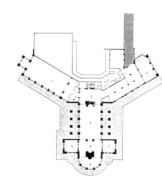

ing. Specifications required that the native granite "be laid with the natural weathered surface exposed and no freshly cut surfaces will be allowed for exterior exposure" and "the largest stone at the bottom gradually reducing the size of the stone to the top." The only part of the structure that is not fireproof is the dining room. Here, Underwood repeated a scheme from his other designs, supporting wooden trusses on paired-log columns under a wooden roof; steel columns were bolted between the log columns, one on the interior of the building, one on the exterior.

The Y-shaped ground floor pivots around the elevator lobby. Underwood deftly created a succession of public spaces beginning at the far corner of the plan, leading from an entrance porte-cochère through a log-and-stone entrance. Decorative Indian patterns, with strong Art Deco influences, predominate a mixture of Rustic and exotic interior motifs. The two-story lobby, delineated by plastered concrete columns, is set off by bands of french doors that open onto the landscape. The floor is decorated with earth-tone rubber tiles, and the cornice is stenciled in Indian designs. The unique lighting – triangular wrought-iron chandeliers and wall sconces – repeats designs used throughout the building.

Small rooms off the "nave" of the Grand Lounge complete the cathedral plan of this wing. The "apse" is a solarium overlooking the southern meadow. One of the "transepts" is the California Room, with memorabilia from the Gold Rush days. The other is the Writing Room, featuring a wall-length oil painting on linen by Robert Boardman Howard depicting the flora and fauna of Yosemite Valley. Public spaces are also provided on mezzanine levels at each end.

The succession of public spaces is a prelude to one of the grandest rooms in any of our national parks, the 130' x 51' dining room. Light pours in from the 25-foot-

▷ *Ruins at Soda Spring Cabin near Parsons Memorial Lodge. The inspiration for John Muir's "Range of Light" came while he was in the area shepherding a flock of 2,000 sheep in the summer of 1869. When he returned twenty years later, he became alarmed at the devastation from overgrazing and uncontrolled camping and vowed to fight for the protection of the entire Yosemite valley. Muir's writings inspired the forces that were successfully mobilized in 1890 to establish the national park.*

▽ *An abstract mural above the huge stone fireplace in the Ahwahnee Hotel lobby is based on Indian basketry designs.*

▷ *The gable-roofed ceiling of the dining room is supported by row after row of 34-foot-high sugar pine peeled columns and log trusses.*

△ *The hotel's solarium faces Yosemite's southern meadow.*

high south-facing windows and from the alcove at the west end of the room, and triangular wrought-iron chandeliers and wall sconces provide warm light after dark. Over-scaled Indian patterns on the uppermost wall sections above the wood wainscoting are echoed in the linen curtains and on the china. Granite piers flank the alcove, framing splendid views of the valley and Yosemite Falls.

Underwood began designing the 150,000-square-foot building in 1925, and ground was broken the next summer. Construction was a logistical nightmare. Battles erupted between the contractor and architect about cost overruns, design changes, and schedules. Convoys of trucks bringing logs, stone, and concrete to the site traveled over marginally improved roads. Steel beams that were to be hauled in over the recently built road from Merced were judged too heavy for the new road, so the contractor had them cut into smaller lengths, which were later reconnected with plates.

As the interior began to take shape, the Yosemite Park and Curry Company hired Drs. Phyllis Ackerman and Arthur Upham Pope, experts in art history, to guide the interior decoration. They commissioned Jeanette Dyer Spencer to create stained-glass windows for the Great Lounge and the basket-design mural for the elevator lobby, and Robert Boardman Howard to paint the mural for the writing room. They also personally chose the Kilims and Oriental rugs used in the interiors.

Ansel Adams was commissioned for promotional work for the hotel, and wrote: *On entering The Ahwahnee one is conscious of calm and complete beauty echoing the mood of majesty and peace that is the essential quality of Yosemite.… Against a background of forest and precipice the architect had nestled the great structure of granite, scaling his design with sky and space and stone. To the interior all ornamentation has been confined, and therein lies a miracle of color and design. The Indian motif is supreme.… The designs are stylized with tasteful sophistication; decidedly Indian, yet decidedly more than Indian, they epitomize the involved and intricate symbolism of primitive man.*

When the building opened, on July 14, 1927, the consensus was that it was worth the wait. Stephen Mather's press release proclaimed: "The Ahwahnee is designed quite frankly for people who know the delights of luxurious living, and to whom the artistic and material comforts of their environment is important." Over the years, the Ahwahnee has greeted heads of state, from presidents to kings, as well as movie stars and international celebrities. But more important than the list of famous guests is the hotel's place in architectural history: it epitomizes

▽ *White Wolf Lodge in Tuolomne Meadows is a favorite starting point for hikers or mountaineers. It is part of the Yosemite Park and Curry Company High Sierra camp system, offering a lodge with dining room, a store, cabins, and tent platforms. The simple, white clapboard frame building with a broad porch is a lingering example of Yosemite's early visitor accommodations. Originally a residence in the center of a lush meadow area used for summer pasturage, the lodge opened in 1926 to serve the increasing traffic on the Tioga Road.*

▽ *The tent platforms, cabins, and nearby campgrounds at White Wolf Lodge were added as improved roads attracted more travelers to Tuolomne Meadows.*

△ *Tioga Road bridge in Tuolomne Meadows. The NPS undertook a bridge construction program in Yosemite Valley between 1921 and 1923 and added eight bridges across the Merced River. All were of similar design, with one to three arches, made of concrete faced with native granite.*

the Rustic ideal and enhances the aesthetic experience of visiting this magnificent national treasure.

Parsons Lodge

Soda Springs has been a landmark and favorite camping site since the earliest travelers came to Yosemite. Using Soda Springs as a base, the Sierra Club organized their first outings in the Tuolumne Meadows area in 1901. They acquired 160 acres to protect the springs and provide access into the high country. When Sierra Club director Edward Taylor Parsons died, a memorial fund was established for a single-room building with a fireplace to serve as headquarters and a meeting place, and it was constructed in 1915.

Parsons Memorial Lodge is a simple building, 1,040 square feet, symmetrical, and rectangular. Some uncertainty exists about who designed the lodge – Bernard Maybeck or his brother-in-law, Mark White.[31] Perhaps they both collaborated with the structural engineer, Walter Huber. Maybeck's building values, stressing harmony with the landscape, are expressed in the use of local pink feldspar granite, peeled logs, a low-rise shed roof, and many hand-crafted touches.

The lodge's interior is an open space with exposed stone walls and a peeled-log roof. The stone fireplace on

▽ *Parsons Memorial Lodge. The rubble-stone masonry walls, deep door and window openings, and shallow-pitched roof visually tie the building to the contours of the nearby granite peaks. The stone walls, battered from three feet thick at the base to two feet at the eaves, are laid on a concrete core. The roman arch at the south entrance frames a sturdy, arched door of heavy planks bound with wrought-iron straps. The voussoirs and keystone are dressed, as are lintel and jamb stones throughout the building. All the windows are protected by shutters, heavily studded with nails to make them bear proof. The massive stone fireplace chimney rises above the roof line into a gentle, flat-topped arch.*

▽ *The original design for Tioga Pass Entrance Station, showing the entrance gateway and compact, one-bedroom ranger station. Plans called for a roof that was strong and shallow-pitched, composed of local stone and timbers. Refinements in the NPS Rustic style can be seen in the whittled-end log rafters that support the shingled roof. The front roof line extends downward to form a porch, supported by peeled-log columns and stone pillars, and the gable roof pitch parallels the ground and flows into the entrance gates.*

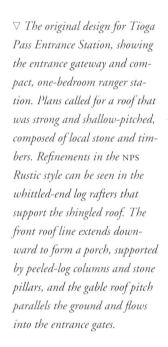

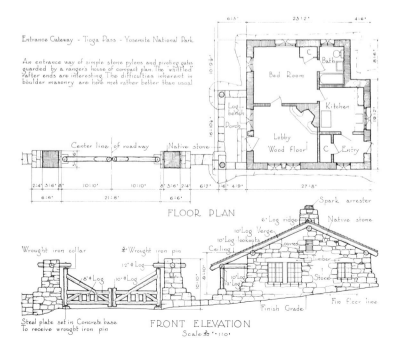

FLOOR PLAN

FRONT ELEVATION

△ *Ranger's house and comfort station at the Tioga Pass Entrance gateway.*

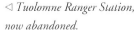
◁ *Tuolomne Ranger Station,
now abandoned.*

▽ *The Tuolomne Meadows Visitor Center, originally built as a mess hall, exemplifies* NPS *Rustic style in form and materials. The building has typical intersecting gabled forms, a steeply pitched roof, and stone base. Paired, peeled-log columns at the* *entrance patio and projecting whittled-end log rafters represent the best of Rustic detailing. Planked siding runs in a horizontal lower band, then vertical from window sills to eaves, and back to horizontal at the eaves.*

the north wall provides a focus on summer evenings. Stone benches under the windows have thick, wooden plank seats. Diagonal log braces on both the interior and exterior rest on low stone buttresses on the east and west walls. Rafters, 1½ feet in diameter, and flattened on top, carry a roof made of peeled logs 6 to 9 inches in diameter with rafter outlookers projecting 2 feet beyond the roof's edge.

Tuolumne Meadows and Tioga Pass

In the early 1930s, the NPS expanded services at Tuolumne Meadows and the Tioga Pass Entrance Station. In rapid succession, a ranger station, campgrounds, comfort station, and Visitor Center were constructed at the meadows. The CCC added manpower to the construction crews in 1933 and increased the number of buildings in the area over the next few years.

Badger Pass Ski Area

The earliest residents in Yosemite Valley cultivated winter sports to help them through the long, cold season when they were isolated from the rest of the world. Skating areas were shaped from frozen rivers and ponds. When the year-round highway was opened in 1927, Yosemite became accessible to tourists in the winter. In 1929, Yosemite made a strong bid for the 1932 Olympics. Ironically, Lake Placid was chosen instead but was forced to truck in snow due to a light winter, while Yosemite was groaning under twelve feet of snow along the Glacier Point Road.

Seeking additional revenues through winter use, the

◁ *Heavy masonry in the Tuolomne Meadows Campground comfort station relates it to the local geology. The shingled roof with jerkinhead ends rests on massive, battered granite walls.*

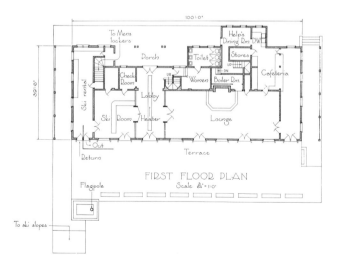

▽ *Carleton Watkins' photograph taken at Cedar Cottage records the festivities surrounding the opening ceremonies for the Mariposa Road on July 22, 1875.*

▷ *Original plan of the Badger Pass Ski Lodge. The interior furnishings, decorations, and artwork follow Nordic and skiing themes.*

Yosemite Park and Curry Company received NPS approval in 1935 for a ski area at Monroe Meadows. Although this meant an intensive use and a whole new type of structure, the only NPS guidelines were these: "New facilities for winter sports use … should not be built until provision is made for their proper maintenance and supervision."

Architect Eldridge (Ted) Spencer[32] designed the project, which included a lodge and ski lift, and the lodge opened in December 1935. A simple, Swiss Chalet character is derived from a shallow pitched shed roof over the entire building. Dressed timbers, exposed over the lounge, form trusses that support the roof and heavy snow loads. French doors open from the lounge onto a broad terrace, and a second floor provides access to a balcony that faces the ski area. A wide overhang supported by truss extensions, along with the balcony and terrace, add to the chalet's character.

The Wawona Hotel

The Wawona Hotel is the oldest resort complex in the national park system. Opened in 1876, the charming, two-story white clapboard buildings with porches, verandas, and Victorian trim harken back to an earlier era of travel. Unlike park hotels built by the railroaders, the seven-building Wawona complex began as a stagecoach stop on a passenger and freight line. Passengers going from Mariposa Grove to Yosemite Valley paused for rest and refreshment at the Victorian resort with its browsing deer and tranquil meadows. The Wawona offers a quiet, reflective setting after the titanic drama of Yosemite Valley.

The complex is on the edge of a rolling hill that overlooks Wawona Meadow and a nine-hole golf course. A circular drive with a centered cobblestone fountain leads to the main building.

Constructed over a period of forty years, the architecture is of less interest than the integrity of the whole complex. Unity is achieved through formal placement of the buildings on the rural landscape, by the principal building material, and by form and massing and color. The porches and verandas around all the buildings further unite them and encourage an airy connection with the landscape.[33] The buildings share other common elements, such as the cornice returns on Washburn Cot-

▽ *The main building at the Hotel Wawona complex, which has provided visitor services for over a century.*

▷ *In the hotel's dining room, sunlight can beam through two walls of wainscot-to-ceiling windows with 5" x 7" lights separated by narrow mullions. Box beams give the ceiling a coffered appearance; the ceiling light fixtures have giant sequoia cones woven into their suspension chains and used as a decorative fringe around the shades.*

tage. Stick style and Eastlake details appear in porch railings and column brackets. Even Palladian Classical elements can be found, as in the cupola of Moore Cottage.

The earliest hotel on the site was a small log cabin built by Yosemite pioneer Galen Clark in 1857. He expanded a small settlement into Clark's Station and later adopted the name Big Tree Station for the stagecoach stop. When the Grove was ceded to California as part of the 1864 grant, Galen Clark was appointed guardian. Clark's tasks distracted him from running his hotel, and a partnership headed by Henry Washburn, a Merced stageline operator, acquired his holdings in 1870. For the next sixty years, the Washburn family provided hospitality at Wawona Meadows.

Henry Washburn was a Vermonter, and his New England heritage is evident in the buildings he erected. His first lodging for guests, "Long White" (now called Clark Cottage), was built in 1876. A fire two years later destroyed the original Galen Clark stage stop buildings, but Long White survived to become the anchor for the new Wawona Hotel complex.

The main hotel building opened in 1879. The T-shaped plan has a main section 32' x 140' with public spaces on the ground floor and an employee dormitory on the second floor. The nearly symmetrical front elevation appears as two stories of deep porches with a veranda roof surrounding the building under a main, hip roof. Porch railings are in a simple pattern of rectangles. Interiors depict a Victorian character with period furnishings (not original), blocked wallpaper, and light fixtures dating from 1917.

The Manager's Residence, small and L-shaped, was completed in 1884, and is now known as Little White. It is a single-story, wood-frame structure with a veranda wrapping around the building; the veranda and main roof are covered with wooden shakes. Aligned with the adjacent Clark Cottage, the residence repeats the New England arrangement of gabled roof, white clapboards, and a veranda with evenly spaced columns.

The Annex, constructed in 1917–18, is a long, rectangular building with 37 rooms and shared baths. A two-story veranda around the building is covered by an extension of the main shake-shingled roof. A simple railing of vertical balustrades and T-shaped diagonal railings

▽▽▽ Moore Cottage, pictur- esquely sited on a knoll behind the main hotel building, is an elegant guesthouse favored by honeymooners. Built in 1896, the cottage is rich in form and details. It is designed in three equally proportioned horizontal tiers—a first-floor porch, a steep hip roof pierced by oversized dormers, and a cupola with a Palladian window. Gable ends in the dormers are filled with diamond-patterned shingles. On the verandah, fretwork rail- ings between chamfered posts and gingerbread brackets of di- agonal, pendant diamonds and scrollwork add a touch of grace.

▷ Landscape painter Thomas Hill's studio, built around 1886. The steeply pitched shake roof is crowned by a small balustrade simulating a widow's walk. The slender, picket railing and upper brackets recall the delicate filigrees of the perpendicular Eastlake style. After the artist's death, in 1908, the building passed through a variety of uses, including ice cream parlor, dance hall, and recreation room. It has recently been restored as a museum.

▷ *A quiet summer afternoon on the porch at Washburn Cottage.*

◁ *Eastlake-style column brackets at Clark Cottage.*

△ *The Yosemite Transportation Company's 1910 building housed a Wells, Fargo and Company office. The richly detailed Rustic log building was unusual in the Yosemite area at that time.*

△ *Washburn Cottage, left, and Clark Cottage. Washburn was built around 1900, with eight guest bedrooms and a bath on each floor. The verandah has porch railings with brackets in between similar in rhythm to Clark Cottage. Scrollwork eave brackets and baseboards terminate in cornice returns – a Greek Revival detail. Vines draped from the porch brackets add to the pleasant tracing of shadows cast on the porch floor. The verandah at Clark Cottage has diagonal cross-piece railings, and is sheltered by a roof supported by chamfered posts and curvilinear brackets. Shake shingles cover the roofs, with five dormers on each side.*

gives the building a Stick-style appearance. The west end contains a sun parlor on the first floor, overlooking the golf course.

In 1882, a Washburn daughter, Jean, suggested the Indian word *Wah-wo-nah* ("guardian spirit and deity of the Big Trees") as a more fitting name for the hotel complex than Big Tree Station. Today the big block letters HOTEL WAWONA stand out on the building's upper wall, greeting guests as they have for more than a century.

As the number of annual visitors to Yosemite National Park increases, so does the urgency to ensure protection for the remarkable collection of historic buildings set gracefully and conscientiously in this crown jewel of the National Park Service.

Sequoia and Kings Canyon National Parks

Sequoia and Kings Canyon, the twin national parks at the southern end of California's Sierra Nevada, have as diverse an ecosystem as any national park in the country. On a clear day, the snow-capped peaks of the Sierra that bound the parks on the east are visible from Fresno, 55 miles to the west. In between are arid foothills, forest belts that include stands of giant sequoias, and alpine terrain. This land so entranced John Muir that he set out countless times to roam the Sierra heights. His books record the redwood groves ravaged by logging and the foothill grasslands overgrazed by sheep.

Sequoia National Park was established on September 25, 1890, and General Grant National Park on October 1, 1890. Between 1920 and 1940, campaigns to enlarge the parks succeeded in extending the boundaries to the north and east to include more stands of sequoias and high peak country. General Grant National Park was incorporated into Kings Canyon National Park in 1940. The last addition to the twin parks was Mineral King, in 1978, in the southern part of Sequoia National Park, to avoid its being developed as a ski resort on Forest Service lands. As a wartime economy measure, the parks were placed under single administration in 1943, an arrangement so effective that it has been continued.

Access to the parks from the San Joaquin Valley to the west set early patterns of settlement and use, including logging practices that almost decimated the sequoias. Ranchers, settlers, sheepherders, and prospectors all left their mark. Logging, beginning around 1862 and peaking between 1880 and 1920, rapaciously attacked the stately sequoia groves. In 1890, John Muir warned that unless protective measures were taken, "all that will be left of *Sequoia gigantea* will be a few hacked and scarred remnants."

For many years the "Big Trees" attracted only a modest number of visitors; in 1909, the superintendent reported 854 tourists at Sequoia and 798 at General Grant national parks. The number had increased to over 10,000 when the National Park Service was created in 1916. Today, Sequoia and Kings Canyon national parks receive approximately two million visitors annually.

▷ *The giant sequoia (Sequoia-dendron gigantea) is found in 75 groves within the Sierra Nevada; thirty of the largest groves (and the largest individual sequoias) are in Sequoia and Kings Canyon. Although not as tall as the coastal redwoods, the giant sequoias are the most massive trees alive anywhere in the world.*

△▷ *Portions of the Sierra
Nevada in Sequoia and Kings
Canyon National Parks receive
almost 300 inches of snow a
year. Massive snowfields last late
into the summer. The variety of
altitude, terrain, and climate
are a surprise to many visitors,
who expect only big trees and
big mountains.*

◁ A Giant Forest Lodge cabin, showing the characteristic exposed frame covered with sequoia bark and bark filling between the framing members. The use of bark on framing members, around the door and window frames, and the repeated color for trim, follows the traditions of Adirondack Rustic architecture.

◁◁ Israel Gamlin built a cabin out of squared redwood logs in 1872, when he filed a timber claim of 160 acres in Grant Grove.

▷ The seasonal cabins in Grant Grove Village have a woodsy feeling, with log slab siding, shake roofs with double-coursing every fifth row, six-light casement windows, and lichen-green trim.

Historic Structures

The few examples of important historic structures at Sequoia and Kings Canyon are the result of the parks' haphazard growth and development. In contrast to the excellent examples of Rustic architecture found elsewhere in the national park system, it would seem that the extraordinary scenery of Sequoia and Kings Canyon confirmed the Grosvenors' claim in the pages of *National Geographic:* "In that architecture which is voiced in the glorious temples of the Sequoia grove … there is a majesty and an appeal that the mere handiwork of man, splendid though it may be, can never rival."[34]

Well-built, attractive groupings of NPS buildings are nestled among the Sequoia groves. Modest in scale, these simple structures were gradually added over the years along simpler architectural themes than those in other national parks.

The earliest historic structures at Sequoia and Kings Canyon National Parks are a scattering of nineteenth-century settlers' cabins built out of felled sequoias. Summer colonies on private inholdings at Wilsonia, Silver City, and Kings Canyon also contain small-scale rustic buildings, mostly wood-frame cabins on post-and-block foundations.

The influence of railroaders and private entrepreneurs was not felt in these parks, and they contain no rustic grand hotels or extensive tourist complexes. Tent camps satisfied the needs of the early visitors and campers who arrived from the California Central Valley. A day trip provided relief from the heat of the lowlands and satisfied most visitors and self-sufficient hikers. The NPS eventually addressed the issue of visitor facilities and initiated concessioner developments at Grant Grove and Giant Forest.

When Stephen Mather became director of the National Park Service, there were only a few service buildings at the parks. They followed the basic principles of Rustic design, using features that would be incorporated in later developments. The harsh climate of the high country placed special demands on the framing and exterior materials used at Giant Forest, Grant Grove, Lodgepole, and Cedar Grove. These buildings are principally characterized by small-scale designs allowing them to follow the site's natural contours – exposed redwood frames with infilled walls and low-pitched gable roofs. Several utility buildings were soon erected; simple in mass and form, they were compatible with the setting because of the color and texture of the exterior materials and their size and scale.

△ *Even the gas pumps at Silver City, a private community near Mineral King, stand red and tall in the sequoia landscape.*

◁ *The Mineral King area of Sequoia National Park was the scene of a miners' rush in the late 1870s. Mining was unsuccessful but the real treasure – the incomparable scenery – was secured as part of the park in 1978 to avoid recreational development. A twisting, switchback hundred-year-old road ends at a cluster of private camps and trails at the edge of the high country.*

▷ Giant Forest Lodge was part of a development in the 1920s that had an overall character consistent with NPS environmental standards. Simple, rugged buildings with hewn exposed frames and sequoia bark infill, they fit into their surroundings by virtue of compatible materials and appropriate scale.

◁ A massive sign at the Ash Mountain Entrance was carved out of blocks of sequoia wood by CCC craftsmen in 1936. The giant redwood trees — and the park — were named for a Cherokee leader, Seqouyah, who invented an alphabet and taught his people how to read and write.

▷ The Ranger Station at Hockett Meadow, built by CCC crews in 1934. Located in an alpine meadow surrounded by dense stands of lodgepole pine and red fir, the well-executed log cabin departs from the architectural theme at Sequoia by virtue of its log bearing wall construction.

by smaller elements to reduce the overall mass. A narrow foundation of rubble granite masonry over concrete from the ground to the floor line provided continuity with the stone chimneys.

The Future at Sequoia and Kings Canyon National Parks

No clear architectural image emerges at Sequoia and Kings Canyon as it does, for example, in the unified Rustic architecture of Crater Lake, Mesa Verde, or Bandelier. After years of planning, an emphasis on restoring the natural environment has emerged, and many of the buildings from the historic districts at Giant Forest/Lodgepole and Grant Grove will be removed. Although a difficult decision for the NPS, the global significance of the trees has been given precedence over the historic structures.

An important footnote to the cautious deliberation over the future of architecture in the two parks is the NPS' publication of an important study that may accompany *Park and Recreation Structures* and Augustus Shephard's *Camps in the Woods* as basic textbooks on Rustic design. The two-volume *Architectural Character Guidelines: Sequoia and Kings Canyon National Parks* provides an analysis of the existing architecture and guidelines for future designs.[36] Five basic issues are covered in the guidelines: site character, overall building form, roofs, facades, and landscape details.

Albert Good provides a fitting prediction about the future of the buildings in Sequoia and Kings Canyon National Parks: *The structures necessary in a park are naturally less obtrusive if they are reasonably unified by a use of one style of architecture, limited construction methods, and not too great a variety in materials. When a truly inappropriate style of architecture already exists in a park in which new work is contemplated, it is urged that the new buildings do not stubbornly carry on the old tradition. If the new style is the more appropriate one, it will prevail. In the course of time the earlier inappropriately styled buildings, will, in the very fitness of things, be eliminated.*[37]

The newly created NPS Landscape Engineering Division, under the direction of Daniel Hull, began designs for an administrative complex at Giant Forest in 1921. The Administration Building, Superintendent's Residence, and employee cabins were all patterned after the earlier utility buildings. At the same time, concession developments were built at Giant Forest and Grant Grove that included lodges and cabins designed by Gilbert Stanley Underwood and Herbert Maier.

Although no single design dominated the federal work at the two parks, the NPS buildings share common Rustic features. These are most visible in the Giant Forest Lodge Market, by Gilbert Stanley Underwood, the Ranger Residence at Giant Forest (1931) by Merel Sager, and the comfort stations scattered throughout the parks built in the 1930s. The designers are credited with understanding that within the dense forest setting, natural stone would play an unimportant, inconspicuous scenic role.[35] At the same time, it was impossible to erect buildings truly proportional to the setting; even the smallest nearby sequoias were often greater than 10 feet in diameter.

Buildings were framed with 10-inch-square redwood timbers. To give the buildings a proper relationship to the surrounding forest, siding, sometimes of unplaned lap, resawn, or tongue-and-groove planking, or shakes, provided an infill between the timber posts. Multilight casement windows and doors were inserted in the bays between the posts. Central gable shake-covered roofs, with vertical board-and-batten ends, were often joined

The Rocky Mountains and the Plateau Country

Glacier National Park

Wander here a whole summer if you can. Thou-
sands of God's wild blessings will search you and
soak you as if you were a sponge, and the big days
will go uncounted.... You will find yourself in
the midst of what you are sure to say is the best
care-killing scenery on the continent, beautiful
lakes derived straight from glaciers, lofty moun-
tains steeped in lovely nemophilia-blue skies and
clad with forests and glaciers, mossy ferny water-
falls in their hollows, nameless and numberless,
and meadowy gardens abounding in the best of
everything.

John Muir, OUR NATIONAL PARKS

Glacier National Park is located in a magnificent mountain wilderness that straddles the Continental Divide and the Canadian border. The spectacular scenery, set between two mountain ranges of the northern Rocky Mountains and divided by glacier-carved valleys, rivals that of any other national park. Glacier is the southern section of the Waterton–Glacier International Peace Park, in northwestern Montana; the northern section, across the border in Alberta, is Canada's Waterton Lakes National Park. The U.S. park's one million acres contain over 200 lakes, waterfalls, glaciers nestled in mountain cirques, a thousand miles of rivers and streams, and abundant wildlife. Dramatic changes in elevation encompass lush, verdant valleys, meadows ablaze with wildflowers, and deep forests reaching upward toward mountain peaks that rise to over 10,000 feet.

Discovery and Development

The Continental Divide separated Indian tribes and discouraged their passage through the Glacier area. Inaccessibility, few natural resources or minerals, and grazing land in a harsh environment attracted only sporadic settlement between 1855 and 1885. Northern boundary surveys in the 1850s were followed by a transcontinental railroad survey in the 1880s. When reports of Glacier's wilderness beauty began to attract visitors in increasing numbers, the first voices for preservation were raised. One of the military leaders of the railroad exploring team, Lieutenant John Van Arsdale, suggested in a letter of September 1883 to the *Ft. Benton River Press* that the region should become a national park.[1] Two years later, George Bird Grinnell visited Montana and toured the future park area.

Grinnell, the influential publisher of *Forest and Stream,* wrote a long account of his activities in Montana and helped popularize the area.[2] Others followed him, including a group of London bankers in 1886. Returning year after year with his wife and eastern friends, Grinnell became a leading activist in the movement to establish the park. His enthusiasm was matched by that of James J. Hill, the St. Paul railroad builder, who had long dreamed of building a railroad across the northern states.

Hill had pushed his Great Northern Railway as far as

▷ The peaks of the Garden Wall in Glacier National Park were formed when glaciers scoured both sides of the Continental Divide.

Overleaf: Alpine sunflowers at the edge of a mountain meadow, with Teton peaks in the background. In contrast to the stark Tetons, groves of quaking aspen and dense forests of lodgepole pine, spruce, and Douglas fir cover the valley and lower mountain slopes. Rivers and streams are fringed with stands of cottonwood and blue spruce. Wildflowers bloom in profusion from late spring through summer.

▷ Mountain goats range at Glacier's highest altitudes.

△ By 1915 a Grand Tour was available to visitors at Glacier National Park. Here, two of the White Company's famous "Reds" wait at Glacier Park Lodge to carry tourists through the park's scenic grandeur.

◁ Going-to-the-Sun Chalet (since removed) on St. Mary's Lake, July 5, 1933. Some of the staff dressed in dirndls, in keeping with the park's Swiss Chalet theme.

▷ A construction drawing of Many Glacier Hotel. It illustrates the Swiss Chalet theme for Louis W. Hill's dream hotel for Glacier, an area he called "the American Alps."

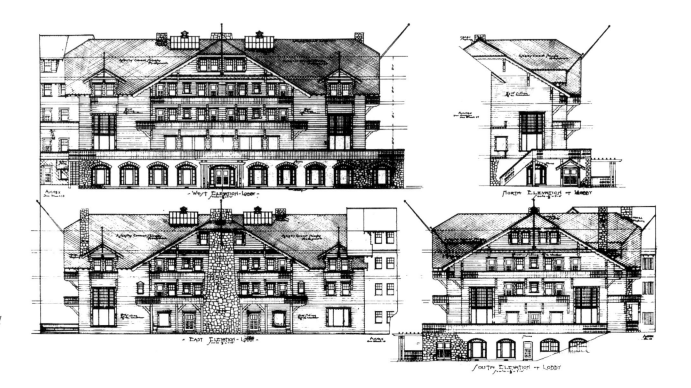

△ *Novelist Thomas Wolfe recorded sketchy journal notes during his whirlwind tour through western national parks in the summer of 1938: "From St. Mary's crossing and the cabins along the Going to the Sun Pass and the stupendous hackled peaks – the sheer basaltic walls of glaciation, the steep scoopings down below, the dense vertices of the glacial slopes and forests – and climbing, climbing to the Logan Pass so down again terrifically, and the glacial wall beside, the enormous hackled granite peaks before, the green steep glaciation of the forest, the pouring cascades, and the streams below – and by the rushing waters, and down and down the marvelous road Mc-Donald Lake."*

Montana but was frustrated in his efforts to reach Seattle by the lack of a suitable pass over the Divide. Marias Pass was the key, and it was finally "discovered" in 1889 by John F. Stevens, an engineer working for Hill, who saw the solution when he walked to the summit on December 11, 1889, in temperatures of -39°F. Hill's dream began to take on reality, and by 1893 the Great Northern Railway had crossed the mountains.

Concerned about inroads by ore prospectors, Grinnell put forth the idea of Glacier National Park in 1901. A National Forest Reserve had been created by purchase of Blackfeet Indian tribal lands on the east side of the Divide but greater protection would be afforded by a national park. Grinnell and various conservation groups, including the Sierra Club, promoted the idea. James J. Hill and his son, Louis W. Hill, who assumed the Great Northern presidency in 1907, saw real advantages for them if the park were created, for they would enjoy a virtual monopoly over access to the area. President Taft signed the Glacier National Park bill in May 1910.

Louis Hill's railroad ran along the southern boundary of the new park. By following the pattern set at Yellowstone, where the Northern Pacific built Old Faithful Inn, and at Grand Canyon, where the Atchison, Topeka, and Santa Fe financed the El Tovar Hotel, Hopi House,

and Hermit's Rest, Hill knew that a destination resort at "his" park would increase passenger revenues along the main railway lines. Hill wanted what the other railroads had achieved: to build resorts whose architectural styles would create memorable images, buildings that would be noteworthy in their own right. The railroaders used architecture as part of their marketing strategy. They deliberately created a sense of place that subtly enhanced the visitors' stay – at destinations accessible only by their railroads.

Glacier's theme, the "American Alps," was promoted by Hill and later by the National Park Service, and provided the architectural refrain for the Swiss Chalet style. The Great Northern Railway planned two large hotels and an extensive backcountry development of smaller chalets at seven locations in the park. Rejecting his competitors' approach – concentration on a single structure or location in a park – Hill's choice of style and a whole system of lodgings gave an architectural unity to an entire region.[3] Hill's development in Glacier was complemented by a Great Northern hotel in Canada's Waterton Lakes National Park (the Prince of Wales Hotel), a privately built hotel on Lake McDonald (Lake McDonald Lodge), and many fine examples of NPS Rustic-style service buildings.

▷ *Early morning mists create a rainbow over Glacier Park Lodge.*

▷ *A rustic gateway made of massive logs greeted early travelers at the Glacier Park Railway Station and hinted at further architectural delights to come. Now gone, it stood halfway between the station and the lodge.*

△ *At Glacier Park Lodge, refinements in the Swiss Chalet style are expressed in arched roof framing at the gable ends, broad overhangs in the shingled hip roofs, and multistoried projecting balconies capped with jerkinhead roofs. The balconies have fretwork railings, which sustain the chalet impression. Balcony railings on the long elevations are made from peeled logs, with panels of horizontals framed with x-crossed pieces next to balustrades. Horizontal emphasis is reinforced by the unbroken line of the main roof and long shed dormers on the main lodge and addition.*

▷ *Architect Thomas D. McMahon set out to recreate the classical volume of the Portland Exposition's Forestry Building in the hotel lobby, and his creation is a marvelous combination of formal and rustic elements. McMahon skillfully enlarged the interior volume of the lobby by placing eight-foot-wide balconies for access to guest rooms around the atrium behind the columns. Skylights interspersed between the kingpost trusses bathe the lobby in natural daylight. At one end of the lobby is the entrance to the dining room, and at the other a passage leading to the annex. An international atmosphere in the original decor included Japanese lanterns, and the staff dressed in lederhosen and kimonos.*

▷ *The westbound Empire Builder arriving at Glacier Park Station, 1930s.*

△ *Construction crews worked steadily for a year and a half to complete the lodge. One of the early challenges was the securing of logs. Timbers that met Hill's specifications were not available in local forests and had to be obtained from Oregon and Washington. Gigantic Douglas fir and cedar logs – from trees 500 to 800 years old – were 52 feet long and up to fifteen tons each, and were shipped to the site by flatcar. Column lintels, trusses, and beams – even the counters at the registration desk – were carved from these massive logs.*

To experience Glacier National Park in Louis Hill's era meant journeying from the east by railroad to the East Glacier Park Station or from the west to Apgar at the park's West Entrance. From these points, travelers could explore the long thumb of the park's mass that projected southward from the Canadian border. An early network of gravel roads and trails radiating from the railheads provided access around the perimeter of the park and into the interior. Working in conjunction with the government, by 1915 Hill had developed a transportation system connecting the Great Northern's hotels and chalets on the east and west sides of the park.

As tourism increased, so did the demand both for convenient crossings between the two sides of the park and for a northern road to Waterton Lakes National Park across the Canadian border. The solution was a trans-Divide highway, which was begun in 1918 and eventually completed in 1933.

Going-to-the-Sun Road is worthy of its long construction period. One of the most spectacular scenic drives anywhere in the United States, 50 miles of narrow roadway loops around lakes, avalanche chutes, wildflower meadows, and glaciers, climbing to Logan Pass at 6,664 feet. Moose and mountain goats can be seen as the road edges toward the Garden Wall and skirts waterfalls and mountain peaks with names like the Weeping Wall, Bird Woman Falls, Haystack Butte, and Heaven's Peak. To connect with Waterton, Chief Mountain Highway was completed from Babb, Montana, into Canada in 1936.

Louis Hill and the Great Northern Railway

Louis Hill wasted little time fulfilling his dream after the park was established in 1910. He envisioned that the visitor from the east would be greeted by a massive lodge of Swiss Chalet design at the East Glacier station just outside the park boundary. This would be no modest hotel, but one whose main lobby recalled the impressive Forestry Building at the Portland Exposition of 1912.

Construction began at East Glacier in 1912, and at the same time, work began on Many Glacier Hotel at Swiftcurrent Lake and on the backcountry chalet complexes at Two Medicine, Cutbank Creek, St. Mary Lake, Gunsight Pass, Sperry Glacier, and Granite Park (the latter two are the only ones that remain today.) By 1915,

after three years of intense building, Hill's plans for Glacier Park's eastern slope were completed.

Glacier Park Lodge

A long journey across the flat landscape in eastern Montana gradually brought the Great Northern traveler to the eastern slope of the Continental Divide. Louis Hill wanted his lodges in Glacier to provide travelers not only with comfort and hospitality but also with a memorable experience in the spectacular scenery. The visitor's arrival was theatrically orchestrated. The introduction to East Glacier was the view from the railroad station of Glacier Park Lodge across a broad lawn filled with an enclave of Indian tepees.

Hill and his architect, Thomas D. McMahon of St. Paul, Minnesota, appreciated the subtleties of proper siting. The long three- and four-story buildings, under a sheltering hip roof, extend across a rise of land at a slightly higher elevation than the railroad station and foreground meadow.

The main section of the lodge, with a lobby, dining room, and 61 guest rooms, was completed in 1913, and a 111-room addition was built the following year. The chalet character is skillfully executed, despite the elongated building plan, by an interesting design device: superimposed on long elevations at regular intervals are chalet gable ends under a hip or jerkinhead roof, and balconies that have jigsawn fretwork railings. The result is repetition of traditional chalet design at different points all around the building.

The interior was originally rich in Blackfeet Indian artifacts. A tepee was set up on the second-floor balcony, and arts and crafts were exhibited on kiosk bases of massive logs in the lobby and throughout the lodge. A 180-foot-long canvas mural painted by Chief Medicine Owl and eleven Blackfeet chiefs hung in the lobby, telling the history of the Blackfeet Nation. Trophy heads were mounted on the log columns, and 24 bearskins were draped over the balcony railings. Mission-style furniture fit in well with the rustic building materials.

Today's visitor can absorb the drama of the space from the comfortable couches on the lobby floor and watch the reactions of other guests as they first enter the huge space and cast their eyes along the rows of massive

▷ A chalet was built nearby as part of the lodge complex to serve as staff housing. Its smaller volume allowed a more direct expression of Swiss Chalet features than the main lodge. Fretwork balconies, a broad overhanging shed roof supported by filigreed brackets, and decorative trim were part of Louis Hill's American Alps design vocabulary.

△ Two Medicine Store, the only building remaining from a complex built by the Great Northern Railway in 1913 to serve horseback riders from Glacier Park Lodge, ten miles to the south. Skilled log craftsmanship is seen in the double saddle-notched corners, cement chinking, projecting purlins and rafters, and peeled-log porch railings.

△ Swiftcurrent Lake, ringed with forested talus bases of glacier-carved peaks, is a stark setting for the 900-foot facade of Many Glacier Lake Hotel. The lake level was artificially raised to create shoreline. Carefully designed to be appreciated from a distance, the hotel is enriched by skillful massing, variations in the roof, and the contrast of white trim against a dark brown exterior.

△ Lowering storm clouds over the Many Glacier Lake Hotel complex.

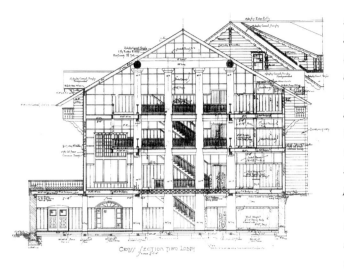

△ *Cross-sectional working drawings of the main lobby at "Many Glaciers Hotel," showing how the column spacing emphasizes verticality.*

△▷ *The wilderness setting of Swiftcurrent Lake is balanced by the spaciousness and comforts of the Many Glacier Lake Hotel interior. A skylit four-story atrium, similar to the one at Glacier Park Lodge, is surrounded by balconies with jigsawn fretwork. Enormous peeled-log columns topped with capitals give the space a formal, classical air. An open hearth on a stone base at one end of the lobby is capped by a large copper fireplace hood with a painted four-story chimney stack suspended by cables.*

columns and upward to the trusses and skylights. Everyone delights in discovering the lobby's decorative elements, for they enhance rather than diminish the powerful space created by the soaring log columns. Tiers of delicate, peeled-log balcony railings are similar in scale to exterior balcony patterns. At the first-floor level, wrought-iron cylindrical lanterns are bracketed onto the face of the columns; three chandeliers suspended from the trusses carry lanterns of the same size and style.

Many Glacier Hotel

Many Glacier Hotel was hailed by Louis Hill as the "Showplace of the Rockies." When it opened, in 1915, it was the largest hotel in the park and the centerpiece of Hill's resort development for Glacier National Park. Located 50 miles from the railroad station at East Glacier, the site on Swiftcurrent Lake offers an extraordinary natural setting where long, narrow lake basins were scoured out by glaciers. Amidst a landscape of valleys, ridges, and pyramid-shaped peaks, pine forests on the shoulders of the lowest ridges provide a green backdrop for the hotel against the stark gray granite ridge walls. Hill planned a design that would sweep along the water's edge. Construction began on the hotel's central portion in 1914. When the dining room and south wing addi-

tions were completed in 1917, the Swiss Chalet complex extended 900 feet along the shore of Swiftcurrent Lake. The lake side of the central unit is elevated on a one-story stone base with arched openings.

McMahon followed the same principles he used at Glacier Park Lodge to assemble long, four-story units into a cohesive image that gives the impression of a series of chalets. The long building mass is skillfully disguised by suggestions of smaller chalets at the ends and along the main elevations.

The original interior expressed Hill's vision of an American alpine resort. Historian James W. Sheire described the Great Northern hotels: *Not simply rows of rooms where the tired traveler spent the night and hurried on the next morning, they were theaters, stages adorned with the props of the wilderness where the guest and participant could assume a role in the frontier past of Jim Bridger, General Custer, Sitting Bull, and Lewis and Clark. They had atmosphere.*[4]

The Indian motif and Japanese paper lanterns have been replaced in recent years by a more alpine atmosphere. Doors to guest rooms have exposed pairs of x-patterned bracing, one above the other, and shields with crosses resembling the Swiss flag.

Construction of the hotel was a formidable challenge.

◁ *Along the trail to Granite Park, visitors may stay overnight at one of the two remaining backcountry chalet complexes built by the Great Northern Railway. The single-story dormitory on the left, 36' x 20', was designed by Thomas D. McMahon and built in 1913. Inside, six bedrooms are partitioned by* *interior log walls. The two-story stone-and-log chalet, right, measures 48' x 36', has a broad shingled roof, and houses the dining room and staff quarters. It was designed by Samuel L. Bartlett and built in 1914.*

▷ *Granite Park Chalet complex promised visitors a hearty meal and warm bed at the end of a long day's hike or trail ride.*

Four hundred railroad employees worked during the building seasons of 1914–15 to complete the project, including employee dormitories, other outbuildings, and corrals. The 50-mile distance from the railhead at East Glacier required a five-day wagon trip over primitive roads to haul construction equipment, the 60 logs for the atrium lobby, and other building materials. Timber for the interior was cut from the surrounding forests, and a sawmill on the site shaped the lumber for the building frame, siding, and some of the furniture. A quarry was developed to provide building stone for foundations and fireplaces and a temporary kiln for making bricks.

When completed, Many Glacier Hotel provided luxurious wilderness accommodations. Road-weary guests, arriving at the remote resort after days of travel, found all imaginable comforts available. They could have rooms with hot and cold running water, private baths, steam heat, and telephones, plus the nearby services of a

barber shop, tailor shop, and even a hospital. Afternoon tea was served by Japanese couples wearing kimonos, and excellent food was served in the dining room by waiters in lederhosen and waitresses in green flowered dirndls with white aprons.

A Many Glacier Hotel tradition that continues today is the entertainment by staff members. To work at the hotel as a waiter, waitress, busboy, maid, or clerk, college-age applicants must qualify through a musical talent audition. Rotating staff performances of musical comedy, light opera, instrumental music, and choral arrangements entertain guests in the spacious lobby througout the summer season.

Granite Park and Sperry Chalets

Among the many rewards of Glacier's backcountry trails are the Granite Park and Sperry chalets. These durable stone-and-timber buildings, representative of the chalet system developed for hikers and horseback trains by the

△ A reminder of the grizzly bear presence at the backcountry chalets.

Great Northern Railway, have managed to escape demolition by either avalanche or the NPS.

Design of the rustic chalet buildings was based on the simple ideals of a hearty meal and warm bed at the end of a long day's hike or trail ride. Gable-roofed buildings – rectangular in plan and constructed of local stone placed as random rubble, peeled-log timbers, and shake-shingled roofs – are rugged in appearance and fit organically into the rugged mountainsides. The interiors retain much of their original character and neither site has been electrified.

Sperry Chalet includes a kitchen and a dormitory. The interior staircase railings, dormer and balcony brackets, and projecting rafter ends are made of peeled logs. The kitchen building is a simple, rectangular, one-story structure. Its windows have intimidating wooden grates with exposed nails—a reminder of local grizzly bears. The two-story dormitory, designed by Kirtland, Cutter and Malmgren of Spokane, has 23 guest rooms and is the most impressive structure in the complex. A chalet is suggested by the broad, shake-shingled hip roof with an overhang supported by projecting log rafters, the dormers on each side of the long elevations sheltering log-railed balconies, and the similar balconies at gable ends.

Lake McDonald Lodge

Louis Hill concentrated on the early tourist development of Glacier National Park on the eastern side of the Divide and the Great Northern Railway, leaving oppor-

tunities for others on the western side of the park. After the railway completed its lines west to Spokane, the Apgar settlement was developed at the western end of the park's largest lake, Lake McDonald. Three miles from the park's entrance, the lake's 11-mile length provided good access to Glacier's interior trails. John Lewis, a land speculator from Columbia Falls, Montana, recognized the benefits of Hill's backcountry development on the eastern side of the park. He purchased the site of the Snyder Hotel at the eastern end of Lake McDonald and commissioned the Spokane architectural firm of Kirtland, Cutter and Malmgren to design a lodge for it, to be named the Lewis Glacier Hotel (the name was changed to Lake McDonald Lodge in 1957).

The architects followed Lewis' instructions to design "something worthy of the park." Their three-and-a-half-story structure called for a stone ground floor and wood framing above, tempered with natural materials. Lewis' lodge provided guest accommodations similar to those of Glacier Park Lodge, but more intimate in feeling. Construction began on the 35-room main lodge and 16 guest cabins in 1913 and took a year to complete. Except for lobby timbers cut near the site, building materials were transported from Apgar by barge in the summertime or across the frozen lake in winter.

Because the only access was by boat until a road was built in 1922, the building's most important elevation faced the lake. Lake McDonald Lodge is on a small rise 100 feet from the shoreline. The symmetrical lakeside elevation is rich in Chalet details mixed with Rustic

▷ Lewis Glacier Hotel, later re-named Lake McDonald Lodge, opened in 1914. The balconies, shingled gable roofs, jigsawn door and window trim, multi-light casement windows, and white trim at each floor level add to the overall chalet character. A framework of unpeeled-log columns, beams, and rafters supports a balcony with a peeled-log railing that runs the length of the first floor; two jerk-inhead-roofed, three-story elements flank the central section. Brown clapboard siding contrasts with bands of white trim at the second and third floors in a fretwork frieze.

△ *Serene Lake McDonald recalls the bygone era when guests arrived by launch or saddle horse. Pictured here is the launch* LEWIS.

8115 LOBBY, LAKE McDONALD HOTEL, GLACIER NATIONAL PARK 5A-H208

◁ *The three-story main lobby at Glacier Hotel is the most architecturally impressive space in the lodge, which was built by John Lewis. A trio of unpeeled cedar logs at each corner extends to the full height of the lobby to support the intricate roof trusswork. John Lewis was a furrier and furnished the lobby with trophies from his private collection. Balconies on three sides of the lobby, supported by log beams and brackets, are embellished by peeled-log railings in Stick-style patterns. The concrete floor is scored to imitate flagstone and has incised messages in Blackfeet, Chippewa, and Cree that translate into "Welcome," "New life to those who drink here," "Looking toward the mountain," and "Big Feast."*

◁ *Six-sided light fixtures decorated with Indian patterns are made of stretched rawhide. They are suspended from the roof trusses, enhancing the verticality of the lobby space.*

embellishments. A one-and-a-half-story dining room and kitchen wing are connected to the main lodge and tied to it visually by siding and roofing materials similar to those used on the main building.

Louis Hill's primary interests centered on the eastern side of the park, and when John Lewis attempted to sell the Glacier Hotel to the Great Northern in 1914, Hill declined the offer. In 1930, the NPS purchased the lodge for $300,000 and leased the facility to the Great Northern Railway.

Prince of Wales Hotel

The Prince of Wales Hotel is the Canadian component of Louis Hill's Great Northern Railway development. The hotel is located in Waterton Lakes National Park, which was created in 1911, a year after Glacier became a national park. In 1932, the United States and Canadian governments established Waterton–Glacier International Peace Park. The idea of a hotel on Waterton Lakes was first conceived by Hill in 1913, but he did not secure a land lease from the Canadian government until 1926.

Construction of the hotel posed a daunting undertaking. The nearest railhead, at Cardston, Alberta, was 30 miles away over unimproved roads frequently plagued by high winds. The domineering will of Louis Hill was

▷ A large inglenook fireplace in the lobby's east wall is made of concrete with scored joints simulating stonework. Indian designs are scored into the lintel and painted above the opening. Unpeeled-log framing similar to that throughout the lobby surrounds the fireplace. Directly above the fireplace is a large, multilight window that splashes light over a moosehead and into the lobby.

△ The Prince of Wales Hotel, Louis W. Hill's venture in Canada's Waterton Lakes Dominion Park. The hotel was completed in 1927 and is perched in the barren landscape at the end of the fjordlike Waterton Lakes. There are few hotels in North America so dramatically sited and surrounded by such magnificent vistas. Situated on a rise more than 100 feet above the lake, it enjoys unobstructed southern views down the lake and along the Continental Divide.

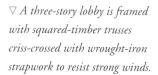

▷ *Balconies with fretwork railings, brackets, jigsawn trim, and sculptured columns decorate the hotel's facade.*

▽ *The seven-story, 65-room hotel is a compact mass with verticality emphasized by exterior decorative work.*

▽ *A three-story lobby is framed with squared-timber trusses criss-crossed with wrought-iron strapwork to resist strong winds.*

△ *A memorable view of Waterton Lakes and Glacier National Park from the lobby windows of the Prince of Wales Hotel.*

another factor to be contended with. His original instructions called for a 200-room hotel, French or Swiss Chalet in character. A plan for a three-story, low-roofed building with a central lobby followed the schemes at Many Glacier and Glacier Park. But Hill changed his mind about the design during construction, and some of the building had to be rebuilt four times, gradually evolving into a compact, seven-story plan.

Work began on the hotel in 1926. The winter that year was severe, and construction was sometimes interrupted by winds so high that the contractor could not record anemometer readings. The entire building was once blown off-center, then corrected. When it happened a second time, work had progressed too far for a perfect realignment. Today's guests in upper-floor rooms can feel the building sway when the winds blow full force. The bedtime experience is truly one of shipboard creaking and rocking.

The view of the park framed by the lobby windows at the Prince of Wales Hotel is memorable. In the comfort of one of the hotel club chairs, safe from the high winds buffeting the upper stories, the entire length of Waterton Lakes and Glacier National Park's mountains unfold in the distance. As chandeliers sway eerily overhead and the old hotel begins to creak and rock, one can only say a silent prayer of appreciation for the determination of Louis Hill and his builders.

△ *The Prince of Wales Hotel*

▽ *The old St. Mary Ranger Station, built in 1913 and restored in 1976, predated the National Park Service. The structures display excellent log-working skills executed by local residents and typify what was later perfected in* NPS *Rustic architecture designs.*

▷ *The Kintla Lake area was the site of oil exploration conducted by the Butte Oil Company at the turn of the century. This simple log structure was built at that time; it was abandoned by the oil company in 1906 and later acquired by the* NPS *for use as a ranger station.*

▽ *The Sherburne Entrance Station is a fine restored example of* NPS *Rustic architecture.*

△ *The early history of the Glacier Park region is preserved in the structures that once served oil and mineral exploration and now serve park visitors. The Polebridge Store is outside the park on the north fork of the Flathead River.*

National Park Service and Other Rustic Buildings

The one-million-acre expanse of Glacier National Park requires that ranger stations for seasonal use be scattered around the interior. Patrol cabins are strategically located eight to ten miles from a permanent ranger station, so rangers can spend several days on patrol duty without returning to the base station for supplies or shelter. The majority of these stations and patrol cabins were built by the NPS in the Rustic style during the 1920s and 1930s.

Each station was an operational headquarters for an administrative district. St. Mary's Ranger Station, one of the earliest in the park, is a restored example of a multi-building complex. The ranger station was built on the site in 1913, but the barn was originally constructed at Lubec Ranger Station and reassembled and restored at the present site in 1976 under the supervision of preservationist Harrison Goodall. Both buildings are excellent examples of log construction. Log walls, saddle notched at the corners, and log rafters and purlins are exposed on the interiors. The ranger station's logs are split vertically, forming a flat interior surface.

The typical ranger station was a one-and-a-half-story building with a living room across the front and bedroom and kitchen at the rear. A narrow stairway led to the loft, usually unfinished. Many of the stations remain in their original locations and are in excellent condition.

Yellowstone National Park

However orderly your excursions or aimless, again and again amid the calmest, stillest scenery you will be brought to a standstill hushed and awe-stricken before phenomena wholly new to you.

John Muir, OUR NATIONAL PARKS

Yellowstone National Park is so rich in scenic, geological, and biological attractions that before 1920 it was nicknamed "Wonderland."[5] Even the most sophisticated traveler is moved by this Rocky Mountain wilderness filled with thermal extravaganzas, mountain ranges that bridge the Continental Divide, pristine lakes, impressive canyons and waterfalls, and plentiful game.

Yellowstone – The First National Park
Explorers first came upon the Yellowstone region in the early nineteenth century, but it was mostly visited only by trappers and prospectors until another exploring party ventured into the region in 1869. Their reports of the extraordinary topography, including geysers, waterfalls, and canyons along the Yellowstone River, inspired further exploration. As a result of vigorous campaigning by the Northern Pacific Railroad, and aided by the photographs of William Henry Jackson and the paintings of Thomas Moran, Yellowstone National Park was established in March 1872. It later became the focus for preservation of wilderness in general. Many of the ideas and ideals of the national park system emerged from this early effort and were spelled out in the Organic Act: "[Yellowstone] is hereby reserved and withdrawn from settlement, occupancy, or sale, and dedicated and set apart as a public park or pleasuring ground for the benefit and enjoyment of the people." Now more than a million travelers visit the park's 2.2 million acres each year.

The challenge of managing the vast preserve and providing services for tourists led to the development of a wide assortment of buildings of varying quality and design. Among them are some of the finest examples of NPS Rustic architecture. The U.S. Army left its mark at Fort Yellowstone. Concessioners built grand hotels, several of which survive today. Yellowstone was a favorite park of Stephen Mather, and under the guidance of the first park superintendent, Horace Albright, the design team of the National Park Service filled Yellowstone with superb structures.

Yellowstone covers an immense landscape – majestic and diverse – that includes 10,000 thermal features, a waterfall twice the height of Niagara, several dramatic canyons, and thousands of elk, bison, and other big game, including grizzly bears. Beginning at Gardiner in

▷ *Old Faithful Geyser has been the official symbol of Yellowstone since the park was founded in 1872.*

▷ *The Grand Canyon of the Yellowstone River is a deep, spectacular chasm 24 miles long. Vibrant red and ochre colors decorate the canyon walls, but the predominant yellows inspired the name of the river and park.*

△ *President Theodore Roosevelt presided over the gala dedication ceremonies and laying of the cornerstone for the gateway arch at Yellowstone's North Entrance on April 24, 1903. Army officers, guests, dignitaries in silk top hats, and a crowd of over 3,000 people watched the president trowel in a stone and then listened to his rousing address.*

the north or Grand Teton National Park in the south, major points of interest are linked by a figure-eight loop road joined to outside highways by five entrance roads. A driving tour on the loop road takes visitors to Yellowstone's highlights, including the buildings of special architectural interest. The following sections are in order counter-clockwise along the loop road, beginning at the North Entrance and ending at the Northeast Entrance, with information about the park's interpretive museums at the end.

Roosevelt Arch

When John Muir arrived at Yellowstone's North Entrance at the turn of the century, he followed the earliest popular tourist route blazed by the Northern Pacific Railroad. A 50-mile spur off the main line from Livingston, Montana, ended at the Gardiner terminus at the park boundary. Visitors traveled by stagecoach on a circular route through the park, a journey of several

days, with each night spent at a different hotel – from Mammoth Hot Springs to Old Faithful, Yellowstone Lake, Canyon, and then back to Gardiner. The park entrance was in a bleak, barren setting, and the impending visit of President Theodore Roosevelt in 1903 set plans in motion for a gateway structure suitable for the nation's first national park.

Captain Hiram M. Chittenden, from the U.S. Army Corps of Engineers, was completing an improved road system to link the park's main attractions when he turned to architect Robert C. Reamer for a gateway design. Reamer, the architect for Canyon and Old Faithful hotels, developed a monumental design from Chittenden's notes. The archway would be tall enough to be seen from the Gardiner railroad depot and wide enough to allow the passage of two stagecoaches. The design called for two soaring 12-foot-8-inch-square columns of basaltic stone 50 feet high, set 20 feet apart, framing an arch with a crown 30 feet above the ground. A concrete

△ The gateway Roosevelt Arch at Yellowstone's North Entrance has a concrete tablet above the keystone, which bears an inscription from the statute establishing the park: "For the Benefit and Enjoyment of the People." Smaller tablets set in the main columns read "Yellowstone National Park" and "Created by Act of Congress, March 1, 1872."

△ Hot water seeps out of the ground at Mammoth Hot Springs, evaporates, and leaves behind deposits of travertine, so that as water breaks through the old terraces, new terraces are formed. Algae tints the limestone and pools with delicate colors. Mammoth Hot Springs Hotel is in the background.

roof, chamfered at the edges, caps the structure. Wing walls of the same stone 12 feet high extend from both sides and terminate in columns similar in proportion to the main columns.

A distinctive feature of the gateway is the use of roughly dressed, oversized stones set in uniform courses with projecting rounded vertical edges at the center of each stone. Reamer's subtle touch directed that the arch be recessed between the columns, so that the stonework and light gray mortar could introduce interesting light-and-shadow play on the rusticated surfaces.

Mammoth Hot Springs and Fort Yellowstone

The sculptured terraces of Mammoth Hot Springs were one of the earliest attractions at Yellowstone. Photographs by William Henry Jackson and Timothy H. O'Sullivan captured the extraordinary scene: hot waters seeping from a hillside, forming white travertine de-

posits, and parasoled ladies in Victorian dress posed demurely in the foreground.

Yellowstone's wonders were quite inaccessible in the early days of the park. Adventurous tourists from the east had two choices. They could take a northern railroad route from Bismarck, North Dakota, for 1,050 miles, followed by 820 miles by steamboat on the Missouri River to Fort Benton and 230 miles by stagecoach (a twelve-to-fourteen-day journey). Or a southern approach route was possible – 1,180 miles on the Union Pacific Railroad from Omaha to Corrine, Utah, and then a dusty ten-day trek over 470 miles by stagecoach via Virginia City, Montana.

The northern route was the easiest, and Mammoth Hot Springs became the site of the park's first tourist accommodations. It was also chosen as the site for Camp Sheridan and then Fort Yellowstone, when the army took over administrative control in 1886. Additional

△ *Yellowstone's first administrative building, constructed under the direction of Superintendent Norris in 1879. Because of the threat of Indian raids, he built a sturdy two-story timber and board-and-batten structure; the cupola was topped with a 53-foot liberty pole. Located at Mammoth Hot Springs, the building was razed in 1909.*

The present Mammoth Hot Springs Hotel and Cabins represent an interesting interlude in the career of one architect and the design tastes of the NPS. The cluster of buildings that included the National Hotel had to be replaced in 1935 with a modern facility appropriate for the automobile era. The successor to the Yellowstone Park Improvement Company, the Yellowstone Park Company, retained architect Robert C. Reamer to design a new Mammoth Hot Springs Hotel, a complex that would incorporate a wing of the old building and add a restaurant, recreation hall, and guest cabins.

Reamer, the designer of Old Faithful Inn and the Roosevelt Arch, displayed his receptivity to new design trends and tastes. Departing from his Rustic triumph at Old Faithful, he created a complex reminiscent of contemporary Scandinavian works. Whether he was following his client's directives or his own inspiration for a "modern" interpretation for the new hotel and cafeteria is unknown. Although totally incongruous in their setting, the buildings are now hailed as mainstream post-modernist.

As early as the 1880s, tourists posed a threat both to the park's attractions and to themselves as well. Whether chipping away pieces of Mammoth Hot Spring's terraces or falling into geyser holes, they required supervision if not containment. Poachers preyed on the park's game, posing a different problem. The failure of Congress to provide funds for the park's administration meant that in 1886 it had to invoke provisions from an 1883 appropriations act, and the Department of the Interior turned to the U.S. Army to send in troops to guard the park.

On August 17, 1886, troops from the First U.S. Cavalry arrived at Mammoth Hot Springs from Fort Custer, Montana Territory, to inaugurate thirty years of army control. By the beginning of the park's most terrible winter (1886–87), five wood-frame buildings had been completed at Camp Sheridan. The establishment of Fort Yellowstone in 1891 led to the removal of the Camp Sheridan buildings and construction of the permanent structures around the Parade Grounds.

The Corps of Engineers was soon at work constructing roads, sidewalks, and utility systems. Early buildings were utilitarian structures of frame construction with red metal-shingled roofs. Officer's Row had four frame du-

hotels and tourist facilities were built, and the NPS moved its park headquarters there in 1916. Today, the site is rich with representative buildings from successive tourist eras, the U.S. Army, and the NPS.

James McCartney and Harry Horr of Bozeman, Montana, built the park's first hotel and bathhouses in 1871 near Mammoth Hot Springs. A crude log building with an earth-covered slab roof, this early hotel lasted until 1912. The first "baths" were troughs in the ground fed by hot springs. Later, wooden bathhouses with the added comforts of bathtubs were built directly on the hot springs terraces.

The Northern Pacific Railroad formed the Yellowstone Park Improvement Company in 1883, motivated by the same hopes of attracting tourists that inspired hotel developments in other national parks. Their first venture was the National Hotel at Mammoth Hot Springs. A three-and-a-half-story frame structure that vaguely recalled the Shingle style, with Queen Anne affectations in the form of gables and towers, the green shingled walls and red roof contrasted with the surrounding gray-green landscape. Interiors and furnishings were lavish and included arc lamps in the public areas.

◁ Reamer adopted the fashionable Scandinavian style in his 1935 Mammoth Hot Springs Hotel, anticipating post-modern architecture by 50 years.

◁ Robert C. Reamer returned to Yellowstone almost 40 years after designing the rustic Old Faithful Inn to design a new Mammoth Hot Springs Hotel. Using classical proportions, simplicity of form, large window openings, and stone-colored stucco walls to contrast with wood trim painted a cream color, the design for the main building's exteriors is held together by rhythms of fluted columns without caps or bases. Dormer windows flush with the restaurant's upper walls recall Classical elements, with pediments and fluted columns as , window jambs. The restaurant's green-and-white striped awnings harmonize with the colors, creating a jaunty atmosphere.

▷ The Norris Soldier Station is a remnant from the sixteen stations that existed toward the end of the army's administration at Yellowstone. Built of logs or wood-frame construction, the stations were for summer detachments of four troopers each, although a few were also used as winter stations. The NPS later made over the stations for ranger use, replacing some with rustic log structures and removing others. Norris Station is T-shaped, with peeled-log walls from foundation to roof eaves. Projecting whittled-end corner logs are saddle-notched. White plaster chinking matches the white window and door trim. An entrance porch is framed by a pair of lodgepole pine posts with "grotesque" knots.

plexes built in the same year, which began the distinctive group of buildings facing the Parade Ground.

A departure from the usual frame buildings was the U.S. Engineer's Office, designed by Reed and Stern of St. Paul and constructed in 1903. Cube-shaped, it was called the "Pagoda" because of obvious Oriental influence. The battered sandstone walls, tapering from a thickness of two feet at the ground to one foot at the eaves, the wide overhangs, projecting decorative rafter tails, and hipped green tile roof created an imposing presence at the corner of the Parade Grounds. Skilled craftsmanship is evident in the random ashlar stone dressed at corner quoins and window jambs.

A surge of construction in 1909 added the seven stone buildings that dominate Fort Yellowstone. Scottish masons used sandstone quarried nearby for a bachelor officer's quarters (now the Park Museum), a three-story barracks (the NPS Administration Building), two residences, two large cavalry stables, and a combined blacksmith shop and stable guard. The buildings were symmetrical forms with red clay tile hipped roofs or hipped roofs with monitors. Undressed random ashlar sandstone walls contrasted with dressed stone lintels and sills. The buildings withstood the severe earthquake of 1959, and over eighty years of severe weather exposure has given the stone the same gray-tan coloration of nearby Mount Everts.

The chapel (1913) was the last building constructed by the U.S. Army at Fort Yellowstone. A late Gothic Revival design of coursed ashlar sandstone complements the nearby stone buildings. The steeply pitched slate roof, the stone buttresses, the arched window in the front elevation, the exposed truss system supporting the roof, and the oak furnishings all reflected the popular style.

▷ Fort Yellowstone had grown into a large community of administration buildings and residences by the time the U.S. Army turned over administration of Yellowstone from the National Park Service in 1916. The fort was laid out in typical military alignment with a headquarters building, barracks, stables, residences, and support buildings.

△ The Horace N. Albright Visitor Center, recently remodeled, was originally the administration building. The sandstone walls and red tile roof followed the standard Fort Yellowstone design.

△ A 1905 replacement for the Post Exchange was a striking departure from Corps of Engineers typical sandstone buildings with red tile roofs, and it evolved into an unusual exercise in Palladian design. A colonnaded entrance portico with four evenly spaced columns on piers supports a pedimented gable with a circular window. The main entrance doors and a pair of sidelights are spanned by an elegantly arched transom with a fan pattern in leaded mullions.

◁ *Old Faithful Inn, with its prodigious scale, informal massing, and great, pitched roof architecturally echoes the shapes of the surrounding mountain peaks. A semicircular grandstand faces the most famous geyser in the United States, Old Faithful, and receives a rush of spectators who descend upon the site hourly during the summer season. A building holding its own in this terrain presented a noble challenge.*

◁ *Old Faithful Inn's asymmetrical composition and rich detailing defies criticism. Dormers and unpredictable interior spaces result in an idiosyncratic design. The overall effect is similar to the experience of touring the park – surprises are around every corner. The structure has survived earthquakes and forest fires, and has inspired Rustic design throughout the world.*

▷ *The original porte-cochère and a second-story porch recessed into the main lodge were enclosed as part of the lobby in 1927. Log cribbing on stone bases supports the extended porch that provides a platform for viewing the geyser. Architect Robert Reamer added a 13' x 72' observation platform on the roof ridge, but it is now closed to guests.*

28478 OLD FAITHFUL INN AND GEYSER YELLOWSTONE NATIONAL PARK

Old Faithful Inn

It is fitting that Yellowstone, the first national park, should contain a tour-de-force tribute to Rustic craftsmanship. Situated in a forest clearing atop a gentle rise overlooking the caldera of the Firehole River, Old Faithful Inn is unequivocally tied to its natural surrounding. One of the few surviving log hotels in the United States, the inn is a masterpiece of stylized design and fine workmanship. Its influence on national park architecture is immeasurable, for it embodies what became the three key working principles of national park design: use of natural, local materials, allusions to pioneer building techniques, and strong ties to site.

Architect Robert Reamer was twenty-nine years old when the Yellowstone Park Association hired him in 1902 to design a lodge for the Old Faithful area. As park concessioners, the association's parent company, the Northern Pacific Railroad, had refrained from building a

◁◁ Reamer was unrestrained in his use of logs in all their forms. The soaring, seven-story lobby is unique in architecture – an astonishing, cavernous space to be experienced from many levels and vantage points. The log framing required the skills of railroad trestle builders to assemble the intricate design.

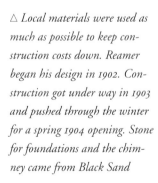

△ Local materials were used as much as possible to keep construction costs down. Reamer began his design in 1902. Construction got under way in 1903 and pushed through the winter for a spring 1904 opening. Stone for foundations and the chimney came from Black Sand Basin and along the road five miles east. Timbers were harvested from a site eight miles to the south, and gnarled lodgepole limbs were culled from nearby forests. Sawmills produced rough boards for floors, walls, ceilings, and the roof.

△ When first installed in 1904, all the interior lodgepole pine railings, brackets, and structural members were unpeeled. In 1940 the bark was removed, and in 1966 the logs were varnished. Those who regretted the loss of the bark were compensated somewhat when the intricate, lacy chiselings of the pine bark beetle were revealed.

◁ Entertainment at the lobby's fireplace in the early 1900s. The chimney is fascinating; it is sixteen feet square at its base, and 500 tons of lava rock frame eight individual fireplaces. An enormous popcorn popper, andirons, and a fourteen-foot-diameter clock designed by Reamer and mounted on the chimney compliment the proportions of the central lobby space.

△ Attention was lavished on the dining room design to coordinate furniture, light fixtures, and exposed structural members.

▷ Rustic stairs assembled from gnarled lodgepole pine and split-log risers.

first-class hotel near the geyser. But in 1901 the NPS altered its policy and shortened the required distance between a building and a natural object of interest from one-quarter mile to one-eighth mile. The Yellowstone Park Association needed lodging for the increasing number of visitors coming to the area by train. They wanted a building constructed at the precise legislated distance from Old Faithful Geyser, built out of local materials to defray expenses, but with an identifiable character. In the end, construction costs would be small in comparison with the positive image they created. Image meant tourists, and tourists meant business.

Reamer provided a unique structure, a building that became a destination in itself. More than any other building in the national parks, Old Faithful Inn met, in fact far exceeded, the concessioner's original hopes. It cost the Yellowstone Park Association $140,000 for construction and $25,000 for furnishings; Charles Adams, noted historian, writer, and former chairman of the Union Pacific Railroad, observed in 1904: "There is nothing in the world like it or to compare with Old Faithful Inn."

Key to understanding the inn is architect Reamer's siting and extravagant use of space and materials. The architect's vision was ingenious. He skewed the inn in relationship to the entry drive to allow an unobstructed view of Old Faithful for the approaching visitor.

From the lobby floor, the massive central chimney rises up past tier after tier of lodgepole columns and twisted log brackets and railings to the shadowy reaches of the 92-foot-high pitched half-log ceiling. By day, dormer windows admit shafts of sunlight that play across the varnished fantasy of beams, columns, and railings. Sparkling rings of wrought-iron chandeliers encircle the columns, and wall sconces cast subtle light through the atrium after dark. The room is a spectacle to be slowly absorbed by gazing upward, then by ascending to the upper balconies to explore the mystery of the extraordinary space.

The architect is described as having "sketched the plans while shakily emerging out of a monumental submersion in malt." Some authorities claim to infer that Reamer had to be "under the influence" by studying the building's unique contours. Whether that was the case or not, the formula worked. Reamer took his cues from the local environment—a valley of smoldering white sinter formed by the evaporating geysers, powerful volcanic rock ridgelines, towering pines, and the on-the-hour majesty of Old Faithful.

Much of the wrought-iron work was forged on the site by a blacksmith named Colpitts. Examples of his work can be seen on the main entrance doors in the grilled peephole, heavy hinges, massive lock and key, and coiled-spring bell ringer.

The building was constructed in three major phases: the 1903 original section with the imposing gable roof,

dining rooms, and kitchen wings to the south, and guest-room wings to the east and west; the 1913–14 east wing; and the 1927 west wing. The building's total length is nearly 700 feet. The foundation of the 1903 portion is stone and concrete with a stone veneer. The first-floor structure consists of load-bearing log walls and log framing. Upper stories are of milled lumber and log framing; exteriors are sheathed in yard-long redwood shingles with the two lower courses sawn into diamond patterns. A harmonious composition is evident in the asymmetrical structure by virtue of chalet overtones, dormers, paired and randomly placed diamond-paned windows, and gnarled lodgepole brackets.

As visitors enter through the huge split-log front door, they are immediately drawn under a low-ceilinged foyer to the edge of the lobby atrium. Ahead, on the left and right, are the reception desk and gift shop; straight ahead are the great fireplaces of the main chimney, with the dining room beyond.

The lobby is surrounded by two balconies built on log framing. The lower balcony encircles the lobby and opens onto a porch; the upper balcony (providing access to guest rooms) is L-shaped. An assortment of oak Mission-style rockers, couches, and easy chairs placed around the balcony provide ample vantage points for viewing the dazzling structure overhead and the lobby activity below. Staircases made of half-logs connect the balconies. Leading up from the second balcony is a "crow's nest," where musicians used to play for the guests far below on the lobby floor. The stairs to the crow's nest and roof have been closed off for safety.

The original dining room was designed with a rustic interior. Wide-planked floors, log walls, and the half-log ceiling supported on log scissor trusses created a woodsy ambience. A large stone fireplace centered on the south wall, of the same masonry as the lobby chimney, was partially destroyed in the 1959 earthquake and was reconstructed in 1985. In the inn's earlier days, guests "dressed" for dinner. Hickory caned-backed chairs and long trestle tables were set with blue dishes for family-style meals.

Hallways at the east and west ends of the lobby lead to guest rooms in the wings of the "Old House." Guest rooms retain much of their original character with rustic log walls or rough-sawn plank paneling. Some rooms still have the original plumbing fixtures: clawfoot bathtubs, wooden water closets, and marble sink tops. Mrs. E. H. Johnson, a guest in 1905, offered these comments about the inn's accommodations and their appeal for the weary traveler: "And then we came to the Inn, the most unique and restful place; it is the craftsman's dream realized. My room alone is a paradise of restfulness though in a rough and rustic fashion."[6]

Several years ago the NPS and the inn's concessioner, TW Recreation Services, began extensive restoration work to both interiors and exteriors. Deteriorating logs and shingles were replaced, along with plumbing and wiring. Safety features were added. The supervising architect, Andy Beck, often had to act as a sleuth uncovering construction secrets not disclosed on available drawings. Old photographs and former guests' recollections helped to solve Reamer's design idiosyncrasies and reveal his implicit intentions. Many of the original furnishings throughout the Old House remain, adding to the integrity of the restoration. Mission-style furniture, leather-topped tables, and hickory chairs are placed in public spaces; some of the bedrooms have original iron bedsteads, dressers, and washstands. Reamer's electric fixtures are still in place, as well as the copper-and-iron chandeliers in the lobby and dining room, and wooden candelabra that serve as capitals on the balcony log-column supports. In 1988 a tragedy was averted through heroic efforts of NPS staff who protected the inn during the massive firestorm that destroyed nearby forests.

▷ *Geyser Hall in Old Faithful Lodge has side aisles under a lowered shed roof, defined by rows of four-log column clusters. The larger columns in each cluster support the main trusses; the three smaller columns end ten feet above the floor at a log lintel spanning the central columns. The truss structure has radial elements of diagonal bracing joined by large black steel plates with exposed bolts. Lower and upper chords are supported by ten-foot-high kingposts; top chords support log rafters and purlins carrying a plank ceiling.*

▷ *Hamilton's Store at Old Faithful, built in 1894. The wood-frame building has gable roofs distinguished by a fantasy of burled pine logs, with decorative branches on the porches and roof brackets.*

The Lodge and Stores

Old Faithful Lodge, designed by Underwood and built in 1923 with additions through 1927, is at the northern end of the geyser area. Rambling in plan, the building exterior is a mixture of stone, timber, and shingles. The lodge provides cafeteria services and contains an extraordinary recreational hall framed in peeled logs.

Approximately 100' x 136' and 75 feet high to the ceiling ridge, the recreation hall (Geyser Hall) is similar in character to the nave in a Gothic cathedral. The ecclesiastical atmosphere derives from the stately rhythm of columns, the proportion and scale of horizontal log placement, and the clerestory windows in the upper side walls. Unlike the cold interiors of stone cathedrals, the lodge's hall is warmed by the use of wood for all its interior surfaces: plank floors, walls, and ceilings are tied together by a tracery of log columns and truss members. A stage at one end of the hall is framed by log columns and crossbracing, and wrought-iron ceiling fixtures light the interior.

The two Hamilton Stores in the Old Faithful area are also of interest. The first was built by Henry Klamer in 1894 and purchased in 1915 by Charles Hamilton—his first concessioner property in Yellowstone. The second store was built in 1929 and designed to be consistent with the NPS design principles. Three gabled entrance porches supported by dressed stone piers join the long gabled roof of the main sales area. Porch roofs are framed in log trusses with projecting whittled-log rafter and purlin ends. Exposed log rafter ends also appear at the main roof eaves. Exterior walls made of concrete look like hewn logs. The interior of the main sales area is framed by peeled logs. A cluster of three columns placed against the interior walls supports hammer trusses with black connecting plates and exposed bolts.

▷ *Recent renovations to Lake Hotel's spacious interiors have reestablished the elegant ambience created by Reamer. Original details like this drinking fountain are integrated with the new furnishings.*

△ ▷ *Yellowstone Lake Hotel, with an extended facade 900 feet long. Early guests found a serenity here that was absent in the more dramatic terrain elsewhere in Yellowstone. Trails through the surrounding woods or along the lakeshore, the quiet waters against a mountain backdrop, and summer evenings that slowly drew the days into lingering twilight provided an unusually restful setting. Recent renovations and refurbishing have restored much of the early elegance of this historic structure.*

◁ Robert C. Reamer was challenged by the Northern Pacific Railroad in 1903 to remodel the nondescript, clapboard Lake Hotel. He transformed it into an elegant neoclassical structure, showing versatility ranging between Rustic and Classical architecture. Three gables on the lake side of the building were extended and converted into Classical porticoes with four 50-foot Ionic columns. Reamer also applied false balconies and decorative moldings and altered the window pattern. The dining room was expanded and a porte-cochère and lobby sunroom added, along with more guest rooms, bringing the total to almost 200.

Lake Hotel

The Grand Tour circuit in Yellowstone's early days proceeded from Geyser Basin and Old Faithful to the shores of Yellowstone Lake. Whether the tourist took a launch across the lake or a stagecoach along its shores, the destination was Lake Hotel. Construction of this permanent structure to replace a little-used tent camp near the lake's outlet into the Yellowstone River was begun in 1889 by the Yellowstone Park Association. The Northern Pacific Railroad backed the venture, hoping to improve park accommodations and increase tourism. There were difficulties in obtaining supplies, transporting them over rough roads, and finding able workers, and the opening of the 80-room hotel was delayed until 1891.

The Lake Hotel's original design was a rather unpretentious four-story frame building. As business increased, more rooms were added and facilities were upgraded. In 1903, Robert Reamer was hired for remodeling and additions. He began the transformation of the nondescript building into an elegant hotel that displays Colonial styling and neo-Classical elements. Inside, Reamer designed the large, tiled fireplace, lobby columns, light fixtures, and a new stairway, substantially altering the floor plan.

By 1923, Lake Hotel had become an imposing structure of Classical beauty extending 900 feet along the lake's shoreline. Painting the exterior clapboard walls a soft yellow unified the old and new wings. White trim and columns added an elegant air to the long elevation facing the lake.

Lake Ranger Station

Development around the Lake Hotel added several nearby structures. An 1887 ranger station was replaced by the NPS in 1922 with a combination Lake Ranger Station and Community Center as part of a program of ranger station replacements. Others built at the same time at Canyon and the Northeast Entrance have since been removed. The design by the Landscape Engineering Division of the NPS was unique providing combined functions for management and visitor education programs. To meet the combined uses, an octagonal community room forty feet across was joined to a residence wing 26' x 38'. A north wing was added in 1930–31.

▽▷ The Lake Ranger Station was built of logs and stone taken from the surrounding area. Its log walls are detailed with saddle-notched projecting whittled ends, and wall joints are white plaster chinking; window and door trim is forest green; the hip and gable roofs are shake covered. A cobblestone chimney rises from the central fireplace and is a distinctive feature of the octagonal-roofed Community Room.

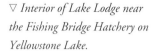

▽ Interior of Lake Lodge near the Fishing Bridge Hatchery on Yellowstone Lake.

The Lake Ranger Station underwent restoration during the summers of 1985–87. Harrison Goodall directed the exterior work and interior renovations performed by NPS staff, and this project provides an excellent model for restoring national park historic structures. Over the years, harsh winter weather had altered the condition and appearance of the structure. Through careful analysis of original materials, the exterior logs were restored, joint chinking replaced, and a new roof applied.

The original chinking was beach sand from the Fishing Bridge area with a binder of elk hair. The restoration used the same beach sand with a binder of upholstery hair. NPS workers removed interior partitions from the octagonal community room and repaired the central fireplace, installed architecturally compatible light fixtures and hardware, and cleaned the exposed logs and rafters. Office space was relocated to the west wing, and the residential addition was remodeled. The structure continues to be used as a combined ranger station and permanent residence, closely resembling its original appearance.

Roosevelt Lodge

The northeast corner of Yellowstone National Park is a country of rolling, sage-covered hills, and rivers and streams draining the pine forests. The land rises to the eastern boundary of the park defined by the 10,000-foot peaks of the Absaroka Range. The principal attractions in the region at the turn of the century were a petrified forest, excellent fishing, and the Lamar Valley Buffalo Ranch. Dude ranches, developed east of the park boundary, laid trails reaching into the park interior.

Tower Junction, near the intersection of the Loop Road and the East Entrance Road, became the site of one of the Wylie Permanent Camping Company sites. Established by a Bozeman, Montana, schoolteacher in the 1890s, the Wylie Way tent camps became an interesting chapter in Yellowstone's history.

Railroad concessioners were dismayed by the substitution of tent camps for hotels, but a park tour that included Wylie Way camps presented a less expensive alternative that quickly took hold with cost-conscious Victorians.

The establishment of the NPS in 1916, combined with Stephen Mather's visions of visitor accommodations, eventually led to the replacement of these popular tent camps with permanent lodges. The first lodge, located near Tower Junction at the reputed site of one of Theodore Roosevelt's overnight stays during his 1903 visit, was planned as a dude ranch. Construction of

◁ Octagonal light fixtures add a touch of rusticity to the Hamilton Store at Yellowstone Lake. Cast-iron simulated logs frame translucent glass and are embellished with squirrels, owls, and an acorn-shaped pendant globe.

▽ The Hamilton Store at Yellowstone Lake has a well-composed form and distinctive octagonal sales area, but execution and detail do not measure up to the NPS work of the 1920s era when it was built. It lacks sensitive integration of exterior and interior materials. Lower interior wall surfaces in the main sales area are horizontal beaded wainscoting, upper walls are planked, and all are painted white. Logs used to outline the wall and exposed peaked roof panel joints are undersized and fail to emphasize the dramatically proportioned interior space.

▷ The nine-building Fish Hatchery complex is carefully unified through Rustic design elements. Exposed peeled-log framing, with reverse board-and-batten vertical siding inside the framing, includes oversized logs used as corner columns and sometimes paired along the wall surfaces. Log trusses are exposed on gable ends with arched lintel logs, and a log sill rests on concrete foundations. All roofs and column-supported porches have the same pitch, with doubled-coursed shake shingles. The buildings are further tied together by brown paint over all the exterior surfaces.

▽ *Roosevelt Lodge, built in 1919, is a center for fishing trips and trail rides. Cabins surround the main lodge and come in a variety of construction types – logs, board and batten, flush plank siding, "logs out," and "studs out."*

▷ *The lodge's porch offers a relaxing Western ambience with nearby rolling hills, sage-covered flatlands, and fish-rich streams.*

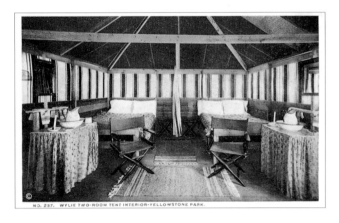

△ *A "Wylie Way" two-room tent. The green-and-white candy-striped tents were neatly arranged, well maintained, usually sited in wooded areas, and offered a pleasant relief from the formality of hotels. The Wylie Permanent Camping Company employed students and schoolteachers during the summer, who generated enthusiastic service, talented entertainment, and educational programs.*

Roosevelt Lodge began in 1919 and was completed the following year. The lodge, serving as headquarters for fishing and saddle-horse trips, was eventually surrounded by 110 cabins.

The Rustic tune of the Roosevelt Lodge complex is sounded loud and clear by the log gateway arch over the entrance road. Although not of the highest NPS Rustic design standards, the one-story log lodge projects a pleasant, welcoming ambience. The wide porch is lined with hickory rocking chairs. Guests use the central lodge building for dining, enjoying the dude-ranch lifestyle of the moderately priced complex, complete with square dancing, cookouts, and stagecoach rides. The lodge was rehabilitated by the NPS in the 1980s, and a kitchen wing was added.

Northeast Entrance Station

Of the various national park building types, the entrance station presented a unique challenge to the talented de-

sign staff at the NPS. The entrance or checking station served several purposes: collecting fees and counting visitors; establishing the presence of the NPS for the visitor; and defining a sense of place and identity for the park. *Park Structures and Facilities* set out the criteria: *Prompt to admit that the entranceway is more sinned against than sinning, we can hope that the artificiality and sophistication will not be too brazenly flaunted.... [It] should at once invite and deter, encouraging use while discouraging abuse of the park by the public. It should be all things to all men, tempting the devotees to Nature and of the past, while warding off and detouring that block of the public primarily bent on a greater gas consumption. A kind of semaphore simultaneously reading "stop" and "go," yet somehow avoiding all accidents to traffic and temperament. Surely, no easy accomplishment, perhaps unattainable.*

The Northeast Entrance Station at the Cooke City–Silver Gate Entrance is a prime example of this Rustic architectural solution in the national park system. The

◁ *A ranger's quiet moment at the Northeast Entrance Station.*

◁ *The Northeast Entrance Station is unified by the gable roofs spanning the entire structure and at right angles to the main roof. A rubble masonry foundation over concrete, lodgepole pine log walls, and shingled roofs make up the limited palette of materials used by the designers. Gable ends are finished with vertical channeled siding.*

▷ *The floor plan of the Northeast Entrance Station is a sample of the early work of the NPS Landscape Engineering Division. The main office is flanked by covered roadways and storerooms.*

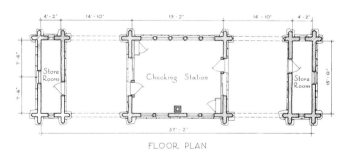

FLOOR PLAN

one-story log structure was built in 1935, at the zenith of NPS Rustic design skills. Close adherence to building specifications produced excellent log work on both exteriors and interiors. The peeled logs were selected for a minimum taper of not more than one inch in fifteen feet and laid with alternating butts and tips. Saddle-coped and projecting at the corners, log ends were cut with two or three bevel faces in random directions. Log rafter ends projecting beyond eaves have similar detailing. The original oakum rope chinking is still in place. A gentle

concave curve at the log ends from the foundations to the eaves adds an elegant touch to the building.

Museums—Norris, Madison, and Fishing Bridge
Stephen Mather and Horace Albright were firm believers in the role of the national parks in educating the public. Their early efforts procured funds from the Laura Spelman Rockefeller Foundation for the museum at Yosemite. Gradually, the emphasis shifted from education through the imparting of information to "interpretation." The intention was not only to convey information about the parks but also to enable visitors to understand and appreciate what they saw. The distinction has been described by Freeman Tilden as "an educational activity which aims to reveal meanings and relationships through the use of original object, by firsthand experience, and by illustrative media, rather than to simply communicate factual information."[7]

The museums at Norris Geyser Basin, Madison Junc-

▽ The Kiosk is described in PARK AND RECREATION STRUCTURES as a Nature Shrine, "an open-air museum-in-miniature … outstandingly representative of individuality achieved by the use of a material which is a phenomenon of the immediate environs…. The novel motif is altogether amiable largely because it has been employed with logic and restraint." The Kiosk was a prelude to Yellowstone's future museums, one of the finest collections of Rustic structures ever built by the NPS.

▽ Norris Geyser Basin is the hottest thermal area in the park, and Steamboat is the world's largest geyser, with eruptions as high as 400 feet.

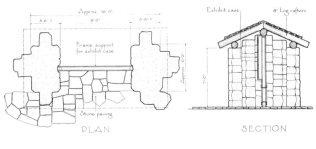

PLAN

SECTION

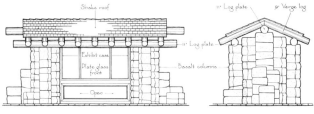

FRONT ELEVATION

END ELEVATION

△ The NPS goals for interpretation of attractions are illustrated by the Obsidian Cliffs Kiosk alongside the road on the way from Mammoth Hot Springs to Norris Geyser Basin. The modest Rustic structure, completed in 1931, was the first wayside interpretive exhibit built in the national park system. Approximately 16' x 6', clustered piers of basaltic rock support a peeled-log framing system capped by a shake roof.

△ At Madison Junction a gable roof covers the exhibition room in the main wing, and an intersecting hip roof covers the two-room Ranger-Naturalist quarters. Both roofs are shake shingled. A bungalow detail used in the gable ends is vertical siding with tree profiles and diamond patterns sawn into the boards. Peeled-log structural framing allows for visible knots and gnarls inside. The floor in the exhibition room is flagstone, and a flagstone terrace, enclosed by low masonry walls at the rear of the structure, overlooks the confluence of the Gibbon and Firehole rivers where they join to form the Madison River.

▽ *Norris Museum floor plan. There is a dramatic transition from the shadowed entrance foyer into the naturally lit exhibition rooms. The building's interiors continue the exterior use of natural materials. Daylight highlights the honey-colored exposed structural framing of peeled-log columns, roof purlins, and rafter beams. Knots and surfaces have been worn smooth by thousands of visitors, who run their hands over them every summer.*

△ *Architect Herbert Maier was at the height of his prowess in Rustic design when he created the Norris Geyser Basin Museum in 1929. The plan is deceptively simple: exhibition space and a small ranger's apartment are contained in a one-story rectangular plan approximately 94' x 20'. A central covered foyer sheltered by a massive jerkinhead roof on trusses of oversized logs rises above the rest of the form.*

△ *Site and structure at Norris Geyser Basin are flawlessly harmonized in the informal building base, made of native stone masonry and bold log work.*

tion, and Fishing Bridge were a happy marriage between Mather's design principles and the extraordinary architectural talents of Herbert Maier. (A fourth museum at Old Faithful was removed in 1971.) They exemplify interpretive principles, using Rustic design, natural materials, exaggerated architectural features, and organic forms. The Norris and Old Faithful museums were associated with thermal geology, Madison Junction with the park's history, and Fishing Bridge with the ecology of the Lake Yellowstone area.

Herbert Maier was trained as an architect at the University of California (Berkeley) and gained his familiarity with museums and parks in New York State. He moved to California in 1923 and for the next ten years divided his time between working at the Western Museum Laboratory of California and the American Association of Museums. During that time he designed the Yosemite museum, the four museums at Yellowstone, and the Yavapai Point Museum at Grand Canyon. He later continued his career with the National Park Service.

During his early years at the NPS, when he espoused Rustic design, Maier's influence on park architecture was overwhelming. His Yellowstone buildings served as models for hundreds of other buildings of entirely different functions in state, county, and local parks constructed under the auspices of the NPS during the work relief programs of the 1930s. Maier's architectural work for the American Association of Museums set a unique standard for interpretive buildings. He described his museums as being *"not mere passive repositories of 'exhibits' but active interpreters and guides to the national and cultural features and historical associations of their parks. They are laboratory manuals … for use not only by the qualified student but by anybody and everybody.… The great thing is to get people to go and see; intelligently, if possible; but by all means to see. And nothing conducive to that end is to be disdained."*[8]

Maier considered buildings in the national parks "necessary evils." His success in minimizing their obtrusiveness was through maximizing the use of indigenous building materials and making structures appear to emerge from the ground. Informal designs were emphasized, using natural materials and horizontal lines. Imbued with an uncompromising strength, the massive size

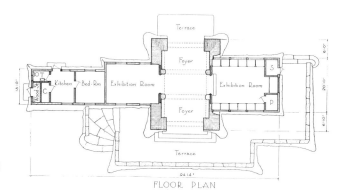

FLOOR PLAN

and irregular shapes of materials reflected the irregularities of nature. Enormous logs, peeled and sawn, with knots left in place, gave a tactile richness to the building form. Boulders in heavily battered walls were left in their natural shapes.

Maier's buildings responded to their sites with pleasing low profiles and jerkinhead roofs, bases of stone to sill height, and wide shingled-roof overhangs. Interiors stressed simple, natural materials as a background to the exhibits. Observation terraces at least half the size of the interior spaces encouraged visitors to enjoy the local features and reflect upon what they had seen and learned inside the museum. All three remaining Maier-designed museums were stabilized under the direction of Harrison Goodall during the 1980s.

Norris Museum

Norris Museum, built in 1929, is the most architecturally imposing of the three remaining Yellowstone museums. It was conceived as a gateway to the overlooks and trails of the geyser basin, and the building's concept, form, and execution of detail make it a masterpiece of Rustic architecture.

Norris Museum's siting skillfully conceals the geyser basin from view until entry into the foyer, which provides access to the flagstone terrace overlooking the thermal springs. "Norris Museum" is spelled out in wrought-iron letters suspended from the entrance truss. The entrance side is a long, low subdued composition of sheltering hip roofs with double-coursed long, wooden shingles on a base of oversized boulders; the overlook side has massive peeled-log brackets to support log lintels and projecting roof rafters.

▷ PARK AND RECREATION STRUCTURES *describes how Maier handled the L-shaped plan of the 700-square-foot Madison Museum: "Minor in size, but not in its contribution to park architecture. The pitch of the roof and the texture of the selected logs conspire with the rakish buttressing of the well-scaled rock work to deserve unqualified acclaim. The spacious 'landscape' window serves to project the outdoors into the museum interior, an illusion to be sought wherever the objective is the interpretation of surrounding Nature."*

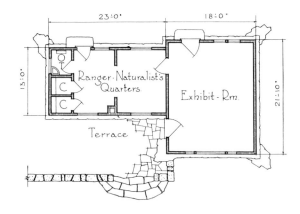

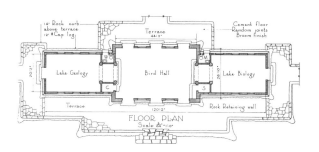

Madison Museum

Madison Museum, also built in 1929, is the smallest of Maier's four museums. Set in a meadow at the point where the Firehole and Gibbon rivers join to form the Madison River, the one-story structure is devoted to the park's history. The site is significant because it was here that the Washburn-Langford-Doane exploration party discussed Yellowstone's future.

One can still hear them, a party sitting around a campfire on the night of September 19, 1870, discussing the wonder-filled region and pondering what should be done.[9] Someone is in favor of seizing the opportunity to secure land claims that would turn a profit from tourists and pleasure seekers. Cornelius Hedges disagrees. He thinks that "there ought to be no private ownership of any portion of that region, but the whole ought to be set apart as a great National Park, and that each of us ought to make an effort to have this accomplished." Nathaniel Langford concurs, and the party resolves to try and have the region reserved as a park. Langford's 1871 lecture tour of the East Coast (sponsored by the Northern Pacific Railroad) set the process in motion, and the Park Act was passed a year later.

The design challenge for Maier at Madison Junction was different than at the other museum locations. The site was a meadow fringed by lodgepole pines that did not offer contours for blending the structure into the landscape, so the Bungalow-style influence is more evident here.

Fishing Bridge Museum

Fishing Bridge Museum, constructed in 1930–31, illus-

△ *The flagstone terrace around most of Fishing Bridge Museum provides a transition from a rock outcrop base to the extremely battered masonry walls. Massive boulders used for the lower walls, some up to 5 feet in diameter, rise to the eaves at the corners. The walls are wood* *framed and covered with cedar shakes, resting on log sills. Multilight casement windows flood the halls with natural light. The central roof is a simple gable; wing roofs have jerkinhead ends.*

trates Maier's skill in adapting a design to a site while at the same time meeting program requirements. *Park and Recreation Structures* describes the *well-planned and well-lighted nature museum [as] a successful example of the principles important in the creating of buildings suitable to natural areas – among these the value of the freehand line, the avoidance of underscale, the pleasing quality of the furrowed and knotted log. The particular stone here used and its sweeping batter from grade to its meeting with the wood superstructure are agreeable details.*

Directly beyond the museum a stone terrace over-

◁ Fishing Bridge Museum interior wall surfaces differ from the earlier museums, where drop siding was used. Walls are white plaster, and window and door frames are milled lumber. Massive peeled-log pole clusters have been sanded smooth and support lintel logs at the entranceways to the exhibit halls. Interior rafters and purlins rest directly on each other, contrasting with exposed exterior log framing with coped joints. The Bird Hall exhibits are in freestanding glass cases. Two large wrought-iron chandeliers decorated with elk and deer antlers and ram's horns are suspended from the ridgepole.

looks Yellowstone Lake. Stone steps lead from the terrace fitting the contours of the site before they drop down to the lakeshore. Stone-and-log railings border walks and trails through the area and protect the site's delicate vegetation.

Maier controlled the environment at each museum location by designing everything from support facilities to the furniture. Service buildings were placed at suitable distances from the museums to avoid any distraction from the site's central interpretive purpose. Comfort stations, naturalists' residences, and amphitheaters all incorporated Rustic design features. Amphitheaters were carefully located to fit into the site contours; permanent stages and the supporting frame for a projection screen were constructed of peeled logs.

Yellowstone's Future

There is much concern about Yellowstone's future. It is threatened by steadily increasing waves of tourists, crime and vandalism, poaching of large mammals, and exploitation of the natural resources in the surrounding ecosystem. Intense controversy has emerged over the NPS policy of "natural regulation" of wildlife; at issue is the fundamental principle of conservation versus use and enjoyment.

As the world's first national park, Yellowstone stands as an acknowledgment that there are places on earth that human beings can't improve upon. There is no more fitting place for the ideals of conservation and preservation to be rethought for the continued "benefit and enjoyment of the people."

△ The amphitheater at Fishing Bridge Museum, together with the comfort stations and landscaping, illustrates the complete treatment that was typically given to park areas.

Grand Teton National Park

There they are again, as breathtaking, heartstopping, in their majesty, and beauty, as if you had never seen them before.

Ansel Adams, THE TETONS AND THE YELLOWSTONE

Grand Teton National Park is often acclaimed as providing the most glorious scenery on the continent. The park covers 485 square miles in northwestern Wyoming. It is connected to Yellowstone National Park on the north by the John D. Rockefeller, Jr., Memorial Parkway, a reminder of the philanthropist's role in creating this magnificent reserve. Smaller than most parks, it contains more scenery, more animals, and more recreational opportunities than many areas twice its size. This is a place rich in the historic lore of Native Americans, trappers, and traders — a witness to the exploration, settlement, and exploitation that characterized the opening of the West. It also chronicles a lengthy struggle that ended in a victory for preservation.

Chartres Multiplied by Six

"There are no adjectives adequate to express the beauty and sublimity of this, the Jackson's Hole–Teton Hole–Snake River Country," said Bernard DeVoto.[10] He was describing the Teton Range, a collection of peaks rising a sheer 7,500 feet above the surrounding plain, and the large, open valley to the east, Jackson Hole, threaded by the Snake River, which flows through Jackson Lake and eventually into the Columbia River. The landscape also comprises dozens of lakes, glaciers in mountain cirques, and tumbling streams. Along the base of the Tetons are seven alpine lakes formed by glaciers: Phelps, Taggart, Bradley, Jenny, String, Leigh, and Jackson. The largest, Jackson Lake – alive with cutthroat and Mackinaw trout – is seventeen miles long and at one point eight miles wide. It was originally a natural lake, but was dammed in 1911 to store water, control the Snake River, and provide irrigation in Idaho.

The Teton Range completely dominates the landscape. Seen from a distance of a hundred miles or more, they appear as a wisp of clouds on the horizon; up close the dramatic mountain forms loom over the valley. The Tetons are spectacularly different from other mountain ranges because they have no foothills, no softening foreground around the four-mile concentration of the tallest peaks. Author Robert B. Betts coined this poetic description: *Composed mainly of the Grand Teton, Middle Teton, South Teton, Mount Owen, Mount Teewinot, and Nez Percé Peak, this cluster is called the Cathedral Group, and*

▷ A private ranch nestled between the Grand Tetons and the Snake River.

*▽ The first light of dawn
brushes the Teton Range and
the Snake River.*

*it takes only one look to see why it was given this name:
Chartres multiplied by six, a choir of shimmering granite
spires soaring high above the transept and nave of the valley
below.[11]*

Block-faulting, erosion, and glaciation formed and
shaped the Teton Range. Ice Age glaciers gouged out the
horn-shaped peaks and the U-shaped valleys. The range,
although the youngest in the Rocky Mountain system,
contains the oldest rock in North America. The granitic
gneisses and schists north and south of the central peaks
are some of the hardest and least porous rocks known.
These qualities, and the accessibility of major peaks,

attract technical rock climbers; handholds are secure and the views breathtaking.

Trappers called the high valleys encircled by mountain "holes." In 1829, Bill Sublette named the irregularly shaped 60-mile-long valley "Jackson's Hole" for David E. Jackson, his trapper partner. Around the turn of the century, local officials decided to shorten the name to Jackson Hole.[12]

The Tetons are truly awe-inspiring mountains. Washington Irving, writing about Wilson Price Hunt leading Astorians west toward the Columbia in 1811, described their joyful sighting of the Tetons: "Three mountain

△ *Cunningham Cabin. The*
"dog-trot" cabin was built in
1895 and was the homestead for
the Cunninghams' cattle ranch
until they left the valley for
Idaho in 1928. A dog-trot cabin
consists of two log squares,
joined and covered by a single
gabled roof, forming a two-
room log cabin with a roofed
verandah in the middle.

peaks glistening with snow … were hailed by the travellers with that joy with which a beacon on a sea-shore is hailed by mariners after a long and dangerous voyage."[13]

The phenomenon of light in the Tetons, where the sun's brilliance combines with the thinness of the air, makes distances deceptive. Jessy Quinn Thornton, who was on the Oregon Trail in 1846, made note in his journal of "a remarkable peculiarity in the atmosphere, which made it impossible for me to judge with any considerable degree of accuracy as to the distance of objects."[14]

Mountain Men and Homesteaders

The history of Jackson Hole has a fascination all its own. Shoshone, Crow, Blackfeet, Gros Ventre, and other Native Americans camped in the valley in summer months, but no tribes made it their permanent year-round home. Winters were unbearable. It was the adventurous spirit of the Lewis and Clark expedition and the pursuit of fur that drew trappers and adventurers from the East to the region. John Colter was probably the first, leaving the homeward-bound Lewis and Clark expedition in the winter of 1807–08 as it passed through Montana. Colter prospected for beaver in Jackson Hole and the Yellowstone country. Washington Irving's saga of Colter and

the solitary trapper's life popularized the romantic folklore of the mountain men. Colter was followed by the Astorians, led by Wilson Price Hunt crossing Teton Pass in 1811. French-Canadian trappers who saw the peaks from the west in 1819 referred to them as *les trois tetons* (the three breasts).

The argonauts, and westward-bound settlers on the Oregon Trail, bypassed Jackson Hole, crossing the Continental Divide at South Pass in southern Wyoming. Until the first survey expedition arrived in 1860, Jackson Hole was all but forgotten. Led by the legendary Jim Bridger, topographical engineer Captain William F. Raynolds conducted surveys to collect data about the Indians, farming and mining possibilities, and potential transcontinental routes. Raynolds rejected the idea of a rail route through the valley, sealing Jackson Hole's fate for development for the next four decades. The 1872 Hayden Survey, led by Professor Ferdinand V. Hayden, explored the Tetons and Jackson Hole. William Henry Jackson was a member of the Hayden team and produced the first photographs of the Teton Range.

Although trappers and pioneers built temporary cabins, the first permanent settlers, John Holland and John Carnes, didn't arrive until 1884. They homesteaded

△ *William D. Menor's homestead, built in 1895, was the first homestead settlement west of the Snake River. His ferry operation served a major crossing of the Snake River until a bridge was built in 1927. The complex was acquired by Rockefeller's Jackson Hole Preserve and restored for NPS interpretive use. Despite its pretentious whitewashed walls and classical column-supported center element, the Menor's Ferry complex is of true log construction.*

north of the town of Jackson. Five families of Mormons built homes on the southern edges of the valley in 1890. Significant settlement came after 1900, as schools, post offices, and churches were built at Jackson, Wilson, Moran, and Kelly. Supplying these towns was always difficult. Pack horses and supply wagons had to cross from Idaho over Teton Pass and then face the turbulent Snake River. Menor's Ferry was built at Moose in 1892 by William D. Menor to handle increased traffic in the valley.

Dude Ranching

Jackson Hole's reputation as big game country had been slowly growing through the 1870s. The spread of railroads and feeder stagelines had opened access, increasing its popularity for western vacations, and more and more travelers were reaching the valley. President Chester A. Arthur led a hunting party through the valley in 1883; memorable for its elaborate profligacy, the group left behind a trail of whiskey bottles.

Across the West, poor market conditions in the 1880s and 1890s made ranching risky. The winter of 1886–87 was especially devastating to ranching in the region. Eventually, the ranchers hired out as guides and opened their cattle ranches to paying guests and sports enthusi-

asts. Living a cowboy life and enjoying the Wild West was a happy vacation prospect for easterners willing to travel great distances and pay fancy prices. Word of the profits to be made from these eager sports must have drifted into Jackson Hole. The dude ranching industry was born when ranchers discovered herding tourists was more profitable if no less challenging than herding cattle.

In 1903, Ben Sheffield catered to wealthy hunters from his headquarters in Moran. Louis Joy started the first ranch in Jackson Hole at Phelps Lake in 1908, the JY Ranch. Many of the early dude ranches evolved as a main house was expanded, and then cabins, corrals, and tack sheds were added for guests and horses. Marginal cattle operations were left in place to give the dudes a feel for the "real" West. Joy's operation was the first conceived as a dude ranch from the start. Conversions of other cattle ranches followed, until tourism had become a thriving industry in the valley. The end of the dude ranch boom was tied closely to changes brought about by the National Park Service and the establishing of Grand Teton National Park in 1929. Some still thrive, operating under long-term leases from the NPS. Others are almost gone, decaying remnants abandoned by the NPS after purchase.

▷▷▽ *The 4 Lazy F guest ranch was built around 1927. The main buildings' rustic features show bearing log walls and exposed-log roof framing. Plumbing and electricity are recent additions. The ranch is owned as a life estate and will eventually revert to the National Park Service.*

▷ *Abandoned ranches dot the landscape, reminders of the Rockefeller acquisitions and their determination to restore the valley's original, unsettled appearance.*

◁ *The Grand Teton Environmental Educational Center, originally the Elbo Ranch.*

Grand Teton National Park

The story of Grand Teton National Park is one of patient determination, a significant conservation victory won by individuals who doggedly fought for the park's establishment. Protection for the Grand Teton area was first ensured in 1897 with the creation of the Teton Forest Reserve, which included most of the lands in today's national park. The Forest Service multiple-use policy tolerated cattle leases and allowed actions that resulted in timber exploitation. By the end of the century, a movement was growing to provide greater protection. These early efforts to protect the complete ecological system of a region, unbounded by artificially drafted boundaries, continue today in the Yellowstone–Jackson Hole region.

In 1898, Charles D. Walcott, director of the U.S. Geological Survey, visited Jackson Hole. He suggested incorporating the Tetons and Jackson Hole either as extensions of Yellowstone National Park or "as a separate park, to be known as the Teton National Park."[15] The Secretary of the Interior joined him with his recommendation for expanding Yellowstone southward. But Congress took no action that year nor in 1902. The number of settlements in the area grew, leading to an alliance between the Forest Service and cattle ranchers to oppose a national park.

The idea of a national park languished until 1916, when Horace Albright, assistant to National Park Service director Stephen Mather, made an inspection of the Yellowstone region. He was so impressed with the Grand Tetons and Jackson Hole that he resolved to make them part of the national park system. He had no idea how difficult a task it would prove to be. Two years later, when Albright visited Jackson Hole again, there were many supporters for park status. When he returned the following year, however, he found himself in a hornet's nest of hostility; an organized opposition had developed uniting the National Forest Service, livestock interests, and some dude ranchers.

Those in favor of a national park continued to rally support, and a historic meeting took place at Maude Noble's cabin on the bank of the Snake River on July 26, 1923. A group of Jackson Hole residents invited Horace Albright to discuss ideas for protecting the area from development. They decided to try and attract wealthy individuals who would purchase privately owned lands north of Jackson: Congress would then reimburse the purchasers, and the land would be added to the national park system. This novel approach would have failed if not for the arrival of a certain visitor in 1924. On a tour of Yellowstone and Jackson Hole, John D. Rockefeller, Jr., traveling under the Davison family name, was shocked by the unsightly dead and downed trees along the roadsides in Yellowstone, and he gave the NPS $50,000 for a cleanup.

The proposal to enlarge Yellowstone highlighted the longstanding rivalry between the Park Service and the Forest Service. To expand Yellowstone southward to include Jackson Hole would cost the Forest Service about 800,000 acres of land. The feud became so bitter that in the winter of 1924–25 the President's Coordinating Committee on National Parks and National Forests was appointed to survey and make recommendations regarding park expansion – of all parks, not just Yellowstone.[16] The committee recommended that Grand Teton Park be established as a separate park, but did not approve including Jackson Hole.

In the summer of 1926, Rockefeller, his wife, and their three youngest sons revisited Yellowstone. Albright took them down to Jackson Hole, where they were greatly impressed by the scenery but appalled by the unsightly commercial development. Albright broached the idea of land purchase, but Rockefeller was noncommittal, only asking Albright to "send me an estimate as to what it would take to buy the land and clear the junk out of this area, and send me a map."[17] When Albright visited the philanthropist in New York City the following winter, he took

△ The Chapel of the Transfiguration was built in 1927 by the Episcopal Church. A bell tower, chapel, and office building were constructed following NPS Rustic guidelines, and design features repeated in other valley structures are evident. A picture window behind the altar frames the Cathedral Group.

along maps of land for purchase on the west side of the Snake River all the way to the base of the Tetons. Rockefeller was displeased, exclaiming, "No, no, this isn't what I had in mind at all." He was interested in land on *both* sides of the river, and to the north: "The family is only interested in an ideal project. And it would please me very much if you could get me data on that."[18]

Over the next few years, Rockefeller's agents quietly bought more than 33,000 acres of land in the valley for less than $1,500,000, intending to turn it over to the NPS when a planned Grand Teton National Park came into being. When locals learned that "outside interests" were trying to "take over" their valley, resentment grew, and the NPS and Rockefeller were depicted as villains bent on taking away their lands. Dude ranchers, the Forest Service, livestock owners, hunters, and even some conservationists aligned to prevent the federal government from accepting Rockefeller's gift.

In 1929, Grand Teton National Park was created, but it protected only the mountains and some of the smaller lakes at their base. The new park was small, only about 150 square miles, from three to nine miles wide and 27 miles long, covering only the eastern side of the Grand Teton Range. It included Leigh and Jenny and a few other lakes, but omitted the much larger Jackson Lake and covered little of the lower land to the east that was needed for a winter elk range and as an area from which to view the mountains.

Political maneuvering continued until finally, after fifteen years of holding the land (and paying taxes), the Rockefellers informed the government that their patience was exhausted. Embarrassed by his inability to get Congress to act, President Franklin D. Roosevelt declared parts of Jackson Hole a national monument, thereby halting further development and opening the way for government receipt of the Rockefeller holdings.

◁▽ *The Joe Pfeiffer homestead is an abandoned turn-of-the-century farm complex, retained by the NPS to illustrate early settlement in the valley. While operating, the farm used no electricity or modern equipment.*

▷ *Mr. and Mrs. John D. Rockefeller, Jr., picnicking at Grand Teton National Park, 1931.*

A partisan fight developed in Congress as a reaction to President Roosevelt's action, and he vetoed efforts for repeal. After several years, a compromise was struck for a new Grand Teton National Park, and it was finally established by President Truman on September 14, 1950. Of the area in the monument, all but 9,000 acres was to be transferred to Grand Teton, which was enlarged from 95,360 acres to 298,738 acres.

The Rockefeller contributions were recognized in 1972 when Congress authorized transfer of 24,000 acres of Forest Service land as the John D. Rockefeller, Jr., Memorial Parkway, serving as a corridor and link between Yellowstone and Grand Teton national parks.

The Park Buildings

The controversial and lengthy struggle to establish Grand Teton National Park has left as diverse a collection of buildings as exist in any national park. Overlays

▷ *One of the first* NPS *buildings in Jackson Hole was the information office and museum at Jenny Lake, seen here in 1930. Log walls, skillfully corner-notched, are typically placed directly on log sills without foundations. Excellent craftsmanship is shown in the corner notching, diagonal logs in the gable end, exposed roof rafters, and roof framing. A simple detail that adds to the continuity of valley architecture is the use of saplings for joint chinking. Sometime after construction the roof was shingled and the chimney faced with stone. A Yellowstone Park stagecoach is at the right.*

△ *Cross-buck and rail fencing at a valley cattle ranch in the forested foothills of the Grand Tetons. This type of fencing did not require post holes, which were difficult to dig in the stony Jackson Hole soil.*

of development took place as homesteaders, dude ranchers, and the NPS played out their roles in the transition of an isolated valley settled under conditions of severe weather to one catering to tourism. Superimposed on the vernacular buildings and architecture are the NPS Rustic style and the Rockefeller influence.

Turn-of-the-century structures, built by homesteaders and ranchers, were utilitarian log buildings. These were sturdy, long-lasting shelters that went up quickly with a minimum of tools and materials. Working and abandoned ranches throughout the valley are faithful to local traditions and building techniques.

Construction methods and detailing in valley buildings are consistent, with few exceptions. There is a pleasing uniformity in the prevailing architecture reflecting a style expedient for the homesteaders and ranchers and later adopted by the NPS and Rockefellers for preserving old buildings as well as new construction. Logs, readily available in nearby forests, provided the primary building materials. Building forms are uniformly gable end. With little time for stonework (and the lack of readily available stone), pioneers produced a log cabin vernacular tradition wisely followed by later builders. Cross-buck and rail fencing carries the Rustic style throughout the valley.

Accommodating visitors while maintaining a wilder-

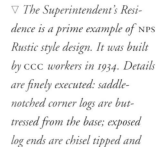

△△▷ *The Jenny Lake Store was originally built by Harrison Crandall in 1931 for his photography concession. The cupola and herringbone-patterned exposed-log ceiling are unique interior features. A new store was recently opened, and the original Crandall Studio is under renovation.*

ness environment challenged the Rockefeller family's goals for preserving the valley. Even as the family's land purchasing agent, the Snake River Land Company, acquired places where tourists could purchase meals and find overnight lodging, they faced new problems. Who would provide guest facilities for the convenience of residents and tourists alike? Through various acquisitions, the Snake River Land Company gradually became involved not only with food and lodging but also in transportation, eventually controlling the tourist business in upper Jackson Hole.[19]

Through Horace Albright's influence, Gilbert Stanley Underwood became the designer of Jackson Lake Lodge for the Grand Teton Company. After his departure from the NPS, Albright continued to support the expansion of Grand Teton National Park to include the Snake River Land Company properties. He had assisted Rockefeller in planning the tourist facilities in Colonial Williamsburg and recommended Gilbert Stanley Underwood for the Williamsburg Lodge design. When park expansion was being finalized, in 1950, the Grand Teton Lodge Company surveyed its lodgings and decided to provide a wide range of accommodations at Jackson Lake and Colter Bay. Albright again recommended Underwood, this time for the design of Jackson Lake Lodge.

The site was selected by John D. Rockefeller, Jr., at a location near Lunch Tree Hill, where he had first viewed the Teton Range in 1926. The building's design, conceived to provide views of the Cathedral Group of mountaintops and the intervening meadow, is unlike any of Underwood's earlier, Rustic log-and-stone structures. Following architectural trends of the day and the

△△▷ *Jackson Lake Lodge. The siting and architecture have stirred controversy since the lodge was completed in 1954. It is difficult to relate this Gilbert Stanley Underwood design to any of his earlier projects, which were traditionally in close harmony with the landscape. To its credit, the lodge's textured and stained wood-formed concrete exteriors and organization of window openings could be heralded as a fine example of Bauhaus-inspired work. But many critics debate the issue of log-and-stone buildings sympathetic with the landscape versus clear statements of contemporary design made of modern materials.*

▷ *Civilian Conservation Corps members were often sent to projects in remote, extraordinarily beautiful settings. Here, at Grand Teton, they are pictured at work on the road at the lower end of Leigh Lake in the summer of 1933.*

△ *Colter Bay Village provides low-priced accommodations for campers.*

prevailing International style, the starkness of the lodge exterior reflects a shift in national park structures to offer efficiency and contemporary expression.

A Preservation Lesson

The efforts of Horace Albright, John D. Rockefeller, Jr., and their many supporters to preserve the beauty of the Grand Tetons and Jackson Hole deserve our eternal gratitude and provide a forceful reminder of the struggles necessary to perpetuate special places in our landscape. An important lesson from the establishment of Grand Teton National Park is the failure of standard congressional procedures. Local interests, buttressed by opportunistic partisan political support, can and do frustrate the protection of scenic areas, often preferring to exploit and despoil them rather than "leaving them unimpaired for the enjoyment of future generations." In all of their dedicated efforts to save this place, Albright and his supporters had to seek the approval of local interest for their plans; and the wishes of a few dude ranchers, hunters, boosters, and developers constantly weighed more heavily than the interests of the people of the United States who, as a matter of fact, already owned most of the land.[20]

Rocky Mountain National Park

In nobility, in calm dignity, in the sheer glory of stalwart beauty, there is no mountain group to excel the company of snow-capped veterans of all the ages which stands at everlasting parade behind its grim, helmeted captain, Long's Peak.

NATIONAL PARKS PORTFOLIO

Rocky Mountain National Park was established in 1915 to preserve the splendid beauty of the area around Long's Peak. More than 100 summits higher than 12,000 feet surround the 14,255-foot landmark in the Southern Rockies, visible at great distances from the plains to the east. Located at the easternmost swing of the Continental Divide in north-central Colorado, the park's high country was shaped by glaciers into deep U-shaped valleys, great rock amphitheaters, and crenellated narrow ridges.

Below the alpine tundra and the tree line are glacial moraines, subalpine meadows, dense woods, serene lakes, rugged gorges, and parks—level valleys between the mountain ranges. Only two hours from Denver, the easily accessible park is besieged by almost three million visitors a year, including 600,000 day hikers.

A Colorful History

The history of Rocky Mountain National Park features Major Stephen Harriman Long's 1820 expedition. His party "discovered a blue strip, close in the horizon to the east—which was by some pronounced to be no more than cloud—by others, to be the Rocky Mountains."[21] The party's journalist noted: "A high Peake was to be plainly distinguished towering above all the others as far as the sight extended."[22] This was the peak later named after the expedition's leader.

In the 1830s and 1840s, fur trappers, explorers, and writers traversed the area—Kit Carson, John Charles Fremont, and Francis Parkman on his journey along the Oregon Trail. Groups of tourists began to visit the region, none more glamorous than the 1854–57 hunting expedition of an Irish baronet, Sir St. George Gore. His "grand hunting party included forty men, two valets and dog handlers, more than one hundred horses, twenty yoke of oxen, fifty hunting hounds, twenty-eight vehicles, and famous mountain men Jim Bridger and Henry Chatillon acting as guides."[23] Gore's travels are a testimony to the developing awareness, even among Europeans, of the adventures to be found in the American West.

When gold was discovered in Colorado, in 1858, the quiet scene changed abruptly under an onslaught of prospectors. Settlement began in 1860, when one of the

▷ *Lupine and sunflowers along Trail Ridge Road. Superlative views await the traveler along this road, the highest paved highway in the nation. For fifteen miles it curves above 11,000 feet through alpine tundra with dazzling snowfields below and the peaks of the Never Summer Mountains in the distance.*

▽ *Bear Lake is one of the few high mountain lakes in the country accessible by car. Trails radiate out from it to Nymph, Dream, and Emerald lakes.*

△ *Stanley Hotel in Estes Park, outside the park boundary. The mountain vacation complex was conceived by F. O. Stanley, inventor of the Stanley Steamer, and the grand opening of the hotel was in 1909.*

gold rush adventurers, Joel Estes, found a broad valley well suited for cattle ranching. Estes Park, as it was later called, also proved an accessible attraction for vacationers.

Attention focused on the area as a result of two overlapping congressionally chartered surveys of the 1870s. The additional geographical and geological surveys of Frederick Hayden and Clarence King, although promoting their personal ambitions, revealed the beauty of the Rocky Mountain wilderness to the public at large. Photographer William Henry Jackson accompanied Hayden, and his record of majestic panoramas reinforced earlier portrayals of the Rockies as a resort to rival Switzerland.[24]

The adventurous and curious generation of Victorian Britons developed a keen interest in the Rockies at a time when the transcontinental railroad, completed in 1869, made the westward trip easier. The Irish baronet Windham Thomas Wyndham-Quin, the fourth Earl of Dunraven, first visited the East Coast on his honeymoon in 1869. He returned in 1871 to hunt in the West with Buffalo Bill Cody as his guide, returning again a year later. Dunraven was so delighted with the Estes Park area on the second hunting trip that he set out to build a great estate and game preserve there, eventually purchasing or controlling 15,000 acres before the courts and homesteaders prevented further acquisition.

F. O. Stanley drove one of his Stanley Steamers from Denver to Estes Park in 1903 and ended up purchasing the remains of the earl's estate, which had been partially sold off. Stanley was suffering from tuberculosis and had been advised by his doctor to visit Colorado. He thrived in the healthful mountain air and stayed to invest in the tourist potential. He planned a luxury resort, and construction of the Stanley Hotel began in 1907.

The credit for establishing Rocky Mountain National Park is due mostly to a man named Enos Mills. He went to Estes Park in 1884, a sickly fourteen-year-old Kansan seeking good health, and eventually became known as the "John Muir of the Rockies" for his conservation advocacy. The experience of climbing Long's Peak in 1887 inspired him to build a cabin at the foot of the mountain and spend his summers guiding tourists. During an 1889 trip to San Francisco, he met John Muir, and the naturalist became a source of encouragement as he instructed the young Coloradan: "You must tell them, tell them that we are cutting down and burning up the forests of the West so fast that we'll lay this continent as waste as China, in a few generations."[25]

Mills dreamed of a national park along the Front Range between Long's Peak and Pikes Peak. A seven-month stay in Yellowstone in 1890 had planted the seed of inspiration. Other travels throughout the West and in Europe reinforced his zeal, and in 1909 he began to crusade in earnest for a national park. His lectures, photographs, articles, and publicizing campaign were all motivated by his passion for conservation. A strong coalition was mounted against Mills, composed of people who saw the potential for economic gain from tourism. Mills' cause found allies in J. Horace McFarland, of the American Civic Association, and the Colorado congressional delegation. A Rocky Mountain National Park bill was introduced in Congress in 1913, and after two years of political maneuvering, the authorizing bill was passed. The original park contained 358 square miles, and was later expanded to 417 square miles by acquisition of inholdings and surrounding acreage.

In the meantime, developers had increased tourism around the proposed park, and the history of the park tells the ironic story of a struggle to reverse this early development and return the park to wilderness. Although

▷ Officials partaking of refreshments after the dedication of Rocky Mountain National Park in September 1915. Left to right, Stephen T. Mather, then assistant to the Secretary of the Interior with responsibilities to supervise the national parks; Robert Sterling Yard, publicist working for Mather in the Department of the Interior; Acting Superintendent C. R. Trowbridge; first official NPS photographer Cowling; and Horace M. Albright, Mather's assistant.

▷ Fern Lake Lodge, seen here in 1936, offered rest to hikers at the end of a four-mile trail. The lodge, built within a mile of the Continental Divide, was demolished around 1975.

it was at one time heavily exploited, years of effort have resulted in the acquisition of numerous inholdings and removal of most traces of the park's early history. For many travelers, the current park experience is the two- or three-hour trans-Divide drive, a trip now unmarred by structures from an earlier era. The principal buildings of interest include a hotel outside the park's boundaries, remnants of the dude ranch and summer home period, and NPS buildings. Among the latter are fine examples of the NPS Rustic style and two recent interpretations of it.

Lodging the Dudes

Unlike other early national parks in the mountainous West, Rocky Mountain does not claim to have been developed as a destination resort by railroaders. The elegant Stanley Hotel just outside the boundary at Estes Park and the modest dude ranches within the park

seemed to adequately meet the tourist demand. Hotels around Grand Lake on the less accessible western side of the Divide were developed in the 1890s. Camp Wheeler, on the North Fork of the Colorado River, north of Grand Lake, opened in 1907 as one of the first dude ranches in that region. Possibly, it was the easy access for day hikers and the lack of roads into the park's interior in the early years that discouraged anything grander than expanded ranches to accommodate visitors.

The railroaders were content to take travelers only as far as Estes Park, and local transportation made the final connections with the dude ranches. As automobile travel increased in the 1920s and the railroads declined to undertake an aggressive advertising campaign, the ranches were able to attract more visitors. For decades the ranches prospered, but improved roads eventually caused their demise. Motor courts and motels geared for shorter stays became more attractive than the ranches. The surge of automobiles also raised alarm that overburdening the park resources would quickly destroy the very qualities that made it attractive in the first place.

An NPS policy of purchasing private inholdings was instituted to restore the park to its original setting. As property was acquired, buildings were either removed or demolished. Although resorts and lodges flourished in Estes Park, Grand Lake, and other boundary areas, the emphasis within the park moved toward outdoor camping for the automobile tourist. The resort industry that helped promote the park's attractions contributed to its own decline by popularizing the park. All of the dude ranches within the park boundaries were eventually acquired, and today only two examples remain, which have been preserved as part of the park's history.

Moraine Lodge and the Holzwarth Homestead

Travelers seeking a taste of the West and the opportunity to fish in the area's clear lakes and streams were accommodated in complexes of small-scale log buildings that had grown up around ranch homesteads. The first dude ranches in the area predated the park by several decades. Long winters and early snows in the Colorado mountains limited the dude business to a short May-to-September season.

A good example of the many lodges throughout the

◁ *Trail riders starting out from the Moraine Park Visitor Center. Dude ranching began in the 1890s and was popular – and profitable – in the park for many years. The NPS purchased the last ranch in the 1970s; some critics have argued that the destruction of the old lodges and resorts represents an undesirable loss of valuable historic structures.*

▽ *This recently restored pioneer cabin was built by Joe Fleshuts in the early 1900s near the Holzwarth Ranch.*

△ *Holzwarth's Trout Lodge and the Never Summer Ranch operated until 1974. Trout catches were limited to twenty pounds; pleasure rides and all-day pack trips explored the western slope of the Continental Divide. The remaining buildings on the western side of the Colorado offer today's visitor a taste of the 1920s dude ranch lifestyle.*

park is what now serves as the Moraine Park Visitor Center. The building was part of Mrs. McPherson's dude ranch, built in 1923 and purchased by the NPS in 1931. A rustic appearance derives from cobblestones faced on a concrete foundation and log veneer on a frame structure. The single restored building is all that remains of the original cluster of cabins.

In 1919, the Fall River Road opened, crossing the Divide, and encouraged tourist travel between Estes Park and Grand Lake, while opening the western side of the park to resort activity. The Holzwarth Homestead and Never Summer Ranch to the north of Grand Lake are well-preserved examples of what dude-ranch life was like in Rocky Mountain National Park.

John G. Holzwarth was a German immigrant who left Denver around 1917 for the mountains when Prohibition abruptly ended his successful saloon business. Along with his wife and three children, Holzwarth built a homestead on the North Fork of the Colorado River. After they tired of hard-drinking friends from Denver taking advantage of their hospitality, the family decided to open a dude ranch and named it the Holzwarth Trout Lodge. Paying guests were pleased to fish, ride, and hike after their long drive from Estes Park.

Prosperity increased, and in 1923 the Holzwarths

moved across the Colorado River and built Never Summer Ranch, named after the adjacent mountain range. A substantial three-story main lodge and cabins added over the years became headquarters for popular fishing and horseback expeditions. After operating for fifty years, Holzwarth's holdings were purchased in 1974 by the Nature Conservancy and transferred to Rocky Mountain National Park the following year.

The Holzwarth buildings on the western side of the Colorado that were part of the original Trout Lodge have been preserved for interpretive purposes. The Never Summer Ranch buildings were removed or destroyed, and the present complex was renamed Never Summer Ranch by the NPS.

Summer Homes

Seasonal residents bought land in the future park and built summer getaways. They began a pattern of generation after generation spending their summers in the Estes Park area. One of the most prominent of these vacationers was William Allen White.[26] His four-building complex near Moraine Park is retained by the NPS as an example of this vacation lifestyle.

White became familiar with the region during early visits in the 1880s and a honeymoon trip in 1893. Later

▽ *William Allen White found Moraine Park a respite from his work as editor of the* EMPORIA GAZETTE *in Emporia, Kansas. He traveled to the park from his home for 60 years and was a regular summer resident.*

As with other private vacation homes in the park, White's camp served as a place for sweet repose and rest in the solitude and tranquillity of the mountains.

▷ *Beaver Meadows Visitor Center, designed in the tradition of Frank Lloyd Wright by Taliesin Associated Architects, used naturally oxidizing steel for structural support.*

△ *A detail of metal cladding imitating concrete block. White appears to have been content with the buildings as he purchased them, making only minimal changes for family and guest comfort.*

▷ *The Ranger Station complex at the Fall River Entrance, built in 1936, is a superb example of* NPS *Rustic architecture. Typical details include carefully selected boulders facing concrete foundations; walls of double saddle-notched logs chinked with saplings; gabled roofs with cedar shakes carried on peeled-log purlins; and rafters that extend beyond the walls. Six-light windows are used in most of the buildings.*

▷ *Fall River Checking Station, 1930, typifying the* NPS *desire to provide a gateway that could "with subtlety and grace project the promise and lure of a region and its offered recreation to the very public highway."*

in the decade, his wife's health and a desire to escape the summer heat of Emporia, Kansas, took the family first to the Colorado Springs area and then to Estes Park. In 1912, White purchased his summer mountain hideaway at Moraine Park—a main cabin, built in 1887, and a studio that had been added around 1900, as well as two additional "bedroom" cabins.

Located in a superb setting, William Allen White's vacation retreat was a log-and-frame construction, typical of local building forms and workmanship. The retreat has been restored for use by an artist-in-residence program.

National Park Service Structures

The NPS structures at Rocky Mountain National Park follow the principles of the Rustic style that was emerging in the 1920s. Designs were created for ranger stations, patrol cabins, shelters, fire lookouts, and a utility district. With a careful eye toward the restoration of the park to a more natural state, structures built from the 1920s until the early 1940s were carefully sited to minimize intrusion on the natural setting. As part of Mission 66, two noteworthy modern buildings for visitor interpretation centers were designed: the Park Headquarters

◁ The Beaver Meadows Visitor Center was one of the better architectural contributions to the national park system from Mission 66. The building represents a successful move to achieve a rustic character using materials other than logs and stone.

◁ Buildings in the park headquarters utility area have a uniform design, although varying in plan for specific functions. "Logs-out" peeled-log framing braced by corner diagonals, vertical reverse board-and-batten plank walls, and multilight windows create well-composed exterior elevations. The single-story complex is unified by shake-covered shed roofs, extended log purlins and rafters, and brown paint on all exterior walls.

at the East Entrance and the Alpine Visitor Center on the Trail Ridge Road.

A three-building complex for the ranger station at the Fall River Entrance is an excellent illustration of the best of what the NPS produced through its Branch of Plans and Design. Similar Rustic elements were used in ranger stations and patrol cabins scattered throughout the park. Native stone and logs were used for foundations, chimneys, and bearing walls, and the buildings are characteristic of those in other national parks in similarly forested, mountainous country.

Beaver Meadows Visitor Center at the park's East Entrance shows a successful use of contemporary forms and materials in the Rustic style. Designed by Taliesin Associated Architects in the tradition of Frank Lloyd Wright, the well-conceived and richly detailed building was completed in 1967. It combines service as the park's administrative headquarters with visitor orientation.

In departing from traditional use of logs and stone,

the architects used two exterior materials (Cor-ten steel and native stone set in concrete) to achieve a design that blends into the surrounding landscape by virtue of a long, low profile set among sheltering pines. The steel, used both structurally and ornamentally, oxidizes naturally to a warm reddish brown and is richly detailed with patterns of mountain profiles. Great care was taken in the selection and placement of boulders into the concrete masses buttressing the steel. The results seem to organically merge the building base from the meadow into the superstructure above. Horizontal scoring in the concrete creates a shadow line and scale for the massive walls while helping to define the deeply recessed rectangular openings for entrances and the windows framing the mountain views.

The Alpine Visitor Center is at an elevation of 11,796 feet on the Fall River Pass at the intersection of Trail Ridge Road and Fall River Pass Road. The two-building complex, located at one of the highest auto-accessible

points in the country, is open only during the summer months. The Mission 66 Center contains exhibits interpreting the tundra; a second, historic structure contains a store and dining room.

The one-story buildings of contemporary Rustic design are sited overlooking a valley. Views sweep out from the terraces toward the glacial moraine and tundra landscape, and paths radiate out into the fields of summer wildflowers. Even on the warmest summer days, icy winds sweep across the site. A strong sense of shelter is conveyed by the massive boulder walls, reinforced by shallow-pitched shingled roofs with wide overhangs.

The Stanley Hotel

The Stanley Hotel, located outside the park boundaries, is a landmark long associated with the Estes Park area. While the Long's Peak region did not see the building of elegant private homes, small hotels were built there for increasing numbers of tourists.

At the turn of the century, the railroads were building elegant hotels at Yellowstone, Glacier, and other parks to stimulate passenger traffic. With Estes Park only 65 miles from Denver, F. O. Stanley could rely on easy access from the main population and rail centers. The same inventive genius that enabled Stanley and his twin brother, Francis, to make a fortune selling sensitive dry emulsion for photographic plates to George Eastman, and later creating the Stanley Steamer, was applied to the design of the hotel.

Acting as his own designer, Stanley chose the Georgian Revival style for his hotel buildings. He realized this was the same time that the railroaders were building massive log hotels, but he sympathized with Robert Reamer's renovations at the Lake Hotel in Yellowstone and his selection of a traditional look familiar to an easterner's background.

Construction began in 1907, and the massive, five-story structure opened in 1909. At the same time, a hydroelectric plant was built on the Fall River, enabling the hotel to proclaim itself the first in the country "to heat,

◁ *Stanley Hotel dining room windows frame views of the Rockies.*

◁ *A recent restoration has returned the Stanley Hotel to its original grandeur. The hotel and accompanying manor, concert hall, carriage house, and guest houses are all clapboard buildings with red-shingled roofs, rich in Georgian Colonial architectural detail and trim: arched fan windows, dentil-trimmed eaves, oriel windows, and columned porches with pediment gable ends.*

▷ *F. O. Stanley at the wheel of a Stanley Steamer in 1913.*

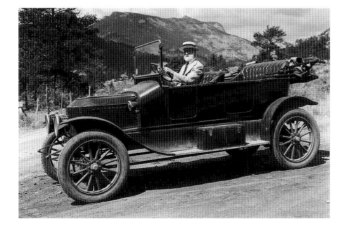

light, and cook meals exclusively with electricity."[27] In 1910, work began on the smaller-scale, 33-room winterized Stanley Manor. A concert hall, carriage house, and guest houses were added later.

Interiors were also richly detailed and furnished. Ground-floor public rooms are spacious, with high ceilings. The main lobby, graced by a grand staircase, is reminiscent of Colonial Williamsburg. An ornate mirror-and-brass hydraulic elevator carries guests to the upper floors. Wide, arched windows in the music and dining rooms are strategically placed to frame views of the mountains. The music room's Steinway piano was occasionally tuned and played by John Philip Sousa. Stanley indulged his fondness for billiards in the heavily paneled billiard room, finished with dark woods and raised benches. Guest rooms, elegantly furnished with period furniture, included four-poster and brass beds.

Stanley's project was an immediate success. Wealthy guests, drawn to the European spa atmosphere and the elegant accommodations, typically stayed for a month or more. The size, conveniences, and scenic location earned it a valued reputation. Stanley catered to his guests by having them greeted at the railheads at Loveland and Lyons and then transported to the hotel in a fleet of eleven-passenger Stanley Steamers. In recent years the hotel has happily regained its former elegance through extensive restorations.

Cedar Breaks National Monument

If Cedar Breaks were anywhere but in this region, it would be picked as one of the world's greatest scenic wonders.

NATIONAL PARK SERVICE GUIDE, 1985

Cedar Breaks National Monument is a brilliantly colored amphitheater carved out of the 10,000-foot-high Markagunt Plateau in southern Utah. A product of the same forces and materials that created the spectacular southwest landscapes of the Grand Canyon, Zion Canyon, and the Bryce amphitheater, it is an original work of nature.

The amphitheater – 2,000 feet deep and more than three miles across – exhibits stone spires, columns, arches, and canyons of intricate design and seemingly endless variety. Eroded by rain, streams, ice, and wind, the layers of stone emanate a multitude of colors as a result of the iron and manganese deposits.

The extraordinary beauty of Cedar Breaks caught the attention of the Union Pacific Railroad engineers in 1922 as they were making plans for a motor coach Loop Tour to originate at Lund, Utah. They scheduled a lunch stop at Cedar Breaks on the first day's drive, 109 miles to Zion National Park. The railroad hired Gilbert Stanley Underwood to design a lodge on the rim of the amphitheater for the midday visitors – one of Underwood's first commissions for the railroad. Over a decade later, after the site was designated a National Monument, the NPS designed and built the two structures close to the same location near the South Entrance to the Rim Road.

Cedar Breaks Lodge

Although no trace of Cedar Breaks Lodge remains today, Underwood's drawings and early photographs, and author Joyce Zaitlin's biography *Gilbert Stanley Underwood,* illustrate how important it was in the development of the Rustic style. The lodge was intended to serve as a dining pavilion for the midday pause in the day's excursion before travelers went on to Zion. The stop provided an opportunity to see the multicolored splendors of Cedar Breaks amphitheater. The building's purpose and Underwood's arrangement of spaces were simple. A long rectangle contained an entrance lobby; on one side was a welcoming fireplace (with restrooms behind it) and on the other, down split-log steps, were a dining room and kitchen. In this simple structure one can see the beginnings of Underwood's Rustic style, his masterful treatment of forms, structure, and materials.

Underwood's preference was for a limited palette of

▷ Cedar Breaks Amphitheater, 2,000 feet deep and 3 miles across, inspired the Indian name "Circle of Painted Cliffs."

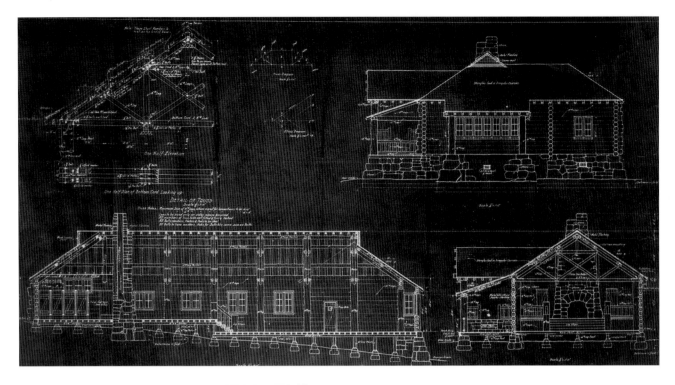

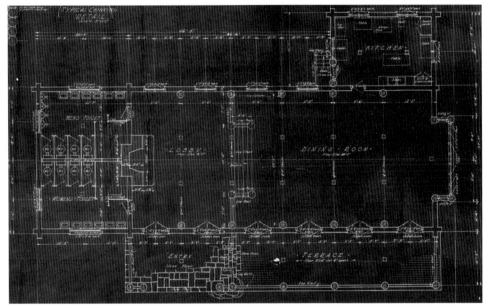

△ This drawing shows Underwood's exceptional skill in using natural materials and forms in a simple building. It was constructed on a foundation of random ashlar stone taken from the site. Foundation corners were battered, and stones diminished in size from the ground up to the log plates of the upper walls. Log purlins and rafters extending at the gable and shed roof eaves were carefully scaled, and the roof dominates the overall form. Traditional-sized windows were specified, which retained the integrity of the log bearing walls, but Underwood refined this technique in later lodges with larger window openings to flood his interiors with natural daylight.

materials, and he was highly selective in his use of stone, unpeeled logs, and cedar roof shakes. The building was log-framed with exposed surfaces for the interior finish. Scale was well defined by the main half-hipped roof covered with cedar shakes in an undulating pattern.

The building entrance illustrated Underwood's distinct, subtle touch. It was defined by a gabled porch that extended to a terrace overlooking the amphitheater. The placement and scale of the porch along the long elevation of the lodge skillfully emphasized the point of entry. Additional focus was provided by the massive, corner paired-log columns supporting the porch roof and by lowering the ridge from the main roof. A horizontal log beam supporting smaller vertical logs in the gable end completed the Rustic version of a Classical pedimented entrance. Massive log columns that supported the terrace roof, and braced log handrails, were spaced in a rhythm to distinguish the terrace from the entrance.

Because the rim is heavily forested, unpeeled logs with saddle-notched exterior corners were used for all the structural framing, creating the predominant design theme. The exterior and interior wall logs were chinked with plaster built up on metal lath.

Working drawings from the project reveal the method for supporting the roof and its heavy snow loads. They also illustrate Underwood's thoroughness, showing that he provided construction details right down to the placement of bolts in the roof trusses. These were no haphazard sketches of vague concepts to be field executed: they were refined architect's drawings. The engineering was developed with structural diagrams to solve the loading problems, as seen in the detailed drawings of building sections and elevations. Unpeeled-log columns placed twelve feet apart along the interior face of the log walls were of sufficient diameter to carry log trusses with paired lower log chords. Exposed log rafters and purlins carried the exposed plank roof deck.

▷ *The Cedar Breaks Visitor Center, built in 1937 as a Civilian Conservation Corps project. Perched on the amphitheater's rim, its form and materials minimize the building's impact on the site.*

△ *Interior of the Visitor Center at Cedar Breaks.*

△ *The Caretaker's Cabin at Cedar Breaks incorporates NPS Rustic details with peeled logs and stonework. Even in the smallest structures like this, careful attention to detailing is evident in the buttressing of the saddle-notched corner logs.*

The dining room was an early example of space and structure used as decoration, a technique that Underwood refined at Ahwahnee and Grand Canyon Lodge. Here, as in later projects, the dining room was lowered several steps as an architectural device to vary floor elevations and emphasize a change in function. A larger volume was created by exposing roof trusses and decking. The rhythm of interior columns against the exterior walls and trusses provided a subtle division in the space. Materials and textures throughout were rough. Wrought-iron chandeliers and Old Hickory furniture completed the special rustic character.

National Park Service Buildings

The three Rustic structures near the South Entrance were designed by the NPS and built by Civilian Conservation Corps crews in 1937. The caretaker's cabin, Visitor Center, and comfort station are simple in form and share common elements of NPS Rustic construction. Single story, with peeled-log walls and shallow-pitched shake roofs, the buildings are in the best tradition of the Rustic-style principles of nonintrusive architecture.

The Visitor Center at Point Supreme Lookout is perched on the edge of the amphitheater – a window to the eroded sandstone formations. The caretaker's cabin is a quarter mile away, visible from the road and closer to the South Entrance. Construction details in both buildings show the familiar NPS treatment of peeled-log walls on a stone foundation.

Zion National Park

Nothing can exceed the wondrous beauty of little Zion Valley.... In an instant, there flashed before us a scene never to be forgotten. In coming time it will, I believe, take rank with a very small number of spectacles each of which will, in its own way, be regarded as the most exquisite of its kind which the world disclose. The scene before us was the Temples and the Tower of the Virgin.

Captain Clarence E. Dutton, U.S. GEOLOGICAL SURVEY REPORT, 1880.

The magnificent Vermilion Cliffs wall is part of a 2,000-foot layer of Navajo sandstone in the western region of the Colorado Plateau in southwestern Utah. The dramatically colored escarpments formed by the earliest sculpting of the Colorado River were named by Major John Wesley Powell for their predominant rock coloring: the Chocolate, Vermilion, White, Gray, and Pink Cliffs. Farther west, the narrow, curving Virgin River carved Zion Canyon through the pink, white, and red sandstone. Eons of erosion created a wealth of dramatic forms, "pyramids, domes, pinnacles, and temples," in a startling array of colors.

Zion Canyon was known to the Anasazi Indians and later to the Paiute. In the 1820s, the trapper Jedediah Smith explored the area, and his stories of travel and adventures incited others to follow and contributed to the development of the Spanish Trail to the Pacific.[28] Two decades later, Captain John C. Fremont explored the region, providing information that guided the Mormons to southern Utah, where they were settling by the early 1850s.[29] Drawn by discoveries of iron ore and coal, fertile valleys, and a warm growing climate, Mormon leaders were inspired to strengthen the southern Utah Mission by a "call" to populate the area. A missionary, Mrs. Nancy Anderson (originally from cotton-growing country), produced a quart of cotton seeds brought from her old home for planting in the Santa Clara Valley, and the "Utah Dixie Country" was born.

Nephi Johnson, a Mormon missionary, entered Zion Canyon in 1858 searching for settlements in the upper Virgin River valley. Permanent settlement began in 1861 and grew to over 800 people by 1864. Homes were log cabins or Mormon-constructed buildings of stone in a vernacular Greek Revival style reminiscent of architecture from their origins in upstate New York. The National Park Service would later incorporate these traditions into their buildings in the canyon.

John Wesley Powell explored the region in the early 1870s, and showed a preference for native names by calling the North Fork of the Virgin River "Mukuntuweap" (straight canyon) and the east fork "Parunuweap" (canyon with a swift stream). In 1909, general interest in preserving the natural scenery resulted in the official enactment of Mukuntuweap National Monument. The

▷ The Great White Throne. Thomas Wolfe visited Zion on June 25, 1938, and recorded his impressions of the landscape: "Fierce blocks of red and temples and kings' thrones and the sheer smoothness of the blinding vertices of soapstone red."

▽ *Tourists in White Company*
coaches leaving the original
Zion Lodge for a drive through
Zion Canyon, 1929.

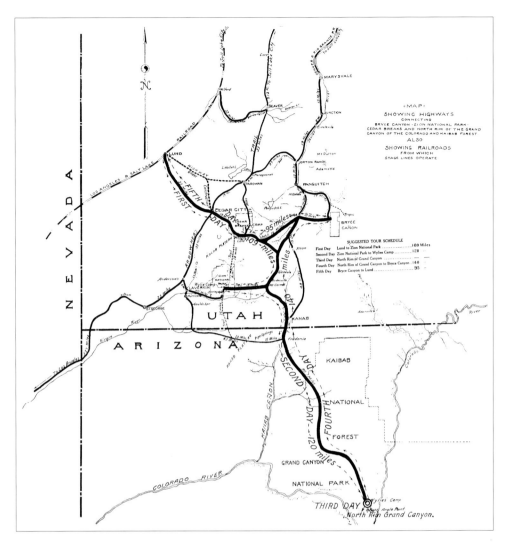

◁ *Map and suggested schedule for the Union Pacific Railroad's carefully planned Loop Tour (1922), which took visitors to five major scenic attractions over the course of five days. Magnificent lodges to accommodate the travelers were built at Zion, Bryce, and the North Rim of the Grand Canyon.*

△ NPS *landscape architects adopted a uniform theme at Zion of roughly dressed native sandstone laid with wide mortar joints.*

National Park Service, through Horace Albright, worked to enlarge the monument and change its name to Zion, and President Wilson's proclamation made it so in 1918. Zion National Monument was five times larger than its predecessor. A year later it became Zion National Park.

Tourists and the National Park Service

When Zion National Monument became part of the fledgling national park system in 1916 it had undergone little commercial development. The NPS and the Los Angeles and Salt Lake Railroad enticed the first tourists to the monuments and parks of southwestern Utah. Entrepreneurs saw opportunities for catering to tourists, and concessions were granted to transportation and lodging companies. Access was important, and the state of Utah began to improve roads into the area. The Wylie Permanent Camping Company followed the formula that had proved so successful in Yellowstone, setting up a tent compound at the base of the east wall of Zion Canyon.

Stephen Mather and Horace Albright brought about the involvement of railroaders, who created access and improvements to the southern Utah parks and the North Rim of the Grand Canyon. Roads were being planned by the NPS, and a concessioner was needed to provide attractive facilities and services. The Union Pacific Rail-

road was seeking additional routes to offset the lull during winter months when heavy snows limited travel in the north. It sought an attraction on the Colorado River's north side to compete with its main western rival, the Santa Fe Railroad, which carried tourists to the South Rim of the Grand Canyon.

Mather urged the Union Pacific to buy the Los Angeles and Salt Lake Railroad and expand access to link Cedar Breaks, Zion, Bryce, the Kaibab National Forest, and Grand Canyon's North Rim. By granting the Union Pacific exclusive concession rights and cooperating with the state of Utah in improving road access, the NPS began development of the parks and monuments in the region. To avoid what looked like the establishment of a monopoly, Mather insisted that a subsidiary company be formed. The Utah Parks Company was created in 1923, and improvements went forward.

The Union Pacific Railroad had extended a spur from Lund, Utah, to Cedar City in 1922 to provide access for their motor coach Loop Tour. The Parks Company's plans for lodges and other tourist facilities went forward in cooperation with the NPS. At the same time, the NPS Landscape Division began planning improved roads, tunnels, and bridges at the parks and national monuments. In later years, additional NPS facilities were produced in harmony with the Utah Parks Company buildings.

A common theme initiated by the Parks Company's architect was adopted by the NPS and became typical of the buildings in the canyon; large blocks of roughly dressed native sandstone were laid with wide mortar joints and combined with overscaled sawn wooden beams and rafters, low-pitched roofs, and wide eaves. Bridges and tunnels were executed with similar materials and careful attention to details. New lodges, opened in 1985 by the concessioner TW Recreational Services, followed the same principles and produced a generally consistent building character throughout Zion Canyon.

Zion Lodge and the Work of Gilbert Stanley Underwood

The original Zion Lodge design reflected the NPS' strong control over site selection for visitor accommodations and its preference for Rustic architecture. The lodge was tragically destroyed by fire and in 1966 was rebuilt on a

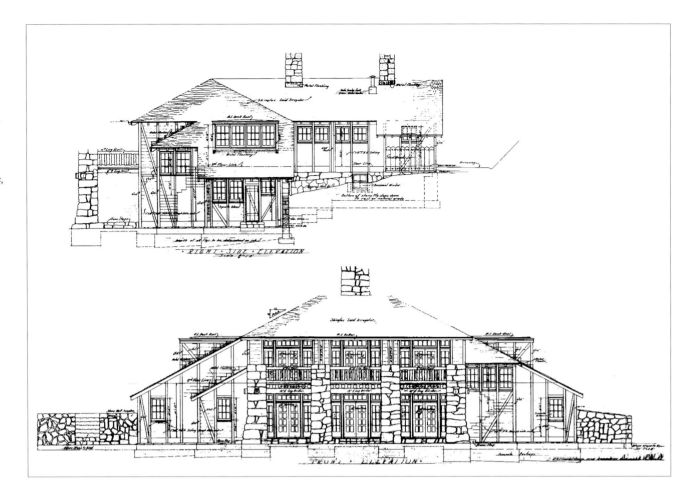

modest scale. In close cooperation with the NPS, TW Recreational Services completed restoration work in 1992 to bring back the character of the original Zion Lodge. The Utah Parks Company's cabins, support buildings, and the Zion Nature Center (originally the Zion Inn) remain as part of Underwood's architectural legacy in the canyon.

Author Joyce Zaitlin recounts the architect's introduction to the Zion project and Stephen Mather's influence on site selection and design of the main lodge.[30] When the Utah Parks Company's original designs were presented to Mather, they were rejected, along with the chosen site close to the Virgin River. Through the influence of Underwood's friend Daniel Hull, then chief of the NPS Landscape Engineering Office and sponsor of the architect's first work at Yosemite, the Parks Company hired Underwood to redesign the project. Underwood continued working on buildings in the canyon until the final cottages were completed in 1934. All his designs were compatible with the NPS Rustic buildings in the canyon.

For the main lodge Underwood conceived a sprawling three-story hotel centered around a central lounge with 75 guest rooms in three radiating wings. The design sketches portray a scheme of modest rusticity with wood exteriors, limited stonework, and wooden roof shakes placed in a straight and regular fashion.

Mather and the federal Fine Arts Commission were impressed by the designs. But Mather rejected the commission's recommendation and expressed a preference for a smaller main lodge with a separate collection of cottages for guest rooms. Underwood's revised design for a small, two-story pavilion with only a lobby, restrooms, office, and store on the first floor, and kitchen and dining room on the second floor, was accepted, and construction began in 1924. Work on the cottages and support buildings began at the same time, with more cottages added over the years. The main lodge was expanded in 1926 to include an enlarged dining room and lobby, a recreation and lecture hall, and a merchandise and curio store.

Working simultaneously on designs for Bryce Canyon, Underwood began to show his flair for using native materials and fitting buildings into their surroundings. His plans typically laid out massive volumes in asymmetrical compositions, punctuated by dramatic roof expressions and stone piers embracing window and door panels. At Zion, four massive stone pillars supported a second-story porch that dominated the facade. The strong vertical lines gave the building a solid appearance and dramatic scale that blended with the neighboring mountains.

The Union Pacific devised a scheme of deluxe and standard cabins to offer visitors a choice of quality and price. The cabins were similar to the nearby main lodge in materials and construction. Deluxe cabins contained two or four rooms that could be combined into suites. The small, rustic structures were placed on rough-dressed stone foundations made with the same stone that was used in ashlar patterns for the chimneys. Standard cabins were simpler in design than the deluxe; wooden stud-out framing was placed outside pine plank walls, and the stone chimneys were omitted.

▷▽ Deluxe cabins designed by Underwood for the Union Pacific Railroad's subsidiary, the Utah Parks Company. Subtle differences are visible in his Zion, Bryce, and Grand Canyon North Rim cabins. Cabins were adapted to the local setting in form and material. The Zion cabins, in a dry climate without nearby forests, used shallow-pitch roofs, dressed native sandstone, milled lumber, and studs-out framing over horizontal pine plank walls. At Bryce and the North Rim, in pine forest settings, logs and boulders were available. Cabins there were designed with high-peaked roofs to shed snow, and logs were used for exterior walls, porch framing, and trim. At each location, the deluxe cabins' small-scale, lively exterior design features and pleasant rustic interiors provided comfortable and attractive lodgings.

△△ On a larger scale, with the same design vocabulary used on the main lodge and cabins, the Men's Dormitory and Zion Nature Center show Underwood's talent for adapting to different building uses. Logs were introduced in the porch framing for the dormitory and to differentiate it from the cabins. The Nature Center implies public use by Underwood's having developed a rhythm of stone piers to frame the walls with either planking infill or windows and doors.

A transition in style and workmanship can be seen when the late 1920s buildings at Grotto Campground and the Pine Creek residential area are compared to the 1930s buildings at Oak Creek, the South Campground, Temple of Sinawava, and the East and South entrances. The 1930s structures reflect pressures on overworked NPS designers to repeat established building plans and adapt to the unskilled labor of CCC work crews. These buildings use smaller stones and smaller beams, purlins, and rafters. Walls are more uniform, with dressed stones and smoother mortar joints, and are placed in a regular, straight-edged pattern.

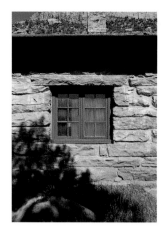 

◁ Overhanging eaves are prevalent, but less pronounced, on service buildings built in the early 1930s.

▷ The 1924 Grotto residence is the earliest example of the NPS Rustic approach adopted at Zion, and is the oldest structure in the park.

▷ The Ranger Residence at the East Entrance and the Oak Creek residence area illustrate the NPS design changes that occurred in the 1930s. Refinements can be seen in the stonework, the use of milled timbers, and the less exaggerated eaves. The Oak Creek residences had pine plank exterior walls, showing the mid- to late-1930s trend toward less-expensive, labor-intensive materials. The residences vary in design and plan, but are unified by the use of stone and repeated wood patterns.

△ *Men's Dormitory, built in 1937.*

◁ *The information kiosk at the Temple of Sinawava is a typical example of the simple building forms and native materials used throughout Zion National Park.*

National Park Service Buildings and Structures
Underwood worked on buildings at Zion for more than fifteen years. His direct involvement in public facilities, service buildings, and residential complexes for park employees is somewhat blurred by his close cooperation with the NPS Landscape Division designers. The Oak Creek and Pine Creek residential areas include early buildings that show consistency in materials and form. All display large blocks of local red sandstone, minimally dressed and laid in random courses with battered block faces. Typical features are six-inch-square projecting beams, exposed rafter ends, and low-pitched roofs with eaves extending two feet beyond the wall.

The Oak Creek residences form a harmonious collection obviously with great variety in scale, design, and plan. They are representative of modifications in NPS

Rustic-style design and construction owing to cost and limited skilled labor. Special care was given to the design and workmanship in the East Entrance residence, built in 1935. The exteriors are smooth-faced sandstone in random ashlar patterns. The corners are buttressed rough-dressed faces, projecting several courses outward at the base. Corner quoins are the largest pieces of masonry in the walls.

A solitary departure from early Rustic design is the Ranger Dormitory, built in 1941 in the Oak Creek area. In this two-story structure with Greek Revival detailing, the NPS opted for the local vernacular building style brought to the area in the nineteenth century by the Mormons from upstate New York and New England.

Overall, the cooperative venture between Underwood and the NPS designers produced a successful collabora-

△△▷ *The Ranger Dormitory is rectangular in plan, with a gable roof and refined masonry work. The smooth-faced sandstone facade is a change from the irregular stone-and-battered walls in Underwood's earlier work. Characteristic Greek Revival details are seen in the wooden cornice under the eaves and returns on the building end walls. Symmetrically placed window openings with double-hung windows and an inset front door with a simple pediment, rectangular transom, and sidelights are typical early nineteenth-century residential details. Authentic to the last detail, all wood trim is painted white.*

tion that yielded an admirable cohesiveness of design, materials, and scale. The same concepts they applied to buildings were used on miscellaneous structures throughout the park, resulting in a harmonious collection of bridges, water fountains, entrance signs, and retaining walls.

The Zion–Mount Carmel Tunnel and the Pine Creek and Virgin River bridges represent formidable engineering feats; they were completed in 1930 to provide easier access to Zion Canyon. Ashlar sandstone facing on these structures is consistent with the overall Rustic theme in the park. The tunnel, over a mile long, provided access from the east and significantly shortened the Loop Tour.

A dramatic series of six switchbacks lined with random ashlar retaining walls lead down to the Virgin River. The Virgin River Bridge is a 185-foot triple span of steel I-beams carried on massive sandstone piers. The steel is covered with redwood planking.

The prewar buildings in Zion National Park are admirable because of their cohesiveness of design, materials, and scale. The use of native sandstone and the traditions of local Mormon vernacular architecture resulted in a collection of structures that illustrate the best of the NPS Rustic style.

Bryce Canyon National Park

Bryce Canyon is an amphitheater—five miles across and, in places, 800 feet deep—with spires and pinnacles, minarets and domes, windows and arches, and fantastic figures and forms in soft reds, pinks, yellows, oranges, grays, and whites. Colors and the changing hues of alternating rock layers dazzle the viewer. The reds and yellows are caused by iron oxides in the rock, the purple and lavenders by manganese. Sun and shadow, summer showers, or dustings of snow play on them and highlight the formations in a colorful display. Glaciers and rivers performed no magic here; the canyon is the result of erosion—wind, rain, ice, and snow working away for centuries at the multicolored limestone layers of the Paunsaugunt Plateau.

The Anasazi Indians first frequented Bryce Canyon, followed by nomadic bands of Paiutes. Spanish missionaries and trappers passed near the area, and Mormon militia were in the vicinity in the 1860s. The first written reports of the canyon came from members of John Wesley Powell's survey team of 1872. Around 1875, Ebenezer Bryce and his family settled on the edge of the natural amphitheater that was to bear his name.

Mormon settlers came to the area to farm and graze livestock. Access into the canyon was difficult; roads were nonexistent and there were no nearby railroads. Settlement gradually promoted improved roads, and after the turn of the century, visitors began to arrive.

In 1915, a U.S. Forest Service employee, J. W. Humphrey, was assigned to manage the Sevier Forest. His efforts eventually led to the creation of Bryce Canyon National Park. Humphrey later declared his role "in introducing Bryce Canyon to the world [as] the greatest accomplishment of [his] life." He promoted Bryce through articles and photographs, and national recognition rapidly followed.

Bryce Canyon National Monument was created in 1923, and in the following year the canyon came into the national park system under the name Utah National Park; it became Bryce Canyon National Park in 1928.

Until the Utah Parks Company (a subsidiary of the Union Pacific Railroad) developed its Loop Tour, in 1923, construction on the canyon rim was severely limited because of inaccessibility. Reuben and Clara Syrett homesteaded 3.5 miles north of Sunset Point in

▷ Bryce's dazzling eroded shale and sandstone landscape, shaped each year by more than 200 cycles of freeze and thaw.

◁▷ *Fantastic hoodoos shaped and reshaped by the elements conjure up all sorts of images. Thomas Wolfe, during a visit on June 26, 1938, described the scene as "a million windblown pinnacles of salmon pink and faery white all fused together like stick candy—all suggestive of a child's fantasy of heaven."*

▽ *Bryce Canyon Lodge, 1929. Gilbert Stanley Underwood skillfully united the original 1924 central portion and the wings added in 1926 by using steeply pitched roofs with half-hips, dormers, and jerkinhead forms. Long, shed dormers interrupt the main roof and reduce the overall scale. The ground-floor walls of the lodge are faced with heavily textured rough stonework with recessed 3-inch-deep raked joints. The lodge's undulating pattern of cedar shingles is a unique feature repeated in other NPS buildings both in Bryce and other national parks.*

1916. Impressed by the fantastic site, the Syretts invited friends from nearby Panguitch to see the canyon, and in 1919 they erected a tent for visitors and began to provide meals. A year later, the Syretts decided to build a permanent lodge and proceeded with verbal approval from the State Land Board. The lodge, named Tourist's Rest, was made of sawn logs and measured 30' x 71'. Eight or ten functional cabins and an open-air dance platform were built near the lodge. The Syretts remained in business until 1923 when they sold the property to the Utah Parks Company.

Historic structures at Bryce Canyon date from the beginning of the national park in 1924. In the next fifteen years the Utah Parks Company and the National Park Service constructed buildings of consistently high quality. They reinforced each other with a design continuity expressed in materials, massing, form, and scale. Buildings were of frame, log, and stone construction; stone foundations and fireplaces, and gabled roofs covered in cedar shakes, were typical. Sites were selected to minimize impact on the natural setting, and the use of local materials produced a collection of buildings that mirrored the highest NPS standards. The integrity of the Bryce Canyon designs represents the peak of the NPS building program from 1925 to 1940.

Bryce Canyon Lodge

Bryce Canyon Lodge and the accompanying complex of deluxe cabins are superb architectural creations by Gilbert Stanley Underwood. On a trip to Zion in the spring of 1923, Underwood and a team of Union Pacific and NPS staff members traveled on to Bryce Canyon for a site reconnaissance. At that time, "the architect concerned himself only with the selection of an appropriate site.... It appears that Underwood was made aware of the fact that the plateau rim would likely be off-limits as a construction site. For this and less well-known reasons, a site was chosen back away from the rim, yet close enough to make it readily accessible."[31] The final choice for the main lodge site was 700 feet from the canyon edge, a location that enhances the element of surprise for the first-time visitor.

Construction at Bryce Canyon began in the summer of 1924, and the central part of the lodge with a lobby, dining room, kitchen, and second-floor sleeping accommodations opened in May 1925. The Union Pacific established a program of meeting immediate visitor needs in the opening year and then adding to the original structure on an annual basis. The short construction season may have had something to do with this approach.

The north and south wings and stone facing on the central portion were added in 1926 and the auditorium in 1927. By then, a complex of 67 wood-framed standard and economy cabins and five deluxe log cabins were grouped around the lodge. Ten more deluxe cabins were added in 1929. The standard cottages cost $900 each to build; the deluxe cabins cost $5,000 each and contained several rooms that could be converted into suites.

Bryce Canyon Lodge is a two-story frame structure with a distinctive profile created by a massive hip roof

△ *Working drawing elevations for Bryce Canyon Lodge, 1924, two years before the wing additions were built. Underwood's original front elevation illustrates the dominance of the massively scaled roof, relieved by dormers to achieve second-story space.*

▷ *A subtle blending of materials and forms in a limited palette of textures and colors satisfied the Union Pacific Railroad's desire for a memorable image of the lodge.*

◁ *Wrought-iron details enhance the lodge's rustic atmosphere.*

with clipped corners. There are references to traditional northern European vernacular designs in the exaggerated main roof, which rises to 36 feet at the ridge and dominates the finished composition.

The 1926 additions were placed at an angle sweeping forward from the central portion to frame the entrance. A portico extends between the wings with massive, paired 20-inch-diameter logs supporting a 52-foot log beam to define the entrance. The portico is paved in a brick pattern repeated on the entrance ramps to the north and south of the portico.

The first floor of the lodge contains the lobby, with the registration desk, offices, small post office, dining room and kitchen, gift shop, and auditorium. Underwood established a uniform interior design with milled timbers in the lobby, exposed roof trusses in the dining room and auditorium, and rough rubble masonry for

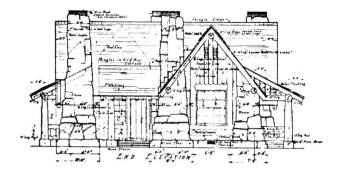

◁ *Working drawing elevation of a duplex cabin. Underwood used full-round logs at the entrance porches, continuing them to the tops of the walls, where they appear to be beams framing the exposed log purlins that extend under the eaves.*

All full-round logs on exteriors and interiors are coped where they intersect, furthering the illusion of true log framing. Log verges, beam ends at the gables, and log window frames complete the image.

△ *Underwood's proficiency can be seen in how he defined the cabins as log structures.*

Only careful inspection reveals that the structures are wood framed, faced with a veneer of half-round logs. The logs are placed horizontally on lower walls and vertically in porch gable ends, and white plaster chinking gives the cabins a striped appearance.

△ *The deluxe duplex and quadruplex cabins at Bryce, a refinement of Underwood's designs at Zion National Park, were masterful creations of Rustic forms and materials. Careful selection and placement of boulders, logs, and "hit or miss" shingles artfully solved the architectural problem of combining multiple units within a single structure.*

the fireplaces. TW Recreational Services and the NPS cooperated recently on an excellent restoration of the building, including conversion of a second-floor employee dormitory to guest rooms.

Duplex Cabins

The duplex and quadruplex log cabins clustered near the lodge are among Underwood's most exquisite designs. Sited in a grove of pines below the lodge, the cabins embody the principles chartered by Stephen Mather for building in the natural environment; they are small in scale, show adroit use of logs and stone, and have steeply pitched roofs. Rubble-stone foundations, chimneys, and corner piers battered at the base are highly textured with raked joints three and four inches deep.

Specified for "hit or miss courses," the roofs are finished with cedar shakes in the same undulating pattern as the lodge roofs. Alternating heights for roof ridges and shed roofs over the porches subtly alter the basic building forms.

Floor plans of the duplexes are 16' x 40' rectangles, each unit consisting of a room with a rubble masonry corner fireplace, a bath, and private porches on the side and end. Interiors are richly detailed with exposed log framing of columns and purlins. The quadruplexes are embellished with rustic log mantelpieces, bookshelves, and twig "braiding" around the bathroom mirrors.

Underwood displayed his strengths as a designer in meeting the challenge to add more buildings at Bryce Canyon while maintaining a unified composition for the project. The dominating mass and larger scale of the lodge is reinforced by the smaller cluster of deluxe cabins. The irregularities of form imitate nature, and the rough stonework and large logs underscore that connec-

tion. The locally quarried stones match the geology, and logs are similar in size to the surrounding pines. Despite the difficulty of designing the Bryce Canyon complex over time, Underwood succeeded in creating a cohesive collection of distinctive buildings.

Men's Dormitory

The Utah Parks Company called upon Underwood for one final project in 1937 – a Men's Dormitory. The site selected was west of the lodge, away from the rim, on the edge of the cluster of standard and economy cabins. The functional requirements for a dormitory to house employees of the Utah Parks Company were met in a rec-

tangular plan with sleeping rooms off a double-loaded corridor, and a lounge and shared bathroom. Proximity to the standard and economy cabins insured the design did not overwhelm the modest cabins.

In his design, Underwood borrowed elements from the lodge and deluxe cabins – stone foundations, exposed stud-framed walls, and massive, cedar-shingled hip roofs. Three horizontal layers of foundation, walls, and roof are in scale with the overall building volume. The building is raised several feet above grade on a rubble-stone foundation. The cedar-shingled hip roof with half-hip ends has overhangs proportionate to the economy and standard cabins.

▷ *Floor plan of the original section of the old Administration Building.* PARK AND RECREATION STRUCTURES *noted: "In parks not accessible to great hordes of visitors, uncomplicated administration functions and a modest museum display can often be housed in one building to practical advantage.... It permits ... one building of suitable size space that as two buildings could hardly avoid seeming trivial and inappropriate in a park of the magnificent distances offered by Bryce Canyon."*

△ *The old Administration Building (original section with 1932 and 1934 additions). The original design incorporated an administrative area and a small museum into a T-shape formed out of two rectangles. Bearing log wall construction is evident from the elongated, whittled-end logs that project past saddle-notched corners. The projections decrease in length from ground to eave. Logs in the gable ends are turned vertically to contrast with the horizontal logs in the walls. A pleasing feature in the cedar-shake roof is the double-thickness shake at every fifth course that creates shadow lines across the roof surface.*

▷ *Now used as the Sunrise Education Center, this building was once the Administration Building. The entrance is clearly defined by the extended gable with unpeeled-log columns and a gable fan.*

▷ *Exposed interior framing and log bearing walls at the old Administration Building.*

△▷▽ *"Study Sketch for Look-out at Inspiration Point, Bryce Canyon Nat'l. Park" (1934). Compared to the Observation Building at Rainbow Point, this sketch shows a more organic approach to architecture.*

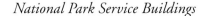

National Park Service Buildings

Although a difficult challenge for NPS designers, their buildings at Bryce Canyon come close to Underwood's high standards. The service structures built in the 1920s adopted Underwood's established forms and details: rectangular plans on a rubble-stone foundation, exposed stud framing over horizontal plank walls, and cedar-shake hip roofs.

The old Administration Building, built in 1932 with additions in 1934, is comparable to other prominent NPS Rustic design projects of the period. Similar buildings from the NPS Landscape Division can be seen at Yosemite, Crater Lake, and Mount Rainier. Its interior continues the outside true-log construction theme: peeled logs form the walls, with white plaster chinking for the interior joints. Plank ceilings on log trusses that support the roof are also exposed. All the logs both on the exterior and interior have carefully coped joints wherever angles intersect.

Several other NPS buildings illustrate the gradual development of Rustic design up to 1940. Staff residences built in 1939 show features of similar form and materials to Underwood's work. Rubble-stone foundations, chimneys, and corner piers, and wide overhangs for cedar-shake roofs in undulating patterns recall the deluxe cabins. The treatment is modified by square-cut timber framing, horizontal shiplapped plank walls, and gable roofs. The changes are subtle but show the transition in design dictated by demands of the economy and unskilled CCC labor.

△ *Staff residences built in the late 1930s at Bryce suggest modifications of Underwood's designs adapted to a constrained economy and inexperienced* CCC *work crews. The importance of protecting landmarks in remote settings from fire danger is underscored by the 1987 fire that destroyed this building.*

Pipe Spring National Monument

The fort complex at Pipe Spring National Monument was built at a time when the Mormons were settling the Dixie Country of southern Utah and northern Arizona. The red-colored sandstone walls of the fort and outbuildings stand today much as they did when completed in the early 1870s, a reminder of the isolated and challenging life of these early pioneers.

Separated from northwestern Arizona by the Colorado River, the grasslands in the midst of this semi-arid country attracted Brigham Young as a possible center for cattle ranching. The Mormons pushed south and west from the Great Salt Lake, exploring the area around present-day Cedar City. In the early 1850s, when iron ore and coal deposits were discovered, settlement began in earnest. As the Mormons advanced into their region, Indians defended against the territorial claims, and the fort at Pipe Spring was built to protect the settlers.

The preserved Pipe Spring complex is a place of abundant water in the vast, thirsty land of the Arizona Strip. Free-flowing water from the sandstone layers to the north provided a cool, tree-sheltered oasis that attracted Indians, travelers, and settlers for centuries. Pipe Spring National Monument is among the few examples in the national park system illustrating the daily life of nineteenth-century ranches.

Founding the Fort—
The Mormon Leatherstocking and Ka-pur-ats
Missionaries under the leadership of Jacob Hamblin were assigned the tasks of reconciling differences with the Indians and exploring the Dixie Country. Hamblin's gentle nature and leadership enabled him to succeed in the role of peacemaker to Indian settlements in southwestern Utah. In addition to protecting settlers, the Mormon missionary explorers searched for crossings in the rugged canyons of the region, including the Grand Canyon.

Hamblin was known as the "Mormon Leatherstocking" and is credited with leading the group that came upon Pipe Spring during an expedition in 1858 into the Arizona Strip between the Utah border and the Colorado River in Arizona. Hamblin's marksmanship gave the spring its name. A story relates his attempt to shoot a suspended silk handkerchief. He became frus-

▷ *The 10' x 12' portals that served as the fort's main entrance contain huge double doors supported by heavy wrought-iron hardware.*

△ *The Pipe Spring fort, named*
Winsor Castle for the ranch's
first superintendent, was an
outpost in the Mormon terri-
tory of the Arizona Strip—the
part of Arizona separated
from the rest of the state by
the Colorado River.

trated at the elusive target and suggested that a pipe be placed on a rock and he would shoot out the bowl without touching its sides. He did it, and the spring was forever after known as Pipe Spring.

Stockmen soon came to the lush grasslands around the desert oases and established ranches. In 1863, James Whitmore began ranching and built a dugout for temporary shelter. Three years later Whitmore and his herder Robert McIntyre were killed by Navajos who crossed the Colorado River to drive off the stock. Companies of militia were sent into the area, and Pipe Spring was selected as the base for holding land north of the Colorado. Brigham Young appointed Anson Perry Winsor in April 1870 to run church affairs, with a promise of a headquarters ranch capable of withstanding Indian attacks.

In September 1870, Hamblin, Young, and Major John Wesley Powell met at Pipe Spring. The adventurous major, called "Ka-pur-ats" (One-Arm-Off) by the Navajos, had traveled with the Mormon leader from Salt Lake City to meet the Indians and try to negotiate a peace treaty. Major Powell was concerned about the safety of his survey team.

Hamblin had been hired as a guide and interpreter, and at Pipe Spring plans were made for a fort to protect the valuable water supply, the grazing grounds, and those called by the church to serve there. A couple of months later, Hamblin and Powell worked out a peace treaty with the Navajos at Fort Defiance. For the time being, peace reigned on the Arizona Strip, and building

began on the fort in late 1870. Winsor was appointed superintendent of the ranch, supervising the construction that began in 1871 and was completed in 1872. The fortresslike structure, more imposing than anything else for miles around, eventually became known as "Winsor Castle."

The Pipe Spring Buildings

An inspection of the restored fort, either from a distance or close-up, gives the clear impression of a complex designed and built with protection in mind. No windows faced toward the outside, and the only openings in the massive, two-foot-thick walls of random ashlar sandstone were pairs of wooden gates in the courtyard walls and gaps between the stones for rifle ports, eight in the north building and fifteen in the south. The tapered gunport openings provided light and served as observation posts. Placing the fort on top of Pipe Spring was a safety feature to protect the water supply. The footings of the northwest wall were built over the mouths of the springs, and the water was channeled in trenches under the floor of the north building into the courtyard and then into a dugout log in the cooler room of the south building and to pools outside the walls.

The twin masonry structures in the fort building are two stories high. They show Greek Revival details that recall the style popular in the 1830s in upstate New York, the original Mormon home. White gable and end-return trim, chimneys at the ends of each building, and a wood-frame clapboard observation cupola on the center of the north building's roof ridge suggest the mixed use of residence and fortress. The fort's interesting architectural profile, reflecting the cliffs behind the building, is an accident of the site. Wintertime excavation for the north building proved difficult and was halted when the floor level was still five feet higher than the south building.

The main roof of each building is extended eight feet to cover second-floor verandahs facing the courtyard. The lower floors are of approximately equal size divided by a stone bearing wall. In the north building, first-floor rooms served as the fort's main kitchen and parlor for family gatherings and social events; the upper floor contained a family bedroom, meeting room, and a guest room with a trap door to the rooftop lookout tower. On

▽ The fort complex, obviously designed for protection, has stone walls 2-feet-thick.

the south building's ground floor were the spring room and cheese room; upstairs were bedrooms, a meeting room, and the telegraph operator's room.

Church members from the territory helped pay their tithes by working on the fort. Brothers Elisha and Elijah Everett were the head stonemasons; both had previously worked on the temple at Salt Lake City. At first, construction moved ahead slowly. Skilled blacksmiths, carpenters, and cabinetmakers had to be brought together, housing created, and tools and other supplies shipped in. Readily available sandstone was excavated from nearby boulders. The masons resorted to the ancient technique of drilling holes along natural fracture lines in the stone, driving in wooden pegs, pouring on water, and letting the swelling pegs split the rock apart. The stones were then drawn to the site, shaped, faced, and hoisted to the top of the walls by block and tackle. Mortar, made from imported limestone, was burned in a kiln on the site. Wagonloads of rough-cut, unmatched pine planks came from the Skutumpah sawmill.

Before the fort was completed, two smaller buildings were added. The stone-walled one-room structure built by the militia in 1868 was extended by adding another room and connected by a breezeway to house the Winsor family during the fort's construction. The buildings later served as the blacksmith shop and bunkhouse. A second stone structure, built west of the fort, served as a bunkhouse for Major Powell's survey crews in 1871. Both were in a state of ruin when acquired by the National Park Service in 1923, but the sandstone masonry walls were rebuilt, and low-pitched log-framed roofs were replaced to match the originals.

National Park Service Acquisition

December 15, 1871, was a day of celebration at the fort: The first telegraph station in Arizona went into service. The line, part of Deseret Telegraph, established by Brigham Young and owned by the church, serviced the state of Utah. When Major Powell's surveyors arrived, they bore the dismaying news that Pipe Spring was not in Utah, as supposed, but Arizona.

At about the same time, Bishop Winsor went into the cheese-making business. This was carried out on the fort's south building lower level and produced 60 to 80

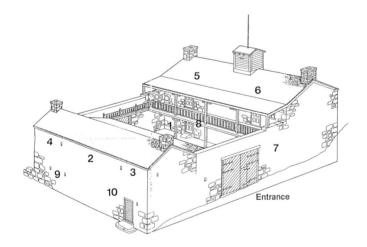

▷ Pipe Spring Fort. North and south buildings are placed parallel along their long axes. Each gable-ended structure is approximately 18' x 43'. A 30-foot-wide enclosed courtyard was created by connecting the residences with stone walls 20 to 30 feet high.

◁ *An upstairs bedroom with original Mormon settler furnishings.*

△ *Wagons and teams could enter the courtyard through the portals, but the massive wooden doors provided secure protection when closed.*

▷ *Drawings of the Pipe Spring*
Fort from the Historic Ameri-
can Building Survey of 1940.
A 2-foot-wide catwalk connects
the upper floors on one side of
the courtyard. Each building
has two chimneys at the exterior
walls rising above the cedar-
shingled, shallow-pitched roofs.
Multilight, double-hung sash
windows face the courtyard,
and raised-panel doors, door-
frame panels, and interior
paneling add to the Greek
Revival ambience.

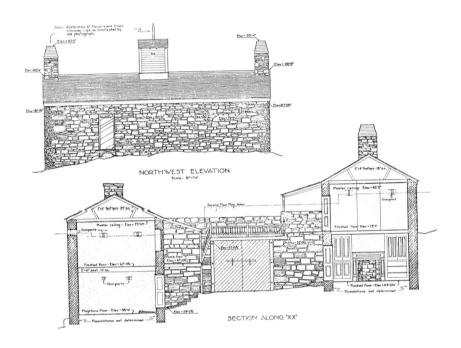

NORTH-WEST ELEVATION

SECTION ALONG "XX"

△ *Eliza Louella Stewart. Her*
telegraph key is on the table,
and above it, a photograph of
her. She was eighteen years old
when she used the telegraph key
to send the first telegraph mes-
sage from the state of Arizona.

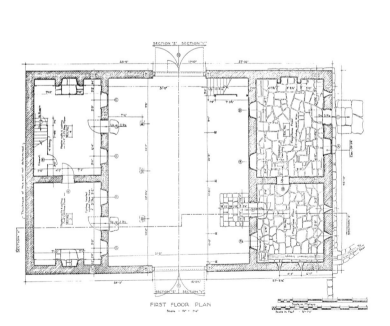

FIRST FLOOR PLAN

▷ *Distinguished visitors at Pipe Spring in 1928. Left to right, Heber J. Grant, president of the Mormon Church; Stephen Mather, National Park Service director; Carl Gray, president of the Union Pacific Railroad; William King, U.S. Senator from Utah; Harry Chandler, publisher of the* Los Angeles Times; *and Charles Heaton, monument caretaker.*

pounds of cheese a day. Brigham Young's plans for self-sufficiency were met with butter, cheese, and beef supplied to St. George, or wherever markets were found. When Winsor left the fort in 1875, the dairy business was being replaced by profits from the cattle herds. When danger from Indians ceased, part of the courtyard walls and the gates were removed, windows were cut in the massive stone exterior walls, and two water-storage pools were dug to irrigate a large garden and orchards.

The importance of Pipe Spring Fort to the Mormons gradually declined, although it became a popular stopping-off place for gold prospectors, cowboys from the surrounding area, and Mormon couples passing on to St. George for marriage in the Mormon temple there. The site was eventually absorbed by the Canaan Cooperative Stock Company of St. George, Utah, in 1879. It was sold to private owners in 1884, and Winsor Castle became the center of a large cattle-ranching operation in the Arizona Strip. The ranch changed hands several times until it was purchased in 1906 by Jonathan Heaton and Sons from nearby Moccasin. The incorporation in 1907 into the Kaibab Paiute Reservation and complications over water rights made ownership burdensome. A fortuitous meeting with NPS director Stephen Mather in 1922 gave Charles Heaton the opportunity to relinquish the property by suggesting Pipe Spring become a national monument commemorating the part the Mormons played in opening the West.

Sites in southwestern Utah had already caught the interest of assistant NPS director Horace Albright. Stephen Mather became interested in Pipe Spring as Zion, Bryce, and Cedar Breaks and other regional parks and national monuments were coming under NPS supervision. In a creative deal, Heaton sold the ranch to the threesome of Mather, Heber J. Grant (president of the Mormon Church), and Carl Gray (president of the Union Pacific Railroad). The new owners deeded the land to the government, and in 1923, President Warren G. Harding proclaimed Pipe Spring a National Monument to serve as a "memorial of western pioneer life." Pipe Spring became the first designated historic site in the national park system, assuring the preservation of this unique remnant of Mormon history and settlement.

The Southwest

Grand Canyon National Park

Good God, something happened here.

Texas cowboy who happened upon the grand canyon

No matter how well prepared by prior photographs or descriptions, the first-time visitor to the Grand Canyon is always awe-struck. The long drive across the sedate landscape of the Colorado Plateau to either the North or South rim, a landscape occasionally forested and broken by gullies, heightens the sense of disbelief; nothing prepares one for the incredible size or dramatic forms of this color-saturated canyon. From the rim down through the depths of the gorge, over 200 million years of geological history unfold.

Capturing the Image and Creating a National Park
For centuries writers have tried to describe the spectacular panorama, which stretches for miles to the horizon. "God's spectacle," wrote John Muir. "No matter how far you have wandered hitherto, or how many famous gorges and valleys you have seen, this one, the Grand Canyon of the Colorado, will seem as novel to you, as unearthly in the color and grandeur and quantity of its architecture, as if you had found it after death, on some other star; so incomparably lovely and grand and supreme, it is above all the other canyons in our fire-molded, earthquake-shaken, rain-washed, river- and glacier-sculptured world."

John Wesley Powell described it this way: "It has infinite variety, and no part is ever duplicated.... By a year's toil a concept of sublimity can be obtained never again to be equaled on the hither side of Paradise."

The canyon as seen by trappers and traders and Spanish missionaries was generally considered a terrible place, almost unworthy of mention. Part of Coronado's expedition entered the region in 1540, and the captain in command reported official dismay at the unbridgeable barrier posed by the chasm. Lieutenant Joseph C. Ives, exploring the lower Colorado River by steamboat in 1857, described its beauty but was pessimistic about its future usefulness. He declared, "The region, is of course, altogether valueless.... Ours has been the first, and will doubtless be the last, party of whites to visit this profitless locality." Ives was a poor historian and a worse prophet.

As a result of his visit to the Grand Canyon of the Colorado in the late 1890s, John Muir became an advocate for its designation as a national park. His journey

Overleaf: Historic architecture at Grand Canyon may seem trivial compared with the dramatic beauty of the setting. John Muir described the canyon as "divinely colored and sculptured buildings.... The vast space between the walls is crowded with Nature's grandest buildings, a sublime city of them, painted in every color, and adorned with the richly fretted cornice and battlement spire and tower in endless variety of style and architecture. Every architectural invention of man has been anticipated, and far more, in this grandest of God's terrestrial cities."

▷ The Indian Watchtower at Desert View was built in 1932 at the eastern end of the Grand Canyon South Rim. A fabricated "ruin" west of the Watchtower illustrates the condition in which most prehistoric Anasazi towers are found, a pile of rubble stone.

△ *Thomas Moran,* CHASM OF
THE COLORADO, *1873–1874.*

▷ *The intrepid explorer and adventurer John Wesley Powell with his Southern Paiute guide, "Man Powell."*

to the rim of the canyon entailed a 75-mile hike from the Atchison, Topeka, and Santa Fe Railroad stop at Flagstaff, Arizona. He marveled at the scene: *After riding through these pleasure-grounds, the San Francisco and other mountains, abounding in flowery parklike openings and smooth shallow valleys with long vistas which in fineness and finish and arrangement suggest the work of a consummate landscape artist, watching all the way, you come to the most tremendous canyon in the world.*

Two decades earlier, John Wesley Powell set forth on one of the greatest exploratory feats in western history. At noon on May 24, 1869, he and his team of nine men pushed off in four boats onto the Green River and began their 217-mile journey down the unexplored canyon. On August 17, they had turned from the Little Colorado into the Grand Canyon. In his journal from the expedition, *The Exploration of the Colorado River and Its Canyons,* Powell recorded his impressions: *We have an unknown distance yet to run and an unknown river yet to explore. What falls there are we know not; what rocks beset the channel, we know not; what walls rise above the river, we know not. Ah, well! we may conjecture many things. The men talk as cheerfully as ever; jests are bandied about freely this morning; but to me the cheer is somber and the jests ghastly.*

Powell's feats were widely broadcast through his published accounts. Subsequent expeditions by Powell and others generated guarded optimism about the tourist potential of the region.[1] As artist Thomas Moran and writers Clarence Dutton and John Van Dyke extolled the beauties of the canyon, national attitudes began to change; the canyon's possibility for enjoyment replaced its potential for commercial exploitation.

By the turn of the century, hotels had been built, tourist tent camps were in place, and several aerial tramways spanned the canyon. An eleven-hour stagecoach ride was soon replaced by rail lines. Travel increased dramatically when in 1901 a spur of the Santa Fe Railway from Williams, Arizona, to the South Rim was completed. Three years later, the railway company built El Tovar Hotel. Twenty years later, the Union Pacific Railroad improved access to the North Rim and Grand Canyon Lodge via their Loop Tour.

Indiana senator Benjamin Harrison introduced a bill that would have secured the Grand Canyon as a national park. The bill was defeated, but in 1883, as president, he signed legislation to establish Grand Canyon Forest Preserve. President Theodore Roosevelt eventually succeeded in securing a transfer to national monument status in 1908, and an act of Congress established Grand Canyon National Park in 1919.[2]

The architects and designers working for the railroads and the National Park Service created architectural legacies of outstanding sensitivity in the park. The North and South rims – separated by only ten air miles but a circuitous 215 miles by highway – are distinctly different places. The South Rim, closer to population centers, was developed first, and the Santa Fe Railway offered direct service to the El Tovar Hotel. The 1923 expansion to Cedar City by the Union Pacific Railroad opened the North Rim, with accommodations at Grand Canyon Lodge.

In many ways, the ecologically different North Rim is more attractive than the South Rim; it is about 1,200 feet higher, cooler, has nearby forests and meadows, and far fewer visitors. The road south from Utah passes through the aspen and pine forests of the Kaibab Plateau; the San Francisco Peaks near Flagstaff can be seen 70 miles to the south and the red mountains and plateaus of Utah to the north. Cut off from the rest of Arizona by the canyon itself, the North Rim enjoys a mere quarter million tourists a year, compared to the South Rim's three million.

South Rim

The architectural attractions of the South Rim cover 32 miles along East Rim Drive and West Rim Drive. At the center is Grand Canyon Village, the Santa Fe Railway

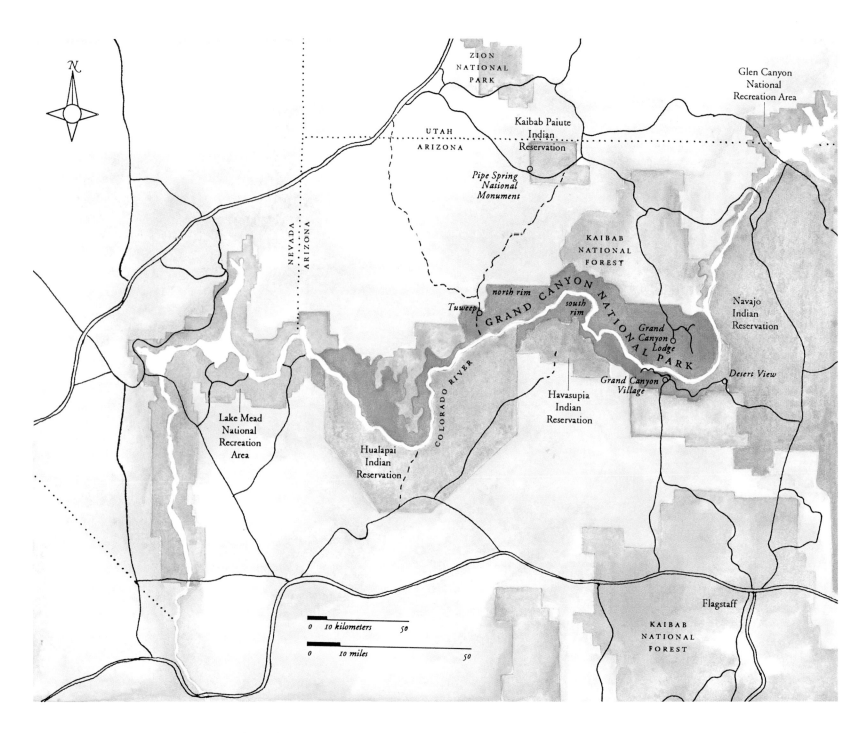

△ *Map of Grand Canyon National Park showing North and South Rims.*

▽ *Grand Canyon Depot is one of three log railroad depots remaining in the United States. Grand Canyon is the only one where logs are used as primary structural materials, rather than as superficial ornament. The depot's architect, Francis Wilson, echoed the exterior of the El Tovar Hotel with log framing, true log construction on the lower floor, and shingled upper walls. The chaletlike massing, projecting eaves, log columns and brackets supporting upper floors, and rows of paired, residential-scale windows combine to provide a warm, rustic atmosphere for visitors.*

▽ *Grand Canyon Depot is the only railroad terminus inside a national park. The building's horizontal line is emphasized by the overhanging upper floor, which has a ridge at right angles to the waiting platform's roof and projecting overhangs. The solid log walls in the lower floor, with false-crowned log ends, were square cut to make them weathertight; shingles on the upper walls were double-coursed every second row for a horizontal shadow line.*

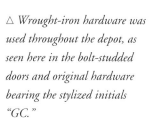

△ *Wrought-iron hardware was used throughout the depot, as seen here in the bolt-studded doors and original hardware bearing the stylized initials "GC."*

depot, and El Tovar Hotel. An architect for the Fred Harvey Company, Mary Jane Colter, designed Hopi House, Lookout Studio, and Bright Angel Lodge. Remnants from the early days of entrepreneurs who catered to the tourist trade are still visible as part of the lodge. The NPS built the Operations Building and Powerhouse, excellent examples of the emerging Rustic style. West Rim Drive ends at Hermit's Rest and Tusayan Museum. The Watchtower is at the end of East Rim Drive.

Grand Canyon Depot

The Santa Fe Railway in 1909 began construction of a railway depot that would be an appropriately rustic gateway to welcome travelers to the El Tovar Hotel. The railroad was promoting the Grand Canyon as a destination resort and wanted visitors to the luxurious El Tovar to be impressed the moment they stepped off the train. "Grand Canyon" in copper letters on the gable facing the tracks and a "Santa Fe" logo centered near the ridge greeted travelers. The last passenger train pulled out of the station in 1968, and the freight office closed a year later, but in 1990 the line was reopened from Williams to the canyon, restoring the steam locomotive service that recalls the early days of travel to the rim.

The depot was designed as a straightforward, functional solution to the demands of handling large volumes of passengers and freight. The first floor of the main building contained a waiting room, ticket office, baggage room, and other public spaces. An upper floor provided the station agent's apartment. A projecting, one-story log entrance porch, sheltered by a gabled roof, is centered on the two-story mass. The two-bay, log-column–supported waiting platform extends a lowered ridgeline from the main structure.

El Tovar Hotel

During the fierce competition for railroad customers at the turn of the century, the Atchison, Topeka, and Santa Fe Railway set out to build a rustic resort that would fulfill passengers' dreams of the romantic western frontier and opened the El Tovar Hotel in 1905. From the mainline junction at Williams, Arizona, visitors traveled an additional eleven miles on the spur running north. The canyon was masked from view by the uphill tilt of the Kaibab Plateau, but El Tovar's long profile, capped by a Victorian shingled turret, lent a sense of heightened anticipation and drama. In such a remote, isolated setting, this manmade structure presented a magnificent sight, with its mixed stone-and-shingle styles and Victorian ornament.

Twenty years earlier the trip to the Grand Canyon was a grueling affair, an eleven-hour stagecoach ride to a small hotel. The Santa Fe Railway had bought the hotel to accommodate railroad passengers, but plans to enlarge it were frustrated by an early local settler who built a competing hotel nearby. To overcome that vexation, the railroad moved its terminal several hundred feet to the east and began plans for a luxury hotel that would command unparalleled views of the canyon. A branch line off the main railroad was completed in September 1901, and tourists soon began to arrive at Bright Angel Point.

▷ The El Tovar Hotel's three-story guests wings radiating from the central section have a modulated exterior treatment, similar in color but varying in texture. On the first floor, horizontal courses of rounded log siding with notched corners provide a warm rustic touch at eye level. Using the same log course width, planks sheath the second floor, and milled lumber was used for the window surrounds. The third floor is a shingled mansard with dormers rhythmically punctuating the roof line. The guest-room layout assured that each would receive direct sunlight sometime during the day and have a view of some portion of the canyon.

△ The Santa Fe Railway built El Tovar Hotel at the South Rim of the Grand Canyon. El Tovar pleased passengers from back East with its western frontier image, and at the same time furnished enough comfort and elegance to meet their sense of propriety. The native materials and massive scale satisfied nineteenth-century romantic tastes. A Victorian rooftop wooden turret, wrapped in shingles, easily identifies El Tovar from a distance.

▷ *The porch lintel at El Tovar is inscribed with wrought-iron letters quoting from "Titans of Chasms," by C. A. Higgins: "Dreams of mountains, as in sleep they brood in things eternal."*

The concept of building grand hotels at great scenic attractions in the West had gained acceptance with the 1903 opening of Old Faithful Inn at Yellowstone. Previously, wood-framed buildings that served as luxury hotels in resort areas were typically sprawling affairs with Victorian overlays. The railroaders sought a different architectural concept, one that contributed to the way people perceived and experienced the natural scenic wonders that would later be set aside as national parks.

Charles Whittlesey's architectural reputation was already well established when the Santa Fe Railway selected him to design their Grand Canyon hotel. He envisioned a distinctive silhouette for the hotel and planned a building over 300 feet long with multiple roofs at different levels to add architectural interest and an identifiable profile.

A railroad brochure dated 1909 described El Tovar as "combining the proportions of a Swiss chalet and the Norwegian villa." The hotel's style remains steeped in the late Victorian predilection for the exotic, complete with roof turret, finials, chaletlike balconies and terraces, and varied exterior wall treatments. Whittlesey's use of a base course of boulders, log veneer siding with notched corners, log detailing on the first floor, and rustic interiors created the frontier atmosphere railroad entrepreneurs were anxious to promote. Logs stained a weathered brown and a roof shingled with wooden shakes merges the building into the gray-green hues of nearby piñon forests and stone outcroppings. The dark exterior color gives architectural weight to the massive volume and silhouette.

A cascade of changing roof forms continues at each end of the three-story wings where one- and two-story roof terraces provide views north to the canyon and south to the railway station. The upper terraces are visually separated from the log or plank-sheathed walls below by a projecting roof deck; sections of fretwork railing divided by ten-foot-high tapered finial posts capped by carved trefoils further define the terraces. The one-story terraced wing on the hotel's rim end is extended by two shingle-roofed gazebos, with rustic benches for silently contemplating the view down into the canyon or across to the North Rim.

The grade at the southern end of the hotel drops off down to the basement level of coursed rubble stone, with arched masonry openings repeated at the entrance porch. The dining room, kitchen, and utility rooms of the west wing stretch out into the lush green lawn. Two stone chimneys on the north and south sides of the dining room are flanked by picture windows facing the canyon. A porch also facing the canyon dates from a dining room expansion and the addition of a cocktail lounge in the 1950s.

Early promotional material from El Tovar described the experience of arriving at the railway depot and proceeding up a winding path, to be welcomed by a Norwegian gabled entrance skillfully scaled against the massive dark bulk of the hotel. Projecting out over the wide porch steps at the entrance is a sign with the coat of arms of the family of Don Pedro de Tovar. The porch, flanked by stone walls, is filled with rustic rocking chairs facing Hopi House.

The Santa Fe Railway intended the El Tovar to be "not a Waldorf Astoria, but more like a big country clubhouse." Promotional material invited the visitor to linger in the entrance lobby, named the "Rendezvous," a room almost 40 feet square and two stories high. "In it the better half of the world may see without being seen – may chat and gossip – may sew and read – may do any of the inconsequential things which serve to pass the time away."

El Tovar's early operator was the Fred Harvey Company. The dark, stained wood walls and timber-and-plank ceiling, emphasizing the hotel's rustic character, were offset by elegant hospitality. As in other locations where the remote setting was tempered by creature

comforts, the guests in the Norway Dining Room were
served with luxurious china, silverware, crystal, and
linen. The railroad shipped in provisions daily, which
were prepared under the supervision of "a capable Italian
chef once employed in New York and Chicago clubs."
Fresh-cut flowers for the dining tables and guest rooms
came from a greenhouse built at Grand Canyon Village.

Appreciation for the scenery and hospitality was often
expressed in the hotel's guest book. A Los Angeles visitor
in 1914 inscribed: "The canyon is beautiful – impossible
of comprehension. El Tovar is in a class by itself. Heaven
bless Fred Harvey." The extensive luxury sometimes led
visitors to confuse El Tovar with the main attraction.
John Burroughs, the famous naturalist, claimed that he
heard one guest exclaim, "They built the Canyon too
near this beautiful hotel."

The hotel began to show its age about the time the
railroad era ended, in the 1960s. The days of long vacations yielded to the short-term automobile tour. Wear
and tear from exposure and generations of visitors began
to add up. When El Tovar was acquired by the Amfac
Resort Company, the new management decided to restore it to its early elegance and completed renovations
and restoration in 1983.

Architects worked from old photographs and blue-
prints to ensure historical accuracy. The original hand-
peeled Oregon log siding had become irreparably
weathered, so the entire exterior was replaced with logs
from an Idaho mill; energy-efficient windows replaced
deteriorated wooden frames; long-absent decorative
finials were restored along with scrollwork and railings,
and the original dark brown stain was reapplied. Original interiors were largely retained, but requirements to
meet safety standards and efforts toward modernization
reduced 100 guest rooms to 77, each with a private bath.

Rebuilding a seventy-five-year-old National Historic
Landmark that sits perched 20 feet from the South Rim
of the Grand Canyon required a good deal of courage
and $11 million. The new operators of the El Tovar
Hotel took on the challenge and succeeded admirably.

Hopi House
Architect Mary Jane Colter's first project for the Fred
Harvey Company at the Grand Canyon was Hopi

House. After her success as the interior designer for the
Harvey Company's Indian Building at the Alvarado
Hotel in Albuquerque in 1902, Colter was called upon
to design an Indian building at Grand Canyon to market arts and crafts. Because the Hopis have inhabited the
Grand Canyon area for centuries, she chose a Hopi design. The approved plans were sent to the Santa Fe Railway's Western Division offices in Los Angeles for the
production of construction drawings, and Hopi House
opened a few days before the hotel, on January 1, 1905.

Located across from the El Tovar Hotel, the building
was modeled after Hopi pueblos at Oraibi, Arizona.
Hopi House gave Colter the "opportunity to re-create
the distinctive dwelling of an ancient culture and to ac-
quaint the public with the richness and beauty of Native
American art."[3] Colter's materials and building massing
were identical to those of a pueblo structure and successfully met the Harvey Company's commercial interest in
marketing Native American arts and crafts in an appro-

△ The design for Lookout Studio was inspired by natural forms in the landscape at the edge of the Grand Canyon. The multilevel structure resembles an indigenous Indian dwelling, with coursed rubble masonry walls that appear to merge into the natural rock outcroppings. An uneven roof parapet flows upward into what look like random piles of stones, but are in fact a chimney and an observation room. The piles of stones between the chimney and tower were removed when the original roof was replaced.

priate setting. Much of the building's stone and timber came from the area, and most of the construction was done by Hopi builders.

The interiors are the same primitive Pueblo style as the exteriors. Massive stone walls were covered with adobe plaster, concrete floors were rough finished to resemble mud floors, and ceilings were made of saplings, grasses, and mud finish resting on peeled logs. Corner fireplaces, small niches in the walls, and small doorway openings framed with peeled saplings were characteristic pueblo touches. Colter introduced authentic Southwestern artifacts, including the Harvey collection of Indian art. A Hopi ceremonial altar, a sand painting, several Indian Rooms, and a Spanish-Mexican room were added to sustain the mood and ambience Colter envisioned.

Initially, Hopi House was an actual dwelling; some of the Hopis who worked in the building lived on the upper floors. Indian artisans were in the workrooms making jewelry, pottery, blankets, and other items that were offered for sale. In the evening, the Hopis sang traditional songs, and their dancing on the patio at five o'clock became a daily event.[4]

Lookout Studio
Mary Jane Colter's second building for the Fred Harvey

Company at Grand Canyon Village was the Lookout Studio. Perched on the edge of the rim west of El Tovar, it was designed to allow visitors to observe the canyon through the Harvey Company's telescopes, with opportunities to take photographs from a porch. Inside, a small studio was centered on a fireplace alcove and a display area where postcards, paintings, and photographs were sold.

Unlike the strict ethnographic interpretation at Hopi House, Colter took a more organic approach and adapted the building to the edge of the canyon, letting the surrounding landscape guide the design. Seen from a distance, Lookout Studio blends into the canyon's walls.

The interior of the structure steps down in several levels. Log framing and stonework are exposed; the original ceiling was made of saplings resting on logs. An uncommon touch for Colter's buildings is the light that floods the interior through the windows on three sides.

Bright Angel Lodge
In 1933, the Fred Harvey Company again called upon the architectural services of Mary Jane Colter, this time to design an economy lodge at Grand Canyon Village. The lodge's location was on the historic site of the old Bright Angel Camp, which was a sprawling complex of

◁ Bright Angel Lodge, 1936.

△ Main fireplace of the lodge. Above the stone fireplace, flanked by recessed benches, is a large painted and feathered thunderbird, the Indian symbol of the "Powers of the Air."

cabins, tent platforms, and the antiquated Bright Angel Hotel, clustered near the head of Bright Angel Trail. Acquired by the Santa Fe Railway to resolve a struggle with local hotel operators over tourist traffic, the concessioner was now under the close scrutiny of the NPS in coming up with a design for the site.[5]

Colter's early design concept was for a series of stone lodges set right on the edge of the rim. The NPS rejected the plan, deciding that visitors should have unobstructed access to the canyon rim. Colter then began designs for a pioneer-style log-and-stone complex away from the rim incorporating historic buildings already in place.

Bright Angel Lodge was designed as a small village of cabins centered around a rustic one-story main lodge with shops, lounges, and dining rooms. The large stone-and-log lodge, under a gable roof and broad overhangs, set the tone for the collection of buildings, some connected to the main lodge by pergolas and walkways. Small cabins built of stone, logs, and adobe, with three or four guest rooms, extended west across the site to the mule corral.

Colter's thoroughness in developing a design concept that skillfully incorporated historic structures was unusual for the national parks. Her rigorous attention to

the ethnographic precedents set at Hopi House showed that meticulous research and faithful adherence to historic examples could produce architecture compatible not only with the surrounding topography but also with local tradition. Producing pioneer-style architecture that would recall the early days, incorporate several historic buildings, and respect the edge of the canyon rim was one of her greatest challenges and illustrated her design versatility. The complex is full of interesting touches that lead the visitor through a rustic complex at a relaxed pace, following the canyon rim to the mule corral at the starting point of the famous trail rides.

The rim side of the main lodge is an inviting single-story face of peeled-log walls and paired-log columns supporting a wide overhang. The main lodge lobby is a two-story space with rough wooden walls, a flagstone floor, and a log ceiling with kerosene lamps hanging from the beams. Colter placed an image of a large thunderbird, the Indian symbol for the "powers of the air," above the fireplace, and it became the trademark for the Fred Harvey Company "Indian Detours."[6]

The results of Colter's meticulous research can be seen in the lodge lounge, where picture windows frame views of the canyon and the "geological" fireplace made

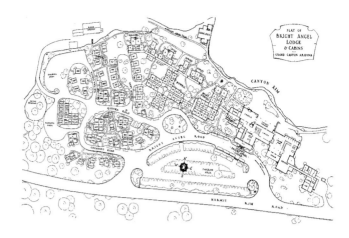

◁ *The site plan for Bright Angel Lodge, which was conceived as a small village of cabins clustered around a one-story rustic main lodge.* PARK AND RECREATION STRUCTURES *thoroughly approved: "Inspired architecturally by surviving structures of stagecoach days, and motivated by a conviction that a group of low rambling structures is the only intrusion to be countenanced in a setting of such magnificence, the results are enormously successful."*

△ *Bright Angel Lodge guest cabin plans.*

◁ *The main lodge's front porch is supported by six peeled-log columns, forked at the top to support the log roof beams. This same device is repeated in the lodge's interior and walkway pergolas.*

△ *Two 1890s log cabins were incorporated into the Bright Angel complex. Grand Canyon's first post office and the Bucky O'Neill Cabin, pictured, were preserved as guest cabins.*

◁ *The famous Grand Canyon mule rides begin near Bright Angel Lodge.*

△▷ The Grand Canyon Power House is the work of a brilliant (and anonymous) architect who capably met the challenge to design an industrial building using styling and materials appropriate for a national park. Clever design techniques create the illusion that the building is smaller than it actually is. The lower two-thirds is stone veneer; the rubble stonework is nearly a foot thick and has deeply raked joints. The upper third combines a sequence of chalet details—an oversized fretwork balcony, a deep cornice with brackets, and wood frames around industrial steel sash— masking an exposed concrete wall simulating stucco. A gable roof with exaggerated eaves furthers the illusion.

△ The park Operations Building compares favorably with similar NPS administration buildings of the 1920s and 1930s at Mount Rainier and Crater Lake. Form, scale, materials, color, and relationship to the site reflect years of experience in evolving the NPS design philoso- phy, and make this building of National Historic Landmark caliber. The juxtaposition of the massive stone foundation and corner piers against log-and-plank walls under a low-pitched roof with wide overhangs could be seen as contemporary "decon-struction." Despite the meager budgets of the time, the native stone and logs are skillfully shaped to merge the structure with the environment.

△ A corner detail of the Park Operations building illustrates the careful attention given to achieving a Rustic character: the massive stone corner pier, decreasing in size as it rises, is stepped like the natural outcrop-pings of the canyon. Stonework texture and recessed mortar cre-ate a play of light and shadow similar to that in nearby nat-ural stone formations. The peeled-log corner post set on top of the pier matches the diameter of the surrounding pine trees.

of stone from the canyon. Relying upon park naturalist Edwin D. McKee's local knowledge, stones in the ten-foot-high fireplace were assembled to begin at the hearth with water-worn stones from the Colorado River and end at the top with Kaibab limestone from the rim. For furnishings, Colter collected authentic pioneer furniture, kerosene lamps, glass shades, and bathtubs. Rare finds were a hobbyhorse belonging to the first pioneer child born in Arizona and the lobby's seven-foot-tall Jenny Lind wooden cigar-store figure.

Bright Angel Lodge opened on June 22, 1935, after two years of construction. The opening celebration featured an evening of ceremonial Indian dances and cowboy songs. Depression-era travelers welcomed the new, attractive, low-cost lodging at the Grand Canyon.

Grand Canyon Power House

A power house was needed to supply power and steam to the Fred Harvey and Santa Fe Railway facilities on the South Rim and steam to heat railroad cars in the rail yards. Although removed from the main visitor traffic along the rim, the building is close enough to El Tovar, the depot, and Bright Angel Lodge to merit attention because of its massive volume and unique design. The building is reinforced concrete and was put into operation in 1926. It managed to combine a straightforward industrial function with the qualities of a Swiss chalet. *Trompe l'oeil* – purposeful overscaling of the windows, balcony, eaves, and exterior masonry – makes the building appear considerably smaller than it actually is. By taking the familiar details of a Swiss chalet and nearly doubling them, the viewer is deceived into believing that the building is half its actual size. Careful adherence to the principle of overscaling reduces the powerful form and large volume to a deceptively modest element in the landscape.

In contrast to the Swiss Chalet exterior, the building's interior is uncompromisingly industrial in character: exposed concrete floors and walls, with steel framing for columns and roof trusses. The two original Fairbanks-Morse diesel generators are still in place, along with an overhead crane for maintenance. The Power House operations were shut down in 1956, and the building is now used for storage.

National Park Service Buildings

The NPS developed a master plan for Grand Canyon soon after the park's creation in 1919. The Santa Fe Railway and Fred Harvey Company buildings had already established their unique architectural character in memorable and distinctive designs. Only a short distance away from the Park Operations building were the "Norwegian-Swiss villa" El Tovar Hotel and the pueblo-inspired Hopi House. In constructing the Operations Building in 1929, the NPS turned to a design in the classic Rustic style. Large enough to have its own identity amid the pyrotechnics of the Santa Fe Railway and the Fred Harvey Company buildings, the Operations Building definitely has its own architectural strength.

The original configuration of the Operations Building was an L-shaped, two-story, wood-framed structure. The building was converted in 1931 into the Superintendent's Residence, with a wing added in 1938. The final composition is a large-scaled residence with many of the elements that would later be refined in other park administration structures at the Grand Canyon and elsewhere in western national parks.

Each element contributes to the Rustic expression of the whole design. Materials appear to have been chosen and placed randomly, belying the designer's subtleties. Each has its own place and importance in the composition. Rows of paired casement windows set in the dark, stained lower walls of horizontal planking and upper walls of vertical board-and-batten read as shadowed planes in contrast with the lighter-colored stone masses. Low-pitched roofs add a horizontal emphasis, and wide overhangs cast shadows onto the already dark walls. Even the choice of dark brown paint for logs and siding and green trim for the doors and windows were decisions made with the utmost care, helping the building blend into its natural environment.

The final step in the development of NPS administrative buildings at Grand Canyon was the Post Office, built in 1934–35. Here, the burden of guiding the many Depression-era projects is evident in the slight degradation of the refined Rustic style. The composition, materials, and building elements of the earlier structures have been diluted. Where stone is used, it is regular in coursing and has finished surfaces; the narrower eaves

▷ As seen from the approach path, Hermit's Rest barely rises above the earth mound it is built on; rarely has a designer so successfully merged a building into the landscape. The approach is through an archway of haphazardly piled stones. Mary Jane Colter brought the bell from a New Mexico Spanish mission.

▷ Tusayan Museum. Herbert Maier shifted his design approach from the traditional forms he used at Yosemite and drew inspiration from Mary Jane Colter's ethnographic interpretation of the Hopi culture.

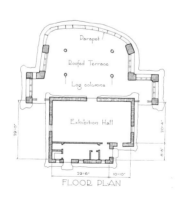

◁ "This little museum, perched on the rim of spectacular Grand Canyon, forms a liaison with its setting by means of its low lines, flat roof, and rugged masonry walls" (PARK AND RECREATION STRUCTURES).

◁ Colter's vision was to create a shelter that would resemble a mountain man's stone-and-timber dwelling.

△ When Hermit's Rest opened, in 1914, the railroad men teased architect Colter about the dingy, cobweb-filled appearance: "Why don't you clean up this place?" Colter answered, "You can't imagine what it cost to make it look this old." Antiques and handcrafted furniture amplify the rustic feeling. Wrought-iron sconces and andirons, kitchen and fireplace tools, chairs made from hollowed-out logs, a European pendulum clock, and bear traps contribute to the building's unique atmosphere.

and projecting log beams carry a roof that more closely resembles a suburban residence than a Swiss chalet. Today it serves as the Magistrate's Office.

The Tusayan Museum west of Grand Canyon Village at Yavapai Point is an example of early NPS efforts at interpretation. The partnership of the American Association of Museums and the Laura Spelman Rockefeller Memorial Foundation that sponsored Yosemite Museum, in 1926, supported the design of a museum at the Tusayan ruins near the rim of the Grand Canyon.

Designed in 1927 and opened in 1928, the museum is a representation of traditional Hopi buildings. The rectangular building (with a 1934 addition) is extended by a roofed observation terrace on the canyon side with a parapet on the edge of the rim. An outdoor exhibit of native plantings supplements the museum proper.

Hermit's Rest

Seven miles west of Grand Canyon Village, at the end of West Rim Drive, is a Colter jewel of ingenious design, uniquely adapted to a special site. Hermit's Rest was built for $13,000 in 1914 and is a testament to the daring Fred Harvey Company and the brilliance of their designer. Fred Harvey ran tours by stagecoach to the end of an old trailhead and wanted a small refreshment stand there for the dusty passengers. Several designs were considered, and Colter's primitive building style was chosen.

The structure appears to be a random jumble of stones with a chimney spire growing out of it. The canyon side of the structure has a log-frame roof protruding from the stonework, covering a patio separated from the rim by a stone wall.

The interior of Hermit's Rest is medieval in character, shaped by the rugged stonework and cavelike space, with dramatic changes in volume and light. On its northern side the central room is covered by the exposed peeled-log flat roof of the porch. The roof height opens up two stories farther into the interior to a flat ceiling of exposed vigas (beams) and latias (poles). The windows facing the canyon and in the upper part of the wall provide a subtle source of natural daylight. A huge semi-dome alcove on the southern end of the space shelters an arched stone fireplace with the flagstone floor stepped up at the alcove for emphasis.

Indian Watchtower at Desert View

Mary Jane Colter returned from Fred Harvey work elsewhere in 1930 to design an observation building at the eastern end of the stagecoach tour. Desert View, with its sweeping vista of the canyons, is 25 miles east of Grand Canyon Village. To take advantage of the site, Colter conceived a soaring tower 70 feet high in the form of an ancient Anasazi watchtower.

Colter's best design work reflects her dedication to archaeology and ethnohistory. For this project she chartered a small plane to gather information on watchtowers, locating ruins and then traveling overland to sketch and study the forms, construction, and stonework. After six months of research she built a detailed clay model to study the design and how it would fit the terrain. Finally, she built a 70-foot-tall wooden tower on the site to test the form and the views she sought from the promontory overlooking the canyon.

The Watchtower's plan provides for two concentric circles connected by gently arched forms. The larger circle and arched portions form the ground-floor lounge; the smaller circle is the 30-foot-diameter base of the tower. Inside the stonework of the tower is a steel framework built by the Santa Fe Railway. This was no random pile of rocks mimicking a ruin; Colter meticulously selected and placed each exterior stone to provide a rich surface texture.

The ground floor of the Watchtower is a large, circular room modeled after an Indian *kiva*. Colter specified large observation windows, a flagstone floor, stone walls,

▷ Colter's design concept for the Watchtower required painstakingly careful selection of stones for the walls. The tower's coursed sandstone alternates with bands of colored stones above a rubble-stone base; a course of triangular stones at the parapet adds visual interest. Oddly shaped stones occasionally protrude from the tower surface to create shadows and give more vigor to the walls. Petroglyphs and animal forms can also be discerned on the wall face. Window openings are irregularly placed and vary in shape; trapezoidal openings filled with plate glass are at the rooftop observation deck.

△ Small windows admit only a minimum of light to the Indian Watchtower, and Indian pots serve as wall sconces for additional, low-intensity light.

▷ The Hopi Room is based on the theme of the traditional Hopi Snake Dance, a rain dance held in August. The Snake Altar features a sand painting by Fred Kabotie. Other paintings portray the God of Germination, the Star Priest, and the Little God. On the ceiling, Kabotie drew symbols of stars and constellations he learned from his grandmother when he was a child. The room was completed with a border design in a circle above the Snake Altar—the Great Snake, parent of all serpents.

a fireplace, and unusual furniture made from tree trunks, rawhide, and burls to create a rustic atmosphere.

From the *kiva* one ascends to the handsomely decorated first floor of the tower interior, the Hopi Room. Here, Colter's intention to link the history of the Hopi Indians with the Grand Canyon was achieved through sand paintings and by murals by two Hopi artists, Fred Kabotie and Fred Greer, depicting Hopi mythology and religious ceremonies.

Above, the tower's open shaft—surrounded by circular balconies around the wall edges—is connected by small staircases leading to the rooftop observation deck.

Benches were placed along the walls for visitors to observe the graceful curves of the balconies and the play of light on walls of soft rust and mauve. The space is filled with tiers of balconies, prehistoric images, and the mystical quality of the Indian Southwest.

Colter designed a "ruin" to the west of the Watchtower to simulate the typical condition of prehistoric towers found in the region. This was the sort of ruin she had studied when designing the tower, and it lends an air of antiquity. The opening of the complex was celebrated with a dramatic Hopi dedication ceremony on May 13, 1933.

▷ *Grand Canyon Lodge in 1936. The lodge was rebuilt after a devastating fire in 1932 destroyed the lodge and several adjacent cabins. It is the most intact Rustic hotel development remaining in the national parks, dating from the era when railroad companies fostered the construction of destination resorts.*

North Rim

Major John Wesley Powell's journey down the Colorado and his explorations of the surrounding area resulted in widespread knowledge about the extraordinary scenery to be found in the territory. Adventurous travelers were soon finding their way to the South Rim of the Grand Canyon. Because of its inaccessibility, the North Rim was an exotic destination. Powell wanted to secure assistance for his continued scientific expeditions in the Southwest and urged Thomas Moran to paint a view of the Grand Canyon from the North Rim that would show the public its majestic beauty. Moran's spectacular painting "The Chasm of the Colorado" hung in the U.S. Capitol until the 1930s; it is now in the National Museum of American Art.

Industrious Mormons worked to attract tourists to "their" north side of the canyon. Jacob Lake is at the junction of the road west from St. George, Utah, and east from the Marble Canyon crossing of the Colorado River. Wagon trips were offered to intrepid adventurers from Jacob Lake southward across the Kaibab Plateau and 45 miles of the Kaibab National Forest. Transporting tourists across the canyon from the South Rim to the North Rim did not seem to be an reasonable prospect, and in 1908 a cable car was installed for a river crossing to reach Bright Angel Point. Travelers who braved the 85-mile stagecoach trip over dusty roads from Kanab, in southern Utah, were accommodated at the Wylie North Rim Tent Camp, built in 1916. Several years later, NPS director Stephen Mather encouraged the development

of improved roads in southern Utah. After the first automobile caravan ventured over the Kaibab Plateau in 1909, tourism on the North Rim began to increase.

Grand Canyon Lodge

In 1926, Gilbert Stanley Underwood was at the height of his architectural powers, working on the Ahwahnee Hotel at Yosemite. The Loop Tour projects at Grand Canyon represented a design challenge of the first order, and the Union Pacific Railroad began its search for a designer who could unite the lodges on their tour with common elements, but who also would avoid exact repetition. The owners understood the importance of establishing a unique image for each site.

The NPS was a willing partner. Joyce Zaitlin describes the situation: "Here there were no constraints at building right up to the edge of the cliff, and the site, which overlooked the canyon, offered one of the most expansive views of the southwest. While the Ahwahnee was built on a valley floor with the best views above it, this lodge was to be perched right at the cliff's edge."[7]

Underwood, the undisputed master of the grand statement, was selected, and he created a true masterpiece at the edge of the canyon rim. Following the format of the lodges in Zion and Bryce parks, Grand Canyon Lodge was not planned to be as large as the Ahwahnee Hotel. Its aim was rather to provide impressive public spaces – guest rooms were never intended to be part of the lodge, for overnight visitors were to stay in nearby cabins.

▽ *In the reconstruction after the 1932 fire, the drama of Gilbert Stanley Underwood's original design was muted by simpler forms. Piers and the irregular roof profile that had effectively related the building to the edge of the canyon rim were eliminated.*

▷ *The original lodge in 1930. The rim side was constructed of battered and buttressed rubble masonry. Kaibab limestone in the foundations, walls, and piers tied the building to the canyon walls, sometimes appearing as natural extensions of the out-croppings. Low-pitched, shingled hip and shed roofs of intersecting gables broken up by shed and gable dormers were stained dark green to match the surrounding piñon forests. Ponderosa logs, log slab siding, and shingled roofs further merge building and site.*

The concept was executed by Underwood with boldness and simplicity. A comparison of the presentation renderings for the Ahwahnee Hotel and Grand Canyon Lodge shows that both are exuberant massings of natural materials set against dramatic landscapes. Overscaled vertical buttresses of local stone ascending to a central tower embrace oversized logs (faux at Yosemite), used as columns in strong rhythms or as infill wall panels. The walls are scaled from ground to upper floors by decreasing the width of bays and sizes of window openings. The wall surfaces are selectively interrupted by projecting balconies and log beam ends.

At Yosemite, the Ahwahnee emphasizes the verticality of the surrounding valley walls; at the Grand Canyon, the Grand Canyon Lodge underscores the sweeping horizontal line of the mesa and layered canyon walls. The lodge's proportions simulate the shapes and sizes of the canyon's outcroppings and mesas; it is uniquely Southwest in concept and execution. The dominating visual line is the horizontal interrupted by massive vertical "fingers of stone."

Underwood began to design the lodge in 1927, and construction was under way late that year, with the first guests welcomed in June 1928. The quick construction was due to the excellent organization of the Utah Parks Company, even though this was the most challenging construction site on the Loop Tour. Until roads were completed over the 200 miles from the Union Pacific Railroad, materials had to be hauled up 4,000 feet from the canyon by aerial tramway. Water also had to be pumped up from the canyon floor.

A fire tragically destroyed most of the original lodge and several adjacent deluxe cabins in 1932. The loss of the main lodge to fire was mourned by Union Pacific officials and the National Park Service. NPS director Horace Albright wrote to the Union Pacific president: *The news came to me as a great shock. It seemed a crime that this wonderful lodge had to be destroyed when there were fully a score of old lodges, hotels, government structures, etc. which we would have been rather pleased to have suffer a fate of this kind. I hope you will find it possible to rebuild the lodge at once, as your operation at the Grand Canyon was the outstanding tourist accommodation of the entire national park system.[8]*

The Utah Parks Company had made a costly decision when they denied Underwood's request to use concrete

▷ *Underwood was a master of the spatial experience on the imperial scale, and he used the canyon rim and vistas to great advantage in his original design for Grand Canyon Lodge. A long, straight entrance drive gradually descended to the U-shaped lodge, passing a hundred standard cabins on the right and twenty deluxe cabins on the left. The lodge tantalizingly screened the canyon from view.*

▷ *The main lodge was rebuilt in 1936–37, retaining Underwood's basic planning concepts.*

▷ *Canyon views from the lounge.*

◁ Exposed roof trusses in the public spaces are actually steel covered by logs. The dining room is typical of the interior treatment throughout the lodge, with verticality emphasized by stone piers and contrasting panels of varnished logs with white chinking, set both vertically and horizontally.

and steel. Choosing to use timber from company-owned forests proved fateful, for only the stone piers remained after the devastating blaze. Although the lodge was rebuilt during 1936–37, under the guidance of Union Pacific engineers, it was not as architecturally spectacular as the original. The second story and dramatic observa-

tion tower were not replaced, and several flat roofs were modified to pitched surfaces.

Despite Underwood's lack of involvement, the reconstruction nonetheless bears his mark. His original plan featured a forecourt with colonnaded porticos – a classical Palladian villa executed with Pueblo-Mission ele-

*Wrought-iron light fixtures,
both exterior and interior,
incorporated Native American
design motifs.*

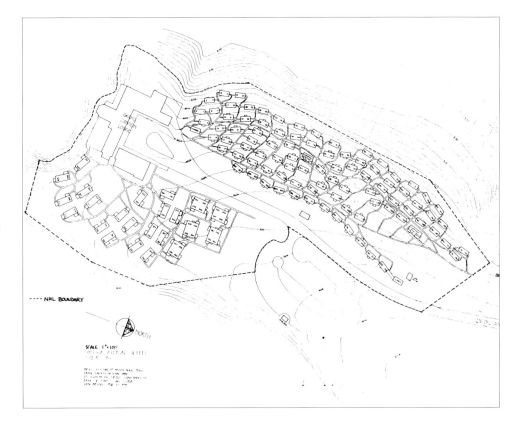

▷ The Union Pacific's concepts for "deluxe" and "standard" cabins were cleverly executed by Underwood. The two cabin enclaves are sited at gentle angles on the slightly hilly terrain, with meandering connecting paths through stands of pine. By avoiding a strictly regulated layout, Underwood reinforced the comfortable rustic atmosphere as a pleasant change from the more formal lodge.

△ Underwood was a perfectionist, right down to the details of composition and selection of materials for the deluxe cabins. They are frame construction, with split-log exterior siding, stone foundations, and stone corner piers. The siding is horizontal on the main walls but vertical in the gable ends, chinked with cement mortar.

▽ Chimneys of textured limestone laid in rough courses vary in placement either as corner piers or at midwall. Shallow-pitched shake roofs have projecting peeled ridgepoles, purlins, and rafters at gables and eaves. Double-hung windows are frequently paired and surrounded by split-log framing. Stonework, log rafters, and purlins are exposed on the interiors.

▽ A distinctive architectural feature of the deluxe cabins is the porches. They are on square, dressed stone foundations with peeled-log columns 2½ feet in diameter that carry shake-covered roofs. Porch railings are four-inch-diameter logs and smaller vertical log posts.

◁ In siting the standard cabins, Underwood followed natural contours to compensate for the dense building arrangement. Materials in the standard cabins are the same as in the lodge and deluxe cabins, except that each cabin is on a stone foundation and shows true log construction with cement chinking. Saddle-notched logs project irregularly at corners and at midwall. Shake-covered gable roofs are shallow pitched. Rather than the elaborate entrance porches on the deluxe cabins, these cabins have simple entrances with a varying number of limestone steps at opposite ends. The cabins are rectangular in plan; log partitions separate the two guest units in each cabin. Log walls, purlins, and rafters are exposed on the interiors.

Today, in the rebuilt lodge, all walls facing the canyon are still filled with large expanses of windows, and interior reflected light radiates from the surfaces of the buff limestone walls. Floor elevations progressively descend to the outdoor terraces that naturally step down to the canyon rim. The recreation room is a few steps above the lobby; the dining room and lounge are a few steps below the lobby. On a terrace outside the lounge, a mammoth fireplace and chimney of rugged stonework rise three stories high.

Interior volumes are light and airy, reducing the transition between inside and outside. Exposed peeled-log roof trusses, a device often used by Underwood, span the public spaces. Large, wrought-iron chandeliers and sconces, parchment fixtures, and painted and carved Indian symbols are found throughout the building. At night, the fixtures provide a warm glow against the limestone piers and dark, stained logs.

Using similar architectural elements, Underwood assembled the deluxe cabins in eighteen duplexes and five quadruplexes, the plans varying in porches, entrances, and interior arrangements.

One of the most exceptional places to stay overnight in any national park in the country is in one of the deluxe cabins (#302 or #306) on the east side of Grand Canyon Lodge; perched at the tip of Bright Angel Point, the cabin entrances are about ten feet above a walk along the edge of the canyon rim. Wide, rustic porches provide private viewing platforms virtually suspended over the canyon's rim, where the fortunate guest can enjoy an unobstructed panorama of the canyon.

The architectural treasures in Grand Canyon National Park are in the contrasting ecological zones of the South and North rims, focused on the spectacular scenery of the canyon. There is great reward in pausing to visit these historic buildings, which are steeped in the history of the earliest Indian inhabitants, Powell's explorations, the railroaders' developments, and the National Park Service's struggle to manage legions of summer visitors. The NPS and concessioners have made commitments to conserve and protect the fragile natural and manmade environment, and they have taken valuable strides to restore and replace important structures that suffer from heavy visitor usage.

ments. The centered entrance was defined by large double gables projecting as dormers from the main roof. The southwestern version of a wide outdoor corridor wrapped around the courtyard, and the two wings housed a "western saloon" and service areas. The shingled roof was supported by heavy stone columns expanded at their bases to form low benches. Public spaces were delineated along the edge of the cliffs, and a spacious lobby offered views of the canyon through large windows. Straight ahead from the entrance was the spacious lounge, to the left a recreation room, and to the right a dining room with peeled-log trusses.

Underwood skillfully varied the treatment from the entrance side of the building to the canyon exposure. The more conservative entrance side was classically proportioned, with a regulated line of identical roof pitches and continuous eave lines to contrast with the dramatic organic stonework of the building's canyon elevations.

Tumacacori National Monument

We had intended to circle back from Tucubavia to Cocospera, but messengers ... from San Cayetano del Tumacacori came to meet us.... The father Visitor said to me that the crosses they carried were tongues that spoke much and eloquently, and that we could not fail to go where they summoned us

Father Kino, January 1691

The white, plastered sanctuary dome of the Mission of San Jose de Tumacacori provides a shimmering landmark at this national monument in southern Arizona. The mission has been only partially rebuilt since its abandonment in 1844. The juxtaposition of the mission ruins and the finely crafted Spanish Colonial museum and visitor service buildings added by the NPS in 1937–39 provides a unique interpretive perspective on the early settlement of the region.

The Mission's History

To establish the church among the Indians, seventeenth-century Jesuit missionaries traveled the desert and Sonora highlands of present-day Arizona and northern Mexico, building churches and establishing villages. Their goals were to convert the Pima Indians and consolidate the king's hold on New Spain. An energetic priest, Father Eusebio Francisco Kino, celebrated mass in 1691 at a site several miles away from the Mission of San Jose de Tumacacori, south of Tucson and twenty miles north of the Mexican border settlement of Nogales. A village grew up around the site, and after the Pima Rebellion of 1751 and the expulsion of the Jesuits, the village was moved to its present location. The Franciscans assumed the Jesuits' work, and around 1772, as a result of continued Apache raids in the Santa Cruz Valley, missionary work was consolidated in the district of Tumacacori.

Construction of San Jose de Tumacacori began around 1800, and the church was in use by 1820. After Mexico won independence from Spain in 1821, most of the frontier missions were abandoned because of the new government's inability to protect them against Indian raids. Lack of government support led to the sale of the mission to a private citizen in 1844. The church was abandoned, and until its designation as a national monument in 1908, its only protection against weather and vandals was its adobe construction, with walls up to nine feet thick.

The Mission

The original mission complex included the church, *convento,* burial ground, and a mortuary chapel (uncompleted). Construction consisted mainly of adobe or

▷ *The powerful entrance facade shows how Spanish Baroque forms were adapted to the traditions of the Sonoran desert. A projecting adobe-brick framework around the edge of the facade focuses attention on the arched entrance, heavily plastered and grooved to simulate stonework. The imposing facade is flanked by pairs of columns—with recesses in between for statuary—that support a beam for the choir loft floor on the interior. The column-and-beam motif repeats on a smaller scale above the beam and supports a broken pediment. A three-dimensional quality was achieved by adding colors to the plaster surfaces along the projections.*

△ *The white lime plaster dome at Tumacacori National Monument has been stabilized as a result of the ongoing restoration work that has been proceeding for years.*

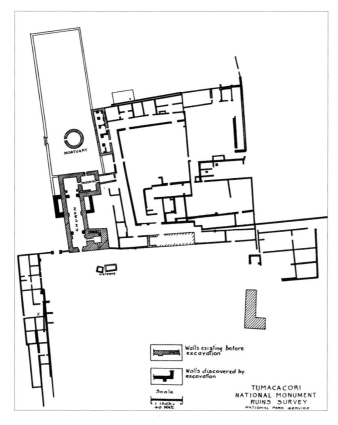

▷ *The mission ruins, showing walls before and after excavation. The plan for the mission complex followed the traditional Franciscan organization of space for spiritual and temporal affairs. A church, residence for the padres, dormitory for young unmarried women (convento), shops, quarters for a military escort, and storerooms all enclosed a courtyard (patio). The church nave was basilican in plan, with an attached barrel-vaulted sacristy (upper right) and a single bell tower over the baptistry (lower right).*

burned bricks. Oriental influences from Spanish mid-sixteenth-century architecture, filtered through Spanish Colonial experiences in Mexico, can be seen in the sanctuary dome and polychrome decoration on the ornate facade. The elaborate facade, unlike those on mission churches farther away from Mexico, was created by modeled plaster decoration over adobe.[9] Massive adobe walls were extended to enclose the Indian village of Tumacacori.

The church interior is a long rectangular nave with a domed sanctuary. The church provided a dramatic transition from the bright outdoors to a dim, mysterious interior. The transition from the City of Man to the City of God was emphasized by the axial composition and careful placement of clerestory windows and lighting. The flat-roofed nave has an exposed ceiling of ponderosa vigas and planks, with a procession of altars, pilasters, and niches along the walls leading to the pulpit. In the nave, traces remain of holy-water fonts at each side of the entrance, oval depressions in the walls for stations of the cross, and symbolic paintings and designs. Small windows above the side altars softly illuminate the nave with morning and afternoon light. A barrel-vaulted sacristy is to the right of the nave.

The Museum and Visitor Center

The ruins of San Jose de Tumacacori Mission came under federal protection in 1908, but minimal restora-

tion or interpretative efforts ensued. The desire to improve the site in the early 1930s raised questions about how to handle the remains of the adobe mission structures. Rather than launching a restoration and reconstruction program based largely on speculation, as the Public Works Administration had done at the Alamo, officials decided to preserve all the mission structures and focus on interpretation. The design and construction of a combined museum–visitor center to implement this concept began in 1935.

The proposed Tumacacori Museum presented an unusual set of problems to the Plans and Design branch of the National Park Service. Up until that time, the major body of Rustic work had been in areas where stone and logs were the appropriate building materials. Following the ethic of using on-site materials and indigenous construction techniques, the designers turned to local culture and Southwestern building traditions for guidance.

The NPS head of Southwestern Monuments, Frank Pinkley, had definite ideas about the design concept and how to proceed with it.[10] He pictured a utilitarian building, low in height to avoid interfering with views of the mission complex, a "pleasing" but not too ornate facade, and construction techniques, materials, and decorations found in other Sonoran missions in the region. Pinkley also proposed a "view room" from which visitors could look out onto the mission complex, and he set the axis of the building at a particular angle so that visitors would see his chosen, knockout, view.

A team of NPS architects, engineers, technicians, and photographers were dispatched to Sonora, Mexico, in October 1935 to record the remaining mission structures in the Kino chain and to study construction techniques and architectural elements, under the direction of the principal designer of the museum, Scofield DeLong. The researchers' stay was cut short because of rebel uprisings in the region. The research nonetheless provided invaluable documentation, and DeLong incorporated many of the elements that he had seen in the Sonoran missions into his design for the museum building.

A seven-foot high adobe wall extending north and south from the museum's west wall screens all but the upper portions of the mission ruins from the road and parking lot and channels visitors toward the museum's

▷ *The interior of the Mission of San Miguel of Santa Fe is spanned by ponderosa beams similar to Tumacacori.*

◁ *The church's domed sanctuary shelters the main altar and the statue of Saint Joseph, patron saint of the church in Franciscan times. The style of Spanish Baroque churches was to focus attention on the altar by means of sanctuary decoration and light streaming through clerestory windows below the dome. The contrast of the light-bathed sanctuary and the dimly lit nave emphasized the mystery of communion and the Mass.*

△ *White plaster on the sanctuary dome contrasts with the unfinished adobe bell tower, which has adobe walls nine feet thick.*

▽ The uncompleted mortuary chapel behind the church in the Campo Sancto, the holy field. The field served as the mission cemetery, but after the mission was abandoned, cattlemen used the enclosure as a roundup corral. Cows destroyed the original graves, and grave looters did further damage. After the Apache wars, settlers gradually came back to Tumacacori, and the sanctified grounds were returned to their original use. The holes around the exterior of the chapel were to support scaffolding for catwalks used by the builders.

main entrance. A T-shaped plan of 5,500 square feet houses the museum. Arcades extend from the east wing – one opening into the garden and the other providing views of the church ruins. The patio garden, begun in 1939, contains plantings similar to those grown in the missions of northern Sonora.

In proper NPS tradition, architect DeLong chose construction materials and decorative elements found in other Sonoran missions. Walls were built of sun-dried adobe bricks, with cornices of fired bricks. The flat-roofed building is surrounded by a parapet with a stepped coping, drained by channels cut into the adobe

piers of the portals. The scallop-shell motif over the main entrance, symbolizing Santiago de Compostela, patron saint of Spain, was patterned after the church entrance at Cocospera, in northern Sonora, Mexico.

The main entrance leads into the museum lobby. The room has a fireplace in the southeast corner and a floor of large bricks laid in a herringbone pattern. Carved corbels and the beamed ceiling are similar to the nave ceiling of Oquitoa, and the lobby counter follows the design of the confessional at Oquitoa. The room also features handmade Spanish Colonial furniture. Of the several museum rooms, the "view room" is architec-

▽ The last burial in the Campo Sancto was in 1916, and a floral wreath is placed on the grave every All Souls' Day.

△ The main entrance door of the museum was carved by CCC craftsmen at Bandelier National Monument. It incorporates floral designs used at San Ignacio in Sonora, Mexico.

▷ The choice of plants for the patio garden was based on plant lists found by historians in mission records.

◁ *The water fountain incorporates a shell motif seen in northern Sonora missions.*

▽ *Tumacacori Mission ruins in 1936, before restoration.*

turally the most important. An arcade on one side, with piers and arches copied from those at Caborca, frames views of the mission. Groin-vault ceilings were often used in Sonoran missions—at San Xavier, Tubutuma, and in the baptistery at San Ignacio. The open-air "room" contains a scale model of the mission for comparison with the stabilized ruins.

Construction began on the museum building in 1937. All work, including the garden, was completed by 1939.

The NPS' goal for the design of the museum building was to replicate the mission architectural style for living and working quarters from around 1800. Rather than follow the archaeological and ethnographic methods used so effectively by Mary Jane Colter, the designers and museum staff instead created a structure to illustrate mission development and act as a model of historic construction techniques and materials. The impressive museum building at San Jose de Tumacacori attests to their success and has been designated a National Historic Landmark.

Petrified Forest National Park

Step out of the car and walk away from the road into the burnished palette of the Painted Desert, into the lunar hills of the Blue Mesa, or among the tangle of fallen logs that marks the petrified forests.

THE SIERRA CLUB GUIDES TO THE NATIONAL PARKS OF THE DESERT SOUTHWEST

Petrified Forest National Park is a marvel of natural wonders forming one of the most unusual landscapes in the United States. The park is in the central Arizona desert highlands. It lacks the dramatic features of the crown jewel parks, and Petrified Forest could easily be missed by the traveler hurtling through the desert on Interstate 40. The park is a tourist's treasure, though, for those who find it. An entrance from the Interstate leads to the nearby Visitor Center. From there a 27-mile road loops southward through the unique terrain of petrified logs, prehistoric ruins, badlands eroded by water and wind, and the Rainbow Forest, taking visitors to the Rainbow Forest Museum at the park's southern end.

Beyond the Visitor Center, a road curves along a wide mesa and rises over the edge of Painted Desert. At Kachina Point, the National Park Service built the superb Painted Desert Inn. A mixture of Spanish and Pueblo styles, this rustic lodge is uniquely representative of Southwestern architecture and bureaucratic ingenuity.

Painted Desert Inn
Painted Desert Inn is a gentle orchestration of building masses set on a flat landscape. From a distance, its earth-colored walls and stepped parapets seem part of the surrounding topography. The inn's stucco surfaces take on different color hues, in perfect harmony with the colors of the Painted Desert. In the early morning hours and at twilight, the walls have an orange cast; at midday the sun has bleached them into flat pink.

The inn comes into view gradually from the approach road. Its irregular plan, multilevel construction, and massing of individual rooms root the inn comfortably in its site. Partial banking into the mesa edge appears to diminish the two-story structure's volume. Terraces on three sides of the building have low walls that define the outdoor spaces, some overlooking the ever-changing colors of the Painted Desert. Exterior walls, pierced by *viga* ends and *canales* (scuppers), drain the flat roofs and create a play of light and shadow on the walls.

The fascinating history of the inn begins with a lodge, the Stone Tree House, privately built in 1924. The lands of the Painted Desert north of the Petrified Forest National Monument, including the original lodge, were acquired by the NPS in 1936. The monument and the

▷ The northern end of Petrified Forest National Park is covered by badlands in layers of limestone and sandstone carved by wind and water. The predominant red in the Painted Desert comes from iron oxides. A dazzling array of reds, pinks, blues, and white vary in hue as light conditions change during the day.

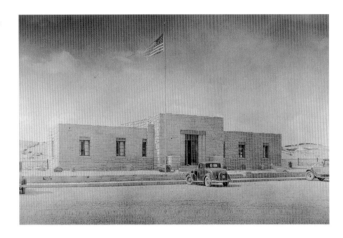

> *The Rainbow Forest Museum, built in 1934, was described in* PARK AND RECREATION STRUCTURES: *"With simple dignity, this building happily succeeds both in capturing the flavor of the architecture of the Old Southwest and in gesturing toward contemporary. This is no mean attainment in itself, and with the added score of an orderly workable plan, it is successful beyond cavil."*

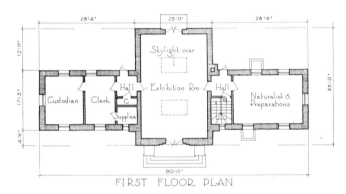

FIRST FLOOR PLAN

> *Human habitation in the Petrified Forest area had ceased by the time a Spanish expedition arrived in 1540. Indian petroglyphs were carved into Newspaper Rock, and elsewhere in the area, centuries ago.*

Painted Desert were assembled into Petrified Forest National Park in 1962. The original lodge was constructed of local adobe and petrified logs and contained a trading post, lunch counter, and the owner's living quarters. Unfortunately, the building was constructed on unstable clay soil that damaged the stone walls.

When the NPS acquired the lodge, Thomas C. Vint, the chief architect of the NPS Branch of Plans and Design, chose to do a major rebuilding. This strategy was a bureaucratic ploy, for funding was easier to obtain for "rebuilding" than for new construction. When construction funds fell short of contractors' estimates, the NPS design staff decided to use the available money to purchase the basic materials and use labor from the CCC camp at nearby Rainbow Forest.[11] Construction began in the fall of 1937 and after considerable travail was finally completed in July 1940.

Under NPS supervising architect Lorimer Skidmore's supervision, CCC crews obtained ponderosa pine and aspen logs for structural members from Sitgreaves National Forest. The crews shaped the logs, carved the corbels, and hewed the beams. In some places, the crews propped up the sagging stone walls, dug underneath

△ *The Stone Tree House, built in 1924 by Herbert D. Lore, was converted into the Painted Desert Inn. The site—off a loop from Interstate Highway 40 at Kachina Point—commands sweeping views of the Painted Desert.*

▷▽ *An artful effect occurs during the day as changing light colors the stucco walls from pale pink to rich red tones.*

△ *Painted Desert Inn was designed in the Pueblo Revival tradition, with a collection of rooms at differing heights. The highest point provides natural daylight through the skylight into the Trading Post room.*

them, and replaced the foundations. Flagstone floors were laid in some rooms, and in others poured concrete was stained soft tints and then incised with patterns inspired by those on Indian blankets. The furniture and interior wall colors repeated the same soft colors. Workers plastered around window and door openings in the two-foot-thick masonry walls, narrowing the width at top and bottom by the sweeping motion of their hands to resemble shapes in old pueblo buildings.

Skidmore described the building's design as influenced by Pueblo Indian dwellings softened by Spanish Colonial decorative touches.[12] The results of thorough study of these influences are evident in the finished building. *Vigas* and split aspen *latias* were used for decorative ceilings in the Indian fashion, along with adzed *vigas*, carved corbels, and brackets of Spanish Colonial origins. Windows, doors, and frames were sandblasted for an "aged" finish before installation.

When the inn opened, it contained 28 rooms divided between the NPS and concessioner's use. The concessioner's space included a lunch room, kitchen, dining room, dining porch, trading post room, six staff sleeping rooms with corner fireplaces, service areas, and the Trading Post Room. Today all the space is used by the NPS.

The Trading Post Room is a magnificent interior space. An enormous skylight with multiple panes of translucent glass painted in designs from prehistoric pottery provides soft illumination over the concessioners' sales items. Six hammered-tin, Mexican-style chandeliers are suspended from ceiling *vigas,* and the posts supporting the corbels and *vigas* are painted in muted Spanish Colonial colors. The masterful combination of the skylight and the highly decorative woodwork on posts, corbels, ceilings, and furnishings makes this building a memorable example of Southwestern design.

The inn officially opened in 1940, but its business

▷ *A variety of volumes and surface finishes, and the decorative use of* vigas, *establishes the inn as a significant example of the Pueblo Revival architectural style.*

△ *The well-composed design for Painted Desert Inn overcame limitations in funding and unskilled labor.* CCC *crews were transported 50 miles a day for 2½ years for the difficult task of rebuilding the existing structure before new construction could begin.*

△ *The inn was at one time divided between National Park Service use and the concession-* *ers' area, each with its own entrance. Today the* NPS *uses all the space.*

◁ The skylight in the Trading Post room is made of multiple panes of translucent glass. Lyle Bennett adapted design patterns from Indian pottery to be applied with opaque paints. Posts and hand-carved corbels in Spanish Colonial designs are painted in muted colors.

▽ A Zuñi "Salt Lake Trip" mural painted by Fred Kabotie. This is one of four murals inspired by Indian blanket designs. Kabotie scored the patterns into the concrete walls and painted them in white, red oxide, and adobe colors.

days were cut short by World War II, after which it no longer offered guest lodging. After the war, the Atchison, Topeka, and Santa Fe Railway's concessioner, the Fred Harvey Company, took over its operation. The company's architect, Mary Jane Colter, was brought to the inn to update the building to Fred Harvey standards. She changed the interior color scheme and hired Hopi artist Fred Kabotie to paint a series of murals. Kabotie was a well-known artist, and Colter had previously enlisted his talents for murals at her Grand Canyon buildings. His Painted Desert Inn murals, completed in 1948, incorporated ceremonial and religious symbolism, and some showed scenes from everyday Hopi life. The dining room was dedicated as the Kabotie Room in 1976.

Many people had a hand in creating the Painted Desert Inn – CCC crews, construction supervisor Skidmore, architect Colter, and artist Kabotie – but the credit for its design belongs to NPS architect Lyle E. Bennett.[13] Bennett's early career with the NPS at Mesa Verde was in the ranger ranks, working elbow to elbow with archaeologists on excavations, unearthing pieces of the past. With pickax, shovel, trowel, whisk broom, and toothbrush, he scientifically dug up bits of pottery, portions of house walls, and various fragments from a vanished civilization. Part of Lyle Bennett's earliest NPS job also included long hours of laboratory work – recording the archaeological data, and cleaning and stabilizing artifacts for future study or museum exhibition. This detailed work led to a strong interest in prehistoric pottery, and Bennett studied the subject further. Years later, he drew upon this knowledge when designing the intricate patterns in the skylight of the Trading Post Room.

At the time Bennett was designing the Painted Desert Inn, he had already completed a number of NPS buildings in the Southwest. His command of the Southwestern idiom was masterful, and he always included design subtleties that made his buildings unique. His talent and experience using only simple building materials, produced an impressive architectural accomplishment in the Painted Desert Inn.

Hubbell Trading Post National Historic Site

Hubbell Trading Post at Ganado is a reminder of the days when the reservation trading post was a center for business as well as social life for the Navajo. Located on the Navajo reservation in northeastern Arizona, the solid stone buildings have changed little since the post's beginnings over a century ago.

The exile of the Navajos from their homeland in 1864 ended with their return on the Long Walk from Fort Sumner, New Mexico, in 1868. As a defeated people, they became dependent upon traders for supplies in exchange for their wool, sheep, rugs, and jewelry. One of the greatest successes and influences in the Indian trade was John Lorenzo Hubbell.

Considered the "dean" of Navajo traders, Hubbell was born in Pajaritos, New Mexico, in 1853. At age sixteen he began his apprenticeship in the trading posts of northern Arizona and southeastern Utah, learning the languages and customs of the local tribes. A settlement at Ganado, founded by an influential chief named Ganado Mucho (Many Cattle), attracted Hubbell, and he built a stone-and-log post near Ganado Lake around 1875. Three years later he bought from William Leonard a group of buildings west of Ganado and moved there, a post from which he traded for the rest of his life.

Hubbell claimed 160 acres of land around the post under the homestead laws. At the time, the property was outside the reservation boundaries. In 1880, an executive order enlarged the reservation, and Hubbell, finding himself surrounded by reservation lands, made several trips to Washington to clear his title. Finally, in 1900, Congress passed a special bill legalizing his claim.

Hubbell operated his trading post for over fifty years, during which he remained merchant, guide, and friend to the Navajo. This was a place where the Navajos came for news, to meet relatives and friends, and to exchange their goods and crafts for food, tobacco, tools, and cloth. Competition among traders was keen; success or failure could hinge on Navajo tolerance of a stranger in their midst. The trader's currency was not merely the supplies that he brought to the Navajos but also the strength of his word. The trader had to learn the natives' language and customs, respect their way of life, and act as an intermediary between them and the white community, supporting them in obtaining government programs.

▷ *The reservation trader served in many roles. As the principal link between the Navajo and the rest of the world, traders like John Lorenzo Hubbell presided over the cultural transition that took place after the settling of the reservations in the 1870s.*

△ *The Rug Room in the Trading Post displays blankets and rugs, jewelry, antique firearms, and a collection of southwestern Indian baskets that hang from the ceiling beams. Today, as over a hundred years ago, Navajo Indians come to the trading post to exchange goods in barter or to purchase supplies.*

By the 1870s, Hubbell's reputation was secure, resting on his honesty, trustworthiness, and initiative. He brought Mexican silversmiths to Ganado to teach the Navajos the craft of making silver jewelry. By the mid-1880s he was encouraging the Navajos to discard careless weaving practices and improve the quality of their work. Under his guidance, they used better wool and developed original designs. The Navajos recognized the benefits of meeting Hubbell's exacting standards, and he gradually assembled the best of the reservation weavers as his suppliers.

Post residence was a solitary life for the trader and his family. Their remote location required a 55-mile wagon trip for supplies from Gallup, New Mexico. Hubbell's substantial income mitigated his circumstances by allowing him and his family to live comfortably and entertain on a lavish scale. Distinguished guests were routine and, at times, as many as forty guests grouped around the immense table in his dining room.

Hubbell's success in maintaining the friendship of the Navajos enabled him to expand his operations to include 24 trading posts, stage and freight lines, a wholesale business in Winslow, Arizona, and other ranch properties and businesses. He died in 1930, and his son Roman carried on the business until 1957; Roman's wife, Dorothy, operated the store until 1967, when the NPS purchased the operation.

The special place that Hubbell Trading Post holds in the history of the Southwest is defined by historian Robert M. Utley as "the most important single trading post in the history of Navajo trading."[14] Hubbell was one of the first traders on the Navajo reservation, and he influenced the character of trade and traders for over half a century. He participated in the evolution of a native economy adapted to the conditions of the reservation and the transition in Native American culture that occurred between 1870 and 1920. The origin and development of Navajo craftwork as a profitable industry owe more to his leadership, vision, and guidance than any other factor.

▷ *Main entrance to the Trading Post. Local sandstone was used for the walls, and ponderosa pine vigas (beams) and aspen latias (poles) from distant forests framed the dirt-covered roofs.*

◁ *The entrance path to the Hubbell residence passes between stone pillars that support a gate decorated with the wrought-iron initials JLH.*

△ *The restored barn, originally built in 1887. Early buildings were constructed of dry masonry, with mud grouting added later.*

▷ *A stone hogan, built sometime in the early 1930s, was in keeping with the tradition in which traders maintained guest hogans for customers from remote regions.*

The Trading Post: A Cultural Bridge

The Trading Post's stone-and-adobe buildings began with the main post building sometime in the early 1880s and have remained substantially the same since 1900. The post looks much as it did in Hubbell's time. Minor modifications to the buildings occurred over the years, as doors were added, roofs replaced, parapets raised, and early chimneys replaced by stovepipes.

The long, stone Trading Post building housed the sales room and storerooms for trading. Built in four phases (the office and rug room first, the adjoining storeroom second, the wareroom next, followed by the wareroom extension), the structure is a fine representation of the typical trading post. Today, a store with massive counters and grocery-lined shelves still serves the Navajos. Small paintings of Navajo rugs line the walls of the rug room, their origin and use a subject of speculation.[15]

The hacienda used as the Hubbell family home was completed around 1900. Until then, the family only summered at the post. The rambling, adobe brick building was expanded over the years and grew into a complex of spaces filled with Hubbell's personal collection of Indian art and artifacts. The long living room and bedroom walls are enriched with artwork, photographs, and an impressive assortment of Indian artifacts.

To the right of the Hubbell home is a stone hogan built as a guesthouse in the 1930s. A restored barn, begun in 1887 and completed around 1900, and the other residences and utility buildings, complete the complex. The adobe bake oven produced nearly 400 loaves of bread a week and stocked the grocery.

Today the National Park Service operates the Trading Post much as it was in the past. The grocery and hardware sales area serve the great-grandchildren of Hubbell's customers and employees across the massive counters where JLH himself once did business. Hubbell Trading Post conveys the remarkable nature of an enterprise that bridged two cultures, the type of man who conducted it, the Native Americans who traded there, and the life they led together.

Mesa Verde National Park

In working out the plans and elevations, we have drawn on the present architecture of the Hopi Indians for practically all details of construction.... This type of construction seems the most logical.... The materials for the most part are right on the ground and easily available. The type will not detract one iota from the ancient dwellings which abound in this Park, both in caves and on the Mesas, but will help preserve the Indian atmosphere which the ruins and environment create.

Superintendent Jesse Nusbaum, 1921

Mesa Verde National Park is in the southwestern corner of Colorado on a mesa 2,000 feet above the surrounding countryside, between Durango and Cortez. Important secrets of our ancient past have been uncovered there in such rich abundance that in 1978 the United Nations declared it a World Heritage Site.

Ancient Cliff Dwellings

The Anasazi, ancestors of the Pueblo Indians, lived in cliff dwellings at Mesa Verde, tucked away in the edges of hidden canyons cut into the mesa.[16] The mesa tops contained fields for growing staple crops of corn, beans, and squash, and were dotted with piñon and juniper trees that provided shade from the hot summer sun. The Anasazi had lived there for generations until their mysterious disappearance in the thirteenth century, perhaps the result of drought or raids. Some walls of the ancient dwellings collapsed, but many remained, sheltered by an overhanging cliff. For centuries the silence might have been disturbed only by the gentle wind, a passing thunderstorm, or the soft scratchings of small animals.

The cliff dwellings were discovered, lost, and then rediscovered at the end of the nineteenth century. Protection and preservation of the ruins became a high-priority issue as the sound of shovels digging through the Anasazi ruins broke the silence. Greedy relic hunters stole pottery and prehistoric household items. They dug up the dead for the items buried with them. For a few dollars, they brought destruction to the remnants of an ancient and precious civilization.

The archaeological community, in particular, fought for federal preservation of places like Mesa Verde. Despite the looting, the cliff dwellings and the surrounding area were continually yielding information about the Anasazi to those who studied the archaeological sites in a scientific manner. In 1906, Mesa Verde finally became Mesa Verde National Park. Archaeological expeditions began to survey the ruins in that same year. In 1908, the Smithsonian Institution, under the direction of Dr. J. Walter Fewkes, began to restore the Cliff Palace in Spruce Canyon. Although park designation technically brought with it appropriate federal protection for the ruins, early administrators often ignored the pot-hunting and vandalism and even profited from it financially.

▷ *Spruce Tree House, with 114 rooms and eight kivas, is notable for its excellent state of preservation. Many of the high walls touch the top of the cave, and original roofs are still intact. The projecting rock shelf created a cave, which has protected the stone walls from wind, rain, and snow for over seven centuries.*

▷ Cliff Palace. Three years after "discovery" of the Mesa Verde ruins by the Wetherill brothers of Mancos, Colorado, in December 1888, a young man from Sweden named Gustaf Nordenskiöld arrived at the Wetherill ranch. He became interested in the ruins, and excavated and collected specimens. His visit resulted in meticulous field notes and photographs, which were published in 1893. A collection of Mesa Verde relics obtained by Nordenskiöld is in the National Museum of Finland.

▷ A party of distinguished visitors at Cliff Palace, 1926. The Swedish royal couple, Crown Prince Gustavus Adolphus (on ladder) and Crown Princess Louisa (behind him in striped dress), with Jesse Nusbaum (kneeling). The Nusbaums' building designs evolved from close study of ruins at the site and the architecture of Hopi Indians.

◁ Jesse Nusbaum in the mid-1920s.

In 1921, the National Park Service appointed Jesse Nusbaum to oversee the management and development of Mesa Verde National Park. Based on his experience as a field archaeologist, including his participation in a 1906 Smithsonian expedition, he looked toward the ancient pueblos for inspiration in choosing a suitable architectural style for the park. He and his wife, Aileen, referred to an 1886–87 Bureau of American Ethnology Report by Cosmos and Victor Mindeleff and concentrated on the sections dealing with Hopi architecture, noting that the Mindeleffs recorded their observations at a time when the "old methods" were still in use.[17]

Jesse Nusbaum requested permission from the director of the NPS to construct his buildings in what he called a Pueblo Revival style, and he justified his choice in several ways. First, he saw that materials for buildings of this type were readily available. Second, Pueblo-style buildings would "help to preserve the Indian atmosphere which the ruins and environment create." Third, he believed that buildings of this style would increase interest in the prehistoric structures and, in the long run, would serve as educational tools. It was Nusbaum's conviction that the style was "best suited to this environment and it is what the Pueblo Indian would build here today if he inhabited the mesa at this time, when the necessity of

▽ *The Community House–*
Natural History Museum
merged with the hillside over-
looking Spruce Tree House.
In a letter to the NPS director,
Jesse Nusbaum described why
he began the research that re-
sulted in his Pueblo Revival
style: "The present buildings
[at Mesa Verde], ranging from
a log cabin to a New England
farm house, are not suitable,

neither do they carry out the
atmosphere which we and you,
wish to create."

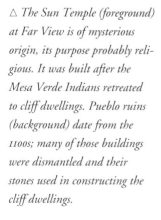

△ *The Sun Temple (foreground)*
at Far View is of mysterious
origin, its purpose probably reli-
gious. It was built after the
Mesa Verde Indians retreated
to cliff dwellings. Pueblo ruins
(background) date from the
1100s; many of those buildings
were dismantled and their
stones used in constructing the
cliff dwellings.

seeking caves for protection was not the determining factor in homebuilding."[18]

The NPS directorate approved Nusbaum's choice of style. A pueblo theme harmonized with the surrounding landscape and showed a genuine concern for the "esthetic value of park lands." His buildings were the new agency's first effort to create an appropriate architecture for park lands set aside for their cultural rather than their natural resources. Instead of following the developing "rustic" philosophy that emphasized the natural environment, Nusbaum chose to have his buildings emphasize a cultural theme. The success of the Mesa Verde buildings is due to the skillful adaptation of traditional building forms, construction techniques, and locally available materials for designs based on historical precedents. The Pueblo Revival style, sometimes with variations, became the standard for the quickly developing southwestern parks and monuments in the 1930s.[19] It is

now part of the mainstream of American Architecture, widely recognized as the "Santa Fe" style.

Nusbaum was superintendent at Mesa Verde until 1931, when he became director of the Laboratory of Anthropology in Santa Fe (an agency of the state of New Mexico). He remained a consultant and maintained strong ties with the park. He continued to review construction drawings for additions and alterations to the buildings he and Aileen designed. He even involved his friend, southwestern architect John Gaw Meem, in reviewing the architectural drawings prepared by the Plans and Design branch of the NPS in San Francisco. Nusbaum's hand guided all of the additions and alterations to his structures; he sent frequent memos about architectural details to the new park superintendent and design team. What Nusbaum created at Mesa Verde provided the impetus for a series of culturally related developments at other national parks and monuments.

△ The Log Cabin Museum was built in 1916 and has the distinction of being the first museum in the national park system. A unique feature of the log construction is seen in the corners: horizontal Douglas fir logs butt into vertical planks attached to a log column.

▷ Early Anasazi pueblo buildings derived their character from coursed sandstone walls similar to those in buildings throughout the region. At Chaco Canyon (a & b), combinations of stones readily available at the site were worked into courses; walls at Aztec Ruins (c) show a refinement, as bands of colored stones were set into the walls. Mesa Verde ruins (d) presented more rugged surfaces from irregular stones.

b

c

d

a

◁◁ *Typical southwestern corner fireplaces, exposed* viga-*and-*latia *ceilings, and pierced-tin light fixtures were used throughout the buildings at Mesa Verde.*

▷ *Administration Building exterior walls have a slight batter, curving inward at the top. They average 18 inches thick overall. The load-bearing walls support* vigas *eight to twelve inches in diameter that project through the masonry to the exterior. Half-round or split* latias *two to three inches in diameter are laid on top of the* vigas, *either perpendicular to the* vigas *or in a herringbone pattern. A layer of juniper bark covers the top of the* latias *for insulation. Wooden decking and the built-up roof protects the interior from the elements;* latias *in these buildings are purely decorative. Parapets surround the flat roofs and are pierced by sheet-metal-covered* canales (scuppers) *projecting a foot from the walls.*

Administrative District Buildings

Jesse and Aileen Nusbaum's legacy at Mesa Verde includes fourteen Pueblo Revival–style buildings. The Nusbaum buildings all contain common architectural elements. The principal building material is sandstone, some reused from prehistoric structures. Masonry is usually laid with the foundation courses set in cement mortar for strength and water resistance. Upper courses are laid with mortar nearly flush with the stone to give the walls a relatively smooth appearance; the mortar was made from local red earth.

Larger pieces of woodwork on the buildings – columns, lintels, squared beams, doors, and jambs – have adze marks that add texture and a pioneer feeling to the structures. Log columns, often capped by bolsters *(zapatas)* with sawn, serrated Indian patterns, support beams with joints carefully centered over the columns. Adze-marked doors are typically paneled; exterior doors often have openings with narrow wooden bars cut in Indian designs. Interiors have masonry walls plastered with either local red earth or modern plaster, rounded plastered corner fireplaces typical of the Southwest, and flagstone floors. Rustic, Franciscan-style built-in benches *(bancos)*, tables, chairs, desks, and closets with hand-chiseled, textured surfaces were designed by the Nusbaums and fashioned on the site during the long winter months. Pierced-tin light fixtures based on Mexican and Spanish Colonial designs contribute to the complement of handcrafted furnishings.

Superintendent's Residence

The first building completed by the Nusbaums in 1921 was the Superintendent's Residence. (This building remains in use as a residence, and the public is not allowed access.) Sited at the edge of the rim of Spruce Tree Canyon, the building evolved in three stages. Begun in 1921 as a four-room residence, two more rooms were added in 1928. During the 1930s the third remodeling added a portal, bedroom, bath, and study.

The stones for the walls of the Pueblo-style structure came from the park. Some with pecked markings came from prehistoric buildings. The building's blocky forms were typical of true Pueblo architecture, and a T-shaped door opening in the basement wall replicates those found in Mesa Verde ruins. Interior plaster walls have small, bull-nosed corners. Exposed *vigas* have gently coved plaster between them. Although Nusbaum owed much to Spanish Colonial architecture, his first venture emphasized the ancient Native American heritage.

Administration Building

The Administration Building (1923 with additions in 1928 and 1939–40) also began as a simple structure. Originally it contained only three rooms, but through the years the expanding staff required larger working space. The additions were all sympathetic to the original design. The adze marks visible on the shaped *vigas* added texture and a pioneer feeling to the building. The *vigas* and *latias* in the portal ceiling reinforced that historical feeling.

▷ *The principal building material at Mesa Verde was sandstone, some of the blocks reused from prehistoric structures. The oldest of the Nusbaum buildings, the Superintendent's Residence, contains some stones that still show pecked markings left by the prehistoric tools used to shape the building stones.*

▽▷ *The Log Cabin Museum was so popular that Nusbaum recognized the need for a larger and safer repository for artifacts from the ruins. When repeated requests for NPS funds were rejected, he solicited contributions from private donors and opened the new museum in 1924. Additions completed in 1936 expanded exhibit space and provided an auditorium.*

◁ *The Superintendent's Residence, built in 1921, was the largest of the staff housing units built at Mesa Verde. Masonry-bearing construction and flat roofs freed the designers to vary parapets and heights in the different spaces. The irregular building plan derived from traditional pueblo structures.*

◁ PARK AND RECREATION STRUCTURES *commended the Administration Building as "that unusual park structure, an administration building that does not accumulate their functions to gain impressive bulk."*

▷ *The entrance portal at the Administration Building incorporates many of the best stylistic elements of the Nusbaums' design work at Mesa Verde. The posts support corbels cut in zig-zag patterns copied from Indian designs. Sandstone courses are more regular than in the earlier Superintendent's Residence, and the finished appearance is smoother.*

Post Office

This small building was originally built as a comfort station (1923) tucked away in the staggered layers of bedrock west of the Administration Building. All the features of the Pueblo Revival style are included in the 450-square-foot structure. After its initial thirteen years of visitor service, the building was remodeled by the CCC and turned into a Post Office. The carefully restored interior lobby looks the same as it did in 1936. The *viga*-and-*latia* ceiling, the tiny writing desk, and the original brass post office boxes retain the building's 1936 ambience.

The Museum

The Mesa Verde Museum began as a small building during the 1920s but underwent a major expansion during the 1930s adding office, exhibit space, and an auditorium. The exterior elements of the completed rambling building closely adhered to the Pueblo Revival style.

The public entrance to the museum is sheltered by a large, L-shaped portal. Its flagstone floor, *viga*-and-*latia* ceiling, and Spanish Colonial *bancos* provide a quiet resting place for visitors. Sawn grilles shade the wood-frame windows. The motif is carried through to the interior, where built-in *bancos* create additional places for visitors to rest and contemplate the exhibits. A small, central courtyard with flagstone walkways and native plantings admits light into the exhibit rooms. The building responds to the surrounding topography by split-level changes through the exhibit rooms, a traditional concept in prehistoric and historic Southwestern architecture.

The most interesting of the interior spaces is the auditorium. Constructed in a configuration vaguely reminiscent of the Spanish Colonial churches of the Southwest, the room has a high ceiling, a rear balcony (choir loft), and a centered double-door entrance. The sawn balcony railing and staircase have visible adze marks. A decorative ceiling treatment has main *vigas* supporting three large *latias,* which in turn support small *latias* parallel to the main *vigas.* While Nusbaum started with a small building that recalled more of a pueblo feeling, major features such as the auditorium were indicative of the 1930s preference for Spanish Colonial.

The Ranger Station

The remoteness of Mesa Verde led the Nusbaums to plan a community building for both visitor and resident use. Construction on the Community House began in

◁◁ *Unusual among the Pueblo Revival–style residences is Residence #8. Originally built as a water storage tower in 1923, around 1935 the two-story round structure was remodeled and a small one-story extension added. The design was probably inspired by the ruins of a round tower at Far View.*

△ *The peeled-log posts supporting the balcony at the museum auditorium are finished smooth and contrast with the mottled texture of the adze marks on the bolsters and massive* vigas *above.*

▷ *The porch of the Community House–Natural History Museum (now serving as the ranger station) allowed visitors to experience Spruce Tree House from a framework of carefully crafted stone-and-timber construction, with* viga *ceiling, zig-zag corbels, and Spanish Colonial furniture. The projecting whittled* viga *ends extend at different lengths in a varied rhythm; distinctively shaped* canales *for carrying water off the flat roofs are above the* vigas.

1927. Its main features were a large upstairs room, a viewing porch, and a partial basement. The public space provided an ideal location for a porch extension to overlook the canyon containing Spruce Tree House. Furnished with handmade benches, the porch is a favorite spot from which to view and photograph the cliff dwelling ruins across the canyon. A stone floor, *viga* ceiling, and serrated bolsters create a frame of reference for the ruins and add to the quality of a quiet, interpretive experience.

The Community House eventually served as a natural history museum, and was converted into a ranger station in 1968.

The Ranger Club

The Ranger Club, built in 1927 to house single rangers, who shared community cooking, eating, and living spaces, is located across the road from the museum. The building, which began as a small structure for seasonal housing, was rebuilt five times through 1952. The original main block of the building has a large U-shaped addition to the north, surrounding a small patio. Seasonal rangers occupied the building until the late 1970s, when it was converted to an art gallery. In 1990–91, the building was again remodeled as the park library.

The Ranger Club is constructed on a relatively flat site but appears taller than other buildings in the complex because it is elevated several steps, exposing the foundation wall. The same vocabulary of forms, materials, and construction in the Pueblo Revival style are repeated. Stone walls are slightly battered, the roof is flat and surrounded by a parapet, and *viga* ends extend out from the exterior walls.

Aileen Nusbaum Hospital–Spruce Tree Terrace

Medical assistance for people in the remote park in its early days was a particular concern of Aileen Nusbaum. The primitive dirt roads to Mancos, Cortez, or Durango took hours to negotiate. A trained nurse with experience in France during World War I, she began plans to build a hospital to serve the needs of the immediate NPS community and the emergency needs of visitors. Her first efforts at providing medical assistance were in 1922, when a tent was purchased with funds donated by visitors, and medical students were hired as summer employees.

Requests for NPS funding for a hospital were fruitless until a congressional delegation visited the park in 1925. The delegation was impressed by Mrs. Nusbaum's activities, and the Interior Department allocation for that year included an item of $7,500 for the construction and equipping of the Aileen Nusbaum Hospital. Mrs. Nusbaum prepared the design drawings herself, but some difficulty arose in getting approval from NPS architects. The problem was resolved when the superintendent pointed out that the project was supported by congressional action. Construction was completed in 1927.

The hospital served the tiny Mesa Verde community for decades, until access to facilities in nearby towns became easier. Eventually the building was used as a first-aid station, until those services were moved to the ranger station (Community Building). In 1968, the NPS turned over the building's management to the park's concessioner. Alterations and additions since that time have changed the building to its present function, housing a snack bar and curio shop.

Residences

The NPS built additional employee housing on the mesa during the 1930s. The buildings followed the design scheme that Nusbaum had laid out in the 1920s. Fine stonework, portals, *viga-*and-*latia* ceilings, parapet roofs drained by *canales,* blocky room masses, and the interplay between solids and voids were evident in all of the houses. (Visitors please note: all residences are off limits to the public.)

The NPS also constructed some buildings unique in the park system. A number of seasonal workers at Mesa Verde were Navajo Indians. In response to their different cultural needs for housing, the NPS produced a series of stone hogans. Over the decades the hogans have been passed down through families to new generations of seasonal workers. This is the only ethnic housing ever built or sanctioned by the NPS.

Bandelier National Monument

The exceptional significance of the Bandelier buildings lies in their impact as a group.... Taken individually, each structure was a well-detailed, solid piece of work. Collectively, the development was a masterpiece combining fine architecture, landscape architecture, and arts and crafts. The unity of design threaded through the landscaping to the buildings and their contents ... and created a sense of place so strong that it predominates today. The whole is greater than the sum of the parts.

Laura Soullière Harrison, HISTORIC STRUCTURES REPORT

Three centuries of Indian culture are compressed into the history of Frijoles Canyon of northwestern New Mexico in the ruins at Bandelier National Monument. The history of this unique site, forty miles west of Santa Fe, and the complex of structures designed by the National Park Service are rare among national monuments and within the entire national park system.

Frijoles Canyon Settlement
The Anasazi Indians deserted their original settlements where they had lived during the ninth to thirteenth centuries, and one splinter group moved toward the upper Rio Grande area west of Santa Fe. The Rio Grande Anasazi settled into the canyon-slashed slopes of the Pajarito Plateau and for the next three centuries built villages in the cliffs of the deep gorges.

Rito de los Frijoles (Bean Creek) is an oasis in the dry country of New Mexico. Extending for approximately two miles on the Frijoles Canyon valley floor and carved into cliff walls of compressed volcanic ash–tuff *(tufa)*– are the ruins of masonry houses and cave rooms. The houses and ceremonial structures were built of blocks of tuff carved from the cliffs and logs carried from the nearby forested mesas. In decline by the time of Coronado's expedition in 1540, the Pajarito villages are not mentioned in the explorer's records. Oral traditions link several present-day Rio Grande pueblos to the inhabitants of Frijoles Canyon.

Bandelier National Monument
At the turn of the century, interest developed in creating a national park in northern New Mexico that would include the Frijoles Canyon ruins. The movement was led by Edgar L. Hewett, an educator and archaeologist, and Iowa Senator John F. Lacey, who was prominent in conservation activities. A struggle ensued over the next three decades for preservation of the site.[20] Not considered important enough for national park status when Mesa Verde was established in 1906, Bandelier National Monument was created in 1916 by President Wilson, who stated: "Certain prehistoric aboriginal ruins ... are of unusual ethnology, scientific, and educational interest ... that the public interests would be promoted by reserving these relics of a vanished people, with as much land as may be necessary for the protection thereof."[21]

▷ *The excavated pueblo of Tyuonyi (foreground) and restored talus house and cave dwellings (background) in Frijoles Canyon.*

▷▽ *A trail from the Bandelier Visitor Center leads to cave dwellings along the northern wall of Frijoles Canyon. The cliff is composed of compressed volcanic ash, called "tuff," and rooms were carved out of it with stone tools.*

Despite difficult access from the mesa down to the Rito Frijoles, the small dude ranch built in 1907 was expanded by George and Evelyn Frey when they purchased the property in 1925. There was no road into the canyon in the national monument's early years.

Supplies were lowered from the mesa by a tramway, and visitors either rode horseback or hiked down a steep trail to the canyon floor. When NPS director Horace Albright wanted to expand the national park system, he succeeded in having Bandelier transferred from Forest Service jurisdiction to the NPS by presidential proclamation in 1932; it retained its national monument status but was enlarged to include additional ruins. The process of protecting the ruins, improving access, and creating visitor services was assigned to the Southwestern Monuments unit of the NPS.

The Frijoles Canyon Development

The design of the Frijoles Canyon development was the product of the NPS Branch of Plans and Design, whose architects and landscape architects worked under the direction of Thomas C. Vint. Construction work was performed by CCC crews, and the final structure in the 31-building complex was completed in 1941.

The building group provided a complete development for a national monument: visitor services, lodging for guests, and office space and residences for employees. Lodging was necessary because the nearest accommoda-

△ *Tyuonyi pueblo ruins set in the deep canyon gorge, seen from the talus houses at the base of the cliff. Anasazi Indians lived here from the thirteenth to sixteenth centuries.*

tions were in Santa Fe, reached in the 1930s by eighteen miles of rough dirt road and seventeen miles of partially paved highway. The design concept, construction program, and finished architecture represent a fascinating episode in the creation of a cohesive complex of distinctive and exceptional Pueblo Revival design.

Appreciation for the traditional building styles of New Mexico emerged around the turn of the century. The additive, massive forms of the pueblo, with small-scale openings, battered walls made from plastered adobe bricks, flat roofs, and projecting *vigas* and *canales* became fashionable among the artists moving to Taos and Santa Fe. NPS designers referred to the restored Palace of Governors in Santa Fe, the Santa Fe Art Museum, and La Fonda Hotel, which are all excellent examples of the regional architectural style.

The choice of Pueblo Revival style at Bandelier fit perfectly with the goal that national park architecture should harmonize with its environment. It expressed the true principles of Rustic architecture, a national movement rather than a local style, one that could embrace any number of regional styles and still produce consistently individual structures that looked as though they belonged in their setting.

The Frijoles Canyon development was conceived as a building group wrapped around three sides of a central parking plaza. Administrative offices are at one end, the walls of the maintenance yard at the other end, and the buildings of the new Frijoles Canyon Lodge on a connecting side. (The lodge is no longer in service.) The fourth side is bordered by the Rito Frijoles. The two main plaza facades are the lodge lobby and dining room and the headquarters–museum building. The individual guest lodges were reached by a series of flagstone pathways that led up from the lodge lobby through small courtyards and patios that stepped up the hillside on several levels. Outdoor areas were planted with native vegetation. A separate complex of employee residences was placed up the hillside from the entrance road, concealed from visitor view by vegetation and the terrain.

Locally available building materials were used, and the structures reflect local cultural traditions in scale, color, texture, and massing. Handmade furniture and light fixtures grace the interiors. The existing topography was respected – from the flat canyon floor to the steeper terrain toward the base of the cliff – by constructing buildings on several levels. Stepped-roof parapets appropriately reflect these elevation changes. Landscape planning contributed to the final effect, including blasted rocks along the entrance road stained for a weathered appearance.

The completed complex shows an architectural unity

FLOOR PLAN

△▷▽ *The Administration
Building is an expression of
Pueblo Revival style as adapted
by* NPS *designers for the Frijoles
Canyon development. The
building was admired for its
"very simplicity and modest
size." Separate buildings are
unified by a scheme of roofs
supported by peeled-log columns
mounted by carved bolsters carrying hand-hewn beams.*

of theory and style that begins with site and building
design and continues inside with fine interior details.
Collectively, it is a masterpiece combining fine architecture, landscape architecture, and arts and crafts.[22]

Civilian Conservation Corps
Passage of the Emergency Conservation Works Act
(ECW) in March 1933 created the Civilian Conservation

Corps and provided funding and manpower to push
forward on Director Horace Albright's decision to pro-
ceed with the canyon road at Bandelier. Working with
Frank "Boss" Pinkley, of the Southwestern National
Monument office, a team of designers under architect
Lyle Bennett began work on the landscape and build-
ing concepts, and the U.S. Army built a camp for the
CCC workers.

The ingenuity of the designers and managers was
severely tested by the funding constraints of the ECW
program, which had a statutory limit of $1,500 on mate-
rials for any one building constructed in a national park
and a limit of six months for workers' enrollment in the
CCC, although workers could and often did re-enlist.
The solution that successfully overcame this challenge
was the decision to design and build in a modular manner. By building many small projects and connecting
them by portals, courtyards, and walls, the architects
devised a cohesive and pleasing development on a very
human scale. For example, the administrative offices and

◁◁◁ *The Plaza facade provided access to lodge courtyards through entryways set into thick adobe walls.*

△ *Frijoles Canyon development from the mesa, showing the overall design planned around a plaza. Ancient talus houses can be seen at the base of the cliff behind the development.*

▷△ *Bandelier shows both a cultural and physical connection to the Southwest. Planners merged buildings into the landscape with Pueblo-style designs that used a simple approach to massing, wall openings, materials, and color. They used structure as decoration, as when* vigas *create pleasing rhythms of shadows or lintels emphasize openings in contrast with wall surfaces.*

△ Lodges and courtyards are naturally fitted to the terrain. Wall surfaces are completely plastered, and vigas and canales project from the roof line below parapets. These guest quarters, seen as they appeared in 1940, today serve as employee quarters and government offices and are off limits to the public.

museum were constructed as two separate buildings connected by a portal, which resulted in three separate projects. Several years later, an additional room was constructed linking the two buildings together into one large building.[23]

The Frijoles Canyon Lodge followed the same pattern; instead of one large building to house the main dining room and the lobby, two separate buildings were constructed, creating a comfortable patio space between them. The individual buildings are tied together by a series of stone walls, plastered portals, flagstone walkways, and stone-edged planting beds. The consistent use of stone and mud-plastered walls gives a strong sense of unity. The interplay of mass and void, as when a solid building face is relieved by a recessed portal, adds architectural interest to the small building volumes.

The quality of CCC workmanship exceeded all expectations. Unskilled enrollees labored alongside an enthusiastic project superintendent and foremen who were not averse to doing work themselves while teaching. Crews went to nearby forests to cut logs, worked in quarries and shaped stones, and erected the structures. The craftsmanship was excellent; woodworkers became accomplished and were hired for projects in other parks, including crafting of the handsome museum doors at Tumacacori National Monument.

△ The weather has taken its toll on these buildings during the fifty years since they were completed. The original mud plaster finish soon wore off, but was replaced with the same finish used on the original. Projecting vigas and canales with whittled ends have been replaced when they have rotted.

△ CCC workers sawing rock
to be used as building stones,
June 1938.

◁ Tuff walls were gently battered and then washed with a
thin coat of pojuaque mud
plaster, designed to wash off
and eventually give the rough,
coursed ashlar masonry a
weathered, aged appearance.
A characteristic element of
Pueblo style is the projecting
vigaends of round, peeled logs,
axe-hewn for a primitive appearance. Parapets extending
above the asphalt-covered roofs
are drained by canales routed
into the viga ends. Most of the
windows are multilight, with
wood-frame casements, and
some are covered with band-
sawn grilles in zig-zag patterns.
Hand-hewn lintels cap door
and window openings, and
stone sills are used on exteriors.
Column bolsters have been deco-
ratively carved with Spanish
Colonial designs.

△ Ceilings made of peeled half-
round aspen latias, placed perpendicular or in herringbone
patterns on the flat-adzed vigas.

△△▷▷ All of the interior and
exterior light fixtures are Spanish Colonial design, made of soldered tin that was scratched and
then painted. CCC workers
handcrafted them according to
designs prepared by the NPS.

▷ *Furniture throughout the village exteriors and interiors was built with mortise joints and typically hand-pegged. Each piece had hand-carved southwest Indian or Spanish Colonial decorative designs.*

The Buildings

NPS architect Lyle Bennett supervised the overall landscape design and the majority of the building designs. His supervision ensured continuity, for all were designed and constructed with similar architectural elements and materials. Stone, timber, gravel, clay, and sand came from the site or the nearby Santa Fe National Forest. The basic building material was stone cut from the local rhyolite tuff. The soft stone could be rough cut at the quarry and later finished at a building site.

All interiors followed Spanish Colonial and Pueblo Revival themes. Wall surfaces were finished with hard plaster and were often painted with Spanish Colonial and Indian motifs. Most ceilings were exposed *vigas* supporting aspen *latias* placed over the *vigas,* sometimes in herringbone patterns. Traditional corner fireplaces built of tuff and firebrick were placed in many rooms. Interior woodwork was frequently carved in decorative patterns developed by the designers specifically for the project. Typical floors were flagstone, varnished to a high, glossy finish. The additive quality of the Pueblo Revival style was expressed by a one- or two-step change in level between rooms.

The overall unity of the design was completed with a Spanish Colonial theme incorporated into the lodge furniture and light fixtures, designed by NPS architects and built by CCC craftsmen. Exterior and interior light fixtures, switchplates, and mirror frames were of cut tin, scratched, dotted, soldered together, and painted. Federal Arts Project artists Pablita Velarde, Helmut Naumer, Chris Jorgensen, and Raymond Terken all contributed artwork.

The Bandelier project is remarkable for its high-quality craftsmanship. The Frijoles Canyon development employed several thousand people, and everything from stonecutting to interior details and furnishings was executed at a master craftsman level. Many were unskilled workers provided with on-the-job training. Working with traditional techniques, such as broad axes and adzes, the CCC enrollees' work is exemplary. The Bandelier building group is also noteworthy as the largest collection of CCC-built structures in a national park not subsequently diluted by the addition of new buildings.

Southwest Region III Headquarters Building

The Pueblo Style ... a massive-looking archless style. Its special feature is the projecting roof beam, or viga.... Some have battered walls; most have walls with blunt angles and irregularly rounded parapets; walls are always plastered.... Roofs are always flat; when the building is more than one story, the stepped-up roofs of the Indian community house may be imitated. A veranda, or portal, with wooden posts that often have wooden capitals, is a common feature.

Marcus Whiffen, AMERICAN ARCHITECTURE SINCE 1780

The Old Santa Fe Trail winds its way north from Mexico to the historic center of Santa Fe – the Plaza – and then threads a diminishing path into surrounding subdivisions and ranches. A bend in the trail about two miles southeast of the Plaza was selected for the site of the NPS Southwest Regional Offices in 1937. The completed structure, 24,000 square feet, is the largest adobe office building and one of the largest adobe secular buildings in the United States.

Designed by Cecil Doty from the National Park Service and built by CCC and WPA crews, the building's massing, plan, materials, and construction methods exhibit a mastery of the Pueblo Revival style. The interior details, furnishings, and artwork incorporate superior workmanship and carry out themes of the Spanish Colonial era in the Southwest.

The setting, in the Sangre de Christo foothills, was chosen by Acting Regional Director Herbert Maier and shifted NPS headquarters from Oklahoma City to the expanding Southwest Region. Maier was a skilled administrator, and his architectural design talents are evident in his work for the museums at Yosemite and Yellowstone. Cecil Doty was selected as the building designer and Harvey Cornell for the landscape design. This talented team, working with Maier, agreed that the Pueblo Revival style and Spanish Colonial themes were appropriate. Plans were under way when approval to locate the offices near Santa Fe were approved by the Secretary of the Interior. Construction began in the fall of 1937, and the building was completed in 1939.

Early photographs of the building, taken before vegetation obscured the view, illustrate the strong Pueblo and Spanish Colonial influences. The design's focal point is the dominant two-story mass defining the entrance, with the lobby and offices of the regional directorate upstairs. The architects created a controlled progression from the parking lot to the building by screening the view of the main entrance behind an adobe wall. A gate in the wall leads to a flagstone path and the entrance doors. The double doors, sandblasted and etched with adze marks to give a primitive appearance, are flanked by massive buttresses – typical southwestern mission structures.[24]

Textured surfaces on the plastered adobe walls batter

▷ Plantings and brick walkways in the central patio, elements similar to those in early missions and haciendas in the region.

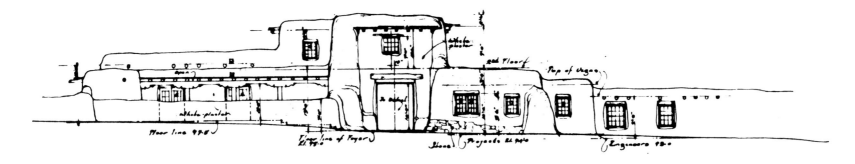

△ *Plastered adobe walls at the entrance facade combine features from southwestern mission structures. The wall surface at the entry is recessed from the buttresses and surrounding walls and painted a cream color, to emphasize the indentations. The two-story entrance is flanked by one-story wings with external buttresses and rows of projecting* vigas.

▷ NPS *Southwest Region Headquarters in 1939, soon after it was completed. Today, the building is an officially designated National Historic Landmark. Its success is due to the superb combination of building and landscape design derived from regional cultural influences.*

from a three-foot-thick base to an irregular roof line of parapets, similar to the massing used in missions at Santa Fe, Taos, Chimayo, and Las Trampas. A contrasting, cream-colored plastered surface, asymmetrically framed by massive buttresses, simulates a mission facade and emphasizes wall thicknesses in the reveals. Massive, double-leaf, carved doors spanned by a hewn lintel beam are further recessed into the surface. *Viga* ends projecting through the upper wall and a glint of hay used as a plaster binder in the wall surfaces illustrate traditional pueblo construction techniques.

The building plan maintains the theme of a Spanish Colonial mission compound. At both sides of the entrance are one-story office wings around central patios, a large one to the west and a smaller one to the east. Most of the interconnected offices in the west wing open directly onto the veranda surrounding the patio. The ground-floor conference room and second-floor

offices of the regional directorate show careful attention to detail, including *viga*-and-*latia* ceilings, corner fireplaces, hammered-tin chandeliers, and hand-carved furniture. The irregularity of the overall plan up or down a few steps and the slight changes in building levels demonstrate the informal qualities of Pueblo Revival and Spanish Colonial architecture.[25]

The patios are open-air outdoor rooms, typical of the architectural style, with peeled-log columns capped by carved bolsters and *viga* ends around the outside. Water flows into a fountain and a nineteen-foot-diameter pool that has built-in *bancos* around it. Plantings add to the serenity of this space, which is favored for work breaks, lunches, and small gatherings.

The combination of the talented NPS designers and the availability of CCC crews and WPA funding accounted for the success of this project. For the finer details of New Mexican architecture, Doty called upon

◁ *The Spanish mission planning concept created a patio at the center of the 24,000-square-foot adobe headquarters building.*

◁ *Desert light at sunset warms the buff plastered surfaces to a rosy hue. Elements from both Pueblo Revival and Spanish Colonial styles are united, as seen in the plastered walls, viga ends, log columns, and carved corbels.*

▷ *Shaded verandas are framed by log columns, carved corbels, and exposed vigas.*

▷ *The main conference room as originally furnished in 1939. The painting of Stephen Mather on horseback in Glacier Park is by Oden Hullenkramer, a Santa Fe artist. The portrait now hangs in the entrance lobby of the Regional Headquarters Building.*

▽ *Conference room furniture, designed by Cecil Doty and handcrafted by Civilian Conservation Corps workers. Several major pieces were patterned after early New Mexican furniture in the Palace of Governors in Santa Fe. Chairs, tables, and patio benches were built of local yellow pine, stained pale gray, rubbed, and then waxed.*

The working drawings called for intricate hand carving and geometric Spanish Colonial designs.

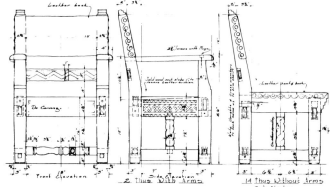

a construction foreman named Carlos Vierra.[26] The CCC crew – 104 workers between the ages of seventeen and twenty-three – had little or no building experience and were paid $30 per month, plus room and board. They dug foundations, formed adobe bricks, cut and shaped timbers, and erected the building. WPA workers installed the heating system and contributed to other portions of the finished work.

Most of the soil for the 10" x 14" x 4" adobe bricks came from the site excavation. In all, 280,000 were made. Specifications directed that the adobe be "mixed with straw in the usual manner."

The building is embellished with fine architectural details, hand-carved furniture, and hammered-tin fixtures. The furniture and light fixtures were designed by Cecil Doty; the hand-hammered, pierced-tin lights are all electrified and vary in size from large chandeliers to small, one-bulb lanterns in the portals. CCC workers built the mortise-and-tenon furniture under the supervision of Vernon Hunter, director of the Federal Arts Project of New Mexico.

Typical Pueblo Revival details are evident in the construction, furnishings, and fixtures. The entrance lobby was given special treatment with exposed hand-hewn ceiling beams and a log staircase (covered with flat risers and treads in 1941). A hand-hammered tin chandelier, massive Spanish Colonial furniture, and a large painting of Stephen Mather fill the lobby space. The office of the regional director is lent an air of special importance by means of an exposed *viga* ceiling, a corner fireplace, windowsills two feet thick, and decorative items that include Navajo rugs, hand-carved furniture, and pueblo pottery.

As the building was being completed, Doty and the landscape architect, John Kell, were granted Federal Arts Project funds to purchase artwork for the building. They visited pueblos in the surrounding area with a $100 limit for each pueblo. The resulting collection of Navajo rugs, signed pottery, and other important artwork is displayed throughout the building.[27]

Doty noted that the building could not have been constructed under any regional director other than Herbert Maier. The magical combination of Maier's administrative brilliance, the immediate availability of a work force and CCC/WPA funding, the use of local materials, and Doty and Cornell's design talents combined to create a truly exceptional building.

Notes

A Sense of Place

1. James Marston Fitch, *Historic Preservation* (New York: McGraw-Hill, 1982), 23. Fitch, as well as other writers on the topic of historic preservation, provides a cultural background for historic preservation of buildings in urban settings, but ignores those in rural landscapes or natural settings.

2. Robin Winks, "Conservation in America: National Character as Revealed by Preservation," in *The Future of the Past* (New York: Watson-Guptill, 1976).

3. Nathan Weinberg, *Preservation in American Towns and Cities* (Boulder, Colo.: Westview Press, 1979), xv.

4. Roderick Nash, *Wilderness and the American Mind,* rev. ed. (New Haven: Yale University Press, 1973). This is a basic reference on the American experience and changing attitudes toward the wilderness.

5. Thaddeus Harris, *The Journal of a Tour into the Territory of the Allegheny Mountains* (Boston, n.p., 1805), 71-72.

6. William C. Everhart, *The National Park Service* (Boulder, Col.: Western Press, 1983), 6.

7. Alfred Runte, *National Parks: The American Experience* (Lincoln: University of Nebraska Press, 1979), 14.

8. Clarence King's Geological Survey of the Fortieth Parallel (1867), Dr. Ferdinand Vandeveer Hayden's Geographical Survey of the Territories (1867), Lieutenant George M. Wheeler's Geographical Surveys West of the 100th Meridian (1869), and Major John Wesley Powell's Geographical and Topographical Survey of the Colorado River (1870).

9. Nash, *Wilderness,* 83. Further documentation of early western photographers is found in Weston Naef, *Era of Exploration: The Rise of Landscape Photography in the American West, 1860-1885* (Boston: New York Graphic Society, 1975), and Karen Current and William R. Current, *Photography in the Old West* (New York: Harry N. Abrams, 1978).

10. Runte, *National Parks,* 29.

11. *Statutes at Large,* 13 (1864): 325.

12. Runte, *National Parks,* 57.

13. Gifford Pinchot, *The Fight for Conservation* (New York: Doubleday, Page and Co., 1910), 45. See also other references on Pinchot: Harold J. Pinkett, *Gifford Pinchot: Public and Private Forester* (Urbana: University of Illinois Press, 1970), and Douglas H. Strong, *The Conservationists* (Menlo Park, Calif.: Addison-Wesley, 1971), 65-89.

14. Runte, *National Parks,* 70.

15. Charles B. Hosmer, Jr., *Presence of the Past* (New York: G. P. Putnam's Sons, 1965).

16. Ibid., 188-295.

17. William Sumner Appleton, *The Colonial Homes of New England, Shall They Be Preserved?* (Boston: Society for the Preservation of New England Antiquities, 1913), 6, 7. See also Hosmer, *Presence of the Past,* 237-59.

18. John Ise, *Our National Park Policy: A Critical History* (Baltimore: The Johns Hopkins University Press, 1961), 143-53.

19. Everhart, *National Park Service,* 11.

20. *Statutes at Large,* 34 (1906): 255.

21. *Statutes at Large,* 49 (1935): 666.

22. *Statutes at Large,* 63 (1949): 927.

23. *Statutes at Large,* 80 (1966): 215.

24. Frederick Law Olmsted, "The Yosemite Valley and the Mariposa Big Trees: A Preliminary Report (1865)," with an introductory note by Laura Wood Roper, *Landscape Architecture 43* (October 1952): 16.

25. Laura Wood Roper, *FLO, A Biography of Frederick Law Olmsted* (Baltimore: The Johns Hopkins University Press, 1973), 285.

26. Bradford Torrey and Francis H. Allen, eds., *The Journals of Henry David Thoreau* (Boston, n.p., 1906), 14:305.

27. Hans Huth, "Yosemite, the Story of an Idea," *Sierra Club Bulletin 33* (March 1948): 65.

28. *New York Times,* August 8, 1864.

29. Harvey H. Kaiser, *Great Camps of the Adirondacks* (Boston: David R. Godine, Publisher, 1982).

30. George Wilson Pierson, *Tocqueville in America* (New York: Doubleday Anchor Books, 1959), 210.

31. Runte, *National Parks,* 9.

32. Phyllis Myers, "The National Park Service as Client," *Architecture,* December 1984, p. 42.

33. Ibid.

The Western Landscape

1. John Muir, "The World Parks and Forest Reservations of the West," *Atlantic Monthly,* January 1898, p. 15.

2. Ansel Adams, *Ansel Adams: An Autobiography* (Boston: Little Brown, 1985), 291.

3. John Wesley Powell, *The Exploration of the Colorado River and Its Canyons* (New York: Dover Publications, 1961), 397.

4. Ibid.

5. Ibid., 394.

6. Wallace Stegner, *Beyond the Hundredth Meridian* (Boston: Houghton Mifflin, 1954), 178–79.

7. The Conservation Foundation, *National Parks for a New Generation: Visions, Reality, Prospects* (Washington, 1985), 32. The quotation is from Robin Winks, "Upon Reading Sellars and Runte," *Journal of Forest History* (July 1983): 142.

8. Wallace Stegner, "The Best Idea We Ever Had," *Wilderness* (Spring 1983): 4.

9. *The National Parks: Index,* available from the Office of Public Affairs, Division of Publications, National Park Service, U.S. Department of the Interior, defines park system nomenclature and describes the units within the system.

10. Gilbert H. Grosvenor, "The Land of the Best," *National Geographic Magazine* (April 1916), 327.

11. R. Elsam, *Essay on Rural Architecture* (London: Bernard Quariteh, 1842), 6-8.

12. Andrew Jackson Downing, *The Architecture of Country Houses* (New York: Appleton, 1850).

13. The acceptance of Rustic design is illustrated in William S. Wicks, *Log Cabins: How to Build and Furnish Them* (New York: Forest and Stream, 1889).

14. Harvey H. Kaiser, *Great Camps of the Adirondacks* (Boston, David R. Godine, Publisher, 1982).

15. Horace M. Albright, *The Birth of the National Park Service: The Founding Years, 1913–1933* (Salt Lake City: Howe Brothers, 1985), 70–71.

16. William E. Tweed, Laura Soullière, and Henry G. Law, "National Park Service Rustic Architecture: 1916–1942" (National Park Service, Western Regional Office, Division of Cultural Resource Management, December 1977), unpublished manuscript.

17. U.S. Department of the Interior, National Park Service, *Annual Report, 1918.*

18. Joyce Zaitlin, *Gilbert Stanley Underwood: His Rustic, Art Deco, and Federal Architecture* (Malibu, Calif.: Pangloss Press, 1989).

19. U.S. Department of the Interior, National Park Service, *Park Structures and Facilities* (1935), 1.

The Far West

1. U.S. Department of the Interior, National Park Service, *Olympic National Park: Historic Resource Study* (1983), 1–2.

2. Ibid., 408.

3. U.S. Department of the Interior, National Park Service, *Park Structures and Facilities* (1935), 1.

4. Department of the Interior, *Olympic National Park,* 299–300.

5. Ibid., 221.

6. U.S. Department of Agriculture, Forest Service Division, *Acceptable Plans Forest Service Administrative Buildings* (1938); U.S. Department of Agriculture, Division of Engineering, *Improvement Handbook* (1937).

7. William E. Tweed, Laura Soullière, and Henry G. Law, "National Park Service Rustic Architecture: 1916–1942," National Park Service, Western Regional Office, Division of Cultural Resource Management (December 1977), unpublished manuscript.

8. Edwin Way Teale, ed., *The Wilderness World of John Muir* (Boston: Houghton Mifflin, 1954), 314.

9. John Muir, *Our National Parks* (Boston: Houghton Mifflin, 1901), 30–31.

10. Alfred Runte, *National Parks: The American Experience* (Lincoln: University of Nebraska Press, 1979), 66.

11. John Ise, *Our National Park Policy: A Critical History* (Baltimore: The Johns Hopkins University Press, 1961), 121–22.

12. U.S. Department of the Interior, National Park Service, *Park Structures and Facilities* (1935), 28.

13. Ibid., 80.

14. Mission 66 was conceived by NPS director Conrad L. Wirth in 1955 to respond to the huge backlog of deferred maintenance and the dramatic post–World War II growth in park visitation. It was a ten-year rehabilitation and capital development program to improve facilities in time for the Park Service's fiftieth anniversary in 1966.

15. E. A. Davidson, "White River Inspection Trip, October 28–31, 1926," Park Development, Construction Programs, Archives, Mount Rainier National Park.

16. See *Fort Vancouver,* Department of the Interior, National Park Service, National Park Handbook 113 (1981), with contributions by Archie Satterfield and David Lavender describing the history of Fort Vancouver, its role in the Pacific Northwest, and the fort's reconstruction.

17. The chief factor at Fort Vancouver was in charge of headquarters for the Hudson's Bay Company in the Columbia district. The position entailed wide authority and responsibility to supervise trading, dispense justice, protect the outpost and its occupants, and oversee relations between Indians and the increasing numbers of settlers.

18. Joyce Zaitlin, *Gilbert Stanley Underwood: His Rustic, Art Deco, and Federal Architecture* (Malibu, Calif.: Pangloss Press, 1989), 132–33.

19. See Linda Greene, *Historic Resource Study: Crater Lake National Park, Oregon* (Denver: National Park Service, Denver Service Center, 1984), for extensive background information on the cultural resources at Crater Lake National Park. The study was used as an invaluable reference source for the history of Crater Lake Lodge.

20. U.S. Department of the Interior, National Park Service, *CRM,* vol. 15, no. 6 (1992), 67–69.

21. Laura Soullière Harrison, *Architecture in the Parks, National Historic Landmark Theme Study,* U.S. Department of the Interior, National Park Service (1986), 344.

22. Ibid., 390.

23. I am grateful to Laura Soullière Harrison for much of the material used in this section on Oregon Caves National Monument. Her work, *Architecture in the Parks, National Historic Landmark Theme Study,* is an invaluable reference.

24. Ibid., 389.

25. Ibid., 390.

26. Laura Wood Roper, "The Yosemite Valley and the Mariposa Big Trees," *Landscape Architecture 43* (October 1952): 13.

27. Ibid., 15.

28. Joyce Zaitlin's *Underwood* is an excellent resource for the

reader interested in a thorough examination of the architect's work. His projects at Yosemite and for the Union Pacific Railroad at Zion, Bryce, Cedar Breaks, and the Grand Canyon's North Rim, and his influence on Timberline Lodge, represent a significant chapter in Rustic architecture.

29. Herbert Maier, "The Purpose of the Museum in the National Parks," *Yosemite Nature Notes* (May 1926): 38.

30. Horace Albright memorandum on the Ahwahnee development (from file containing correspondence to the "Olmsted Brothers," 1927/1928?), Yosemite National Park Research Library.

31. Harrison, *Architecture in the Parks,* 177.

32. Eldridge Spencer designed the later cottages at the Ahwahnee Hotel.

33. Harrison, *Architecture in the Parks,* 28.

34. Gilbert H. Grosvenor, "The Land of the Best," *National Geographic Magazine* (April 1916): 327.

35. Tweed, Soullière, and Law, "National Park Service Rustic Architecture," 57.

36. The *Guidelines* were prepared in a cooperative effort between the National Park Service and the San Francisco architectural firm of Esherick, Homsey, Dodge, and Davis, with George Homsey a principal contributor.

37. Department of the Interior, National Park Service, *Park and Recreation Structures* (1938), 7.

The Rocky Mountains and the Plateau Country

1. James Sheire, *Glacier National Park Historic Resource Study,* U.S. Department of the Interior, National Park Service (1970), 106.

2. Ibid., 107–108.

3. Laura Soullière Harrison, *Architecture in the Parks, National Historic Landmark Theme Study,* U.S. Department of the Interior, National Park Service (1986), 143.

4. Sheire, *Glacier National Park,* 199.

5. *The Sierra Club Guides to the National Parks: Rocky Mountains and the Great Plains* (New York: Stewart, Tabori & Chang), 205.

6. Susan Scofield and Jeremy Schmidt, *The Inn at Old Faithful* (Crowsnest Assoc., 1979), 23.

7. Freeman Tilden, *Interpreting Our Heritage* (Chapel Hill: University of North Carolina Press, 1957); *National Parks Magazine,* vol. 34, no. 91 (October-December, 1947); see also John Ise, *Our National Park Policy, A Critical History* (Baltimore: The Johns Hopkins University Press, 1961), 200–202.

8. Herbert Maier, "The Purpose of the Museum in the National Parks," *Yosemite Nature Notes* (May 1926): 37.

9. The "legend" of the campfire conversation is described in Nathaniel Langford, *Diary of the Washburn Expedition to the Yellowstone and Firehole Rivers in the Year 1870* (St. Paul: F. J. Haynes, 1905), 117–18. The tale is suspect because it did not appear until Langford's diary was published more than thirty years later, prepared from his own notes and those of others. See Aubrey L. Haines, *The Yellowstone Story* (Boulder: Colorado Associated University Press, 1977), 1:130 and footnote 46.

10. Bernard DeVoto, *Across the Wide Missouri* (Boston:

Houghton Mifflin, 1947), 49.

11. Robert Betts, *Along the Ramparts of the Tetons: The Saga of Jackson Hole, Wyoming* (Boulder: Colorado Associated University Press, 1978), 6.

12. Donald Hough, *The Cocktail Hour in Jackson Hole* (New York: W. W. Norton, 1956), 169.

13. Washington Irving, *Astoria or Anecdotes of an Enterprise Beyond the Rocky Mountains* (Philadelphia, 1836), 200.

14. Bernard DeVoto, *The Year of Decision: 1846* (Boston: Houghton Mifflin, 1942), 163.

15. Robert W. Righter, *Crucible for Conservation: The Creation of Grand Teton National Park* (Boulder: Colorado Associated University Press, 1982), 23.

16. John Ise, *Our National Park Policy: A Critical History* (Baltimore: The Johns Hopkins University Press, 1961).

17. Horace M. Albright, *The Birth of the National Park Service: The Founding Years, 1913–1933* (Salt Lake City: Howe Brothers, 1985), 165.

18. Ibid., 166.

19. Righter, *Crucible for Conservation,* 57–59.

20. Ise, *Our National Park Policy,* 492.

21. C. W. Buchholtz, *Rocky Mountain National Park: A History* (Boulder: Colorado Associated University Press, 1983), 34–35.

22. Harlin M. Fuller and LeRoy R. Hafen, *The Journal of Captain John R. Bell* (Glendale, Calif.: Arthur H. Clark Co., 1973), 142.

23. Buchholtz, *Rocky Mountain National Park,* 42.

24. Bayard Taylor, *Colorado: A Summer Trip* (New York: G. P. Putnam and Son, 1867), 165–66.

25. Hildegarde Hawthorne and Esther Burnell Mills, *Enos Mills of the Rockies* (New York: Houghton Mifflin, 1935), 24.

26. White wrote *In the Heart of a Fool* in the summer of 1911 in a tent near a rented cottage at Moraine Park. His *Emporia Gazette* editorials gained him national fame, speaking as the voice of common sense and earning him two Pulitzer Prizes.

27. Florence Johnson Shoemaker, "The Story of Estes–Rocky Mountain National Park Region" (M.A. thesis, Colorado State College, Greeley, 1940), 49.

28. Angus M. Woodbury, "A History of Southern Utah and Its National Parks." Originally published in the *Utah Historical Quarterly,* July-October 1944; revised and privately published by the author, 1950, pp. 128–31.

29. J. C. Fremont, *Narrative of the Exploring Expedition to the Rocky Mountains* (n.p., New York, 1846).

30. Joyce Zaitlin, *Gilbert Stanley Underwood: His Rustic, Art Deco, and Federal Architecture* (Malibu, Calif.: Pangloss Press, 1989), 41–42.

31. Nick Scrattish, *Historic Resource Study, Bryce Canyon National Park* (Denver: National Park Service, 1980), 64. Zaitlin attributes concern about steady erosion at the edge of the cliffs as the probable reason for this decision (*Underwood,* 45).

The Southwest

1. A museum has recently opened at Green River, Utah, at the site of Powell's departure. It provides extensive information about Powell and his explorations.

2. President Theodore Roosevelt is recognized as the first presi-

dent to make conservation a national goal. Acting when exploitation of the nation's resources strongly influenced policy decisions, he broke from the utilitarian viewpoint and promoted landscape preservation. Through the 1891 Forest Preserve Act, he set aside 148 million acres of land for conservation. The 1906 Act for the Preservation of Antiquities provided Roosevelt with the presidential prerogative to set aside sites of outstanding historic, scientific, or scenic interest as national monuments. In all, he designated sixteen national monuments, including the Grand Canyon, until Congress could be persuaded to declare it a national park; John Ise, *Our National Park Policy, A Critical History* (Baltimore: The Johns Hopkins University Press, 1961), 230–38.

3. Virginia L. Grattan, *Mary Colter: Builder Upon the Red Earth* (Flagstaff, Arizona: Northland Press, 1980), 19.

4. Ibid.

5. Ibid., 80–90.

6. Ibid., 84.

7. Joyce Zaitlin, *Gilbert Stanley Underwood: His Rustic, Art Deco, and Federal Architecture* (Malibu, Calif.: Pangloss Press, 1989), 84–100.

8. Ibid., 100.

9. Rexford Newcomb. *Spanish-Colonial Architecture in the United States* (New York: J. J. Augustin, 1937), 19.

10. Laura Soullière Harrison, *Architecture in the Parks, National Historic Landmark Theme Study,* U.S. Department of the Interior, National Park Service (1986), 429.

11. Ibid., 445.

12. Ibid., 446.

13. Ibid., 447.

14. Robert M. Utley, *Special Report on Hubbell Trading Post* (Santa Fe: National Park Service, 1959), 85.

15. Ibid., 81. This notable design collection is often described as what Hubbell used for the patterns from which customers could choose and weavers would work. However, Hubbell's daughter-in-law, Mrs. Roman J. Hubbell, attributes them to visiting artists who gave them to him as tokens of appreciation for his hospitality. She doesn't think he ever used them as examples for the weavers.

16. Robert H. Lister and Florence C. Lister, *Mesa Verde National Park: Preserving the Past* (Mancos, Colorado: ARA Mesa Verde, 1987). For a history of the Anasazi, see "The Anasazi: Riddles in the Ruins," *National Geographic Magazine* (November 1982), 554–92.

17. T. Stell Newman and Harold LaFleur, *Mesa Verde Historical and Administrative District: An Architectural and Historical Study* (Denver: National Park Service, 1974), 20.

18. Ibid.

19. Harrison, *Architecture in the Parks,* 219.

20. Hal Rothman, *Bandelier National Monument: An Administrative History* (Santa Fe: Southwest Cultural Resources Center, National Park Service, Professional Papers, no. 14, 1988). The debate over national park status, the size of the reserve, and description of participants present a colorful story as rich as the Grand Teton National Park controversy.

21. *39 Statute 1764, Presidential Proclamation Number 1322,* February 11, 1916.

22. Harrison, *Architecture in the Parks,* 367–71.

23. Laura Harrison and Randy Copeland, *Historic Structures Report, CCC Buildings, Bandelier National Monument* (Denver: National Park Service, 1984), 49–50.

24. Harrison, *Architecture in the Parks,* 412–13.

25. Ibid., 414.

26. Ibid., 419.

27. Steven M. Burke and Marlys Bush Thurber, *Historic Structure Report: Southwest Region Headquarters Building* (Santa Fe: National Park Service, 1985), 80.

Bibliography

A comprehensive bibliography on the National Park Service, including the sites and buildings described in this book, would be a complete work in itself. Writers, photographers, and painters have been describing and documenting park settings and features for a long time, and there is abundant material available. In this Bibliography, interpretive works are balanced by public documents related to a specific park or national monument. A travel journal, biography, or photograph collection may cover a small region or the entire West; National Park Service handbooks usually describe individual parks; and National Register of Historic Places nomination forms and Historic Structures Reports describe groups or individual buildings. The resources that were most valuable to the author are listed in the General section.

Government documents are primary sources for study of the National Park Service. These provide fascinating reading and depict the sometimes epochal struggles from which public protection of national parks and monuments emerged. Information on the establishment of the parks and national monuments can be found in House and Senate debate records, reports on bills, and committee hearings in the *Congressional Globe* and *Congressional Record. Statutes at Large* include the enabling park legislation. The historical and cultural resource studies prepared under the supervision of the NPS are informative and consistently reliable. Studies prepared by the U.S. Department of the Interior, National Park Service, are usually prepared in a hierarchical format: park history, cultural resources, and then individual structures. Essential references are Laura Soullière Harrison's *Architecture in the Parks, National Historic Landmark Theme Study* and two Department of the Interior publications, *Park and Recreation Structures* and *Park Structures and Facilities.*

The Reader's Guide and *Poole's Index* may be consulted for publications from the Conservation Foundation, Sierra Club, National Parks and Conservation Foundation, National Geographic Society, Wilderness Society, and Audubon Society.

Secondary sources range from seminal works on the appreciation of the natural setting to sweeping treatments of the settling of the West, as well as regularly updated travel guides and magazine and newspaper profiles of the parks. Standard reading on the intellectual idea and history of the parks are Nash's *Wilderness and the American Mind,* Tilden's *National Parks,* and Ise's *Our National Park Policy: A Critical History.* Ise's annotations for the parks and national monuments are

encyclopedic references for congressional debates, reports, and enabling legislation. Shankland's biography of Steven Mather and Horace Albright's reflections on his career in the NPS are excellent resources for NPS history. Roper's *FLO,* Zaitlin's *Gilbert Stanley Underwood,* and Grattan's *Mary Colter* are noteworthy biographies of eminently talented architects who designed many of the park buildings. Several great writers, photographers, and painters are represented in the Bibliography—artists who recorded their enchantment with the scenery and history of the national parks, sometimes decades before the parks were formally set aside "for the enjoyment and benefit of the people."

Readers can embark on their own journey through the West by sampling the work of Washington Irving, Francis Parkman, Wallace Stegner, Bernard DeVoto, and Thomas Wolfe, who have written about the West in fiction, essays, personal observations, and historical narrative. John Muir's writing and Ansel Adams' photographs portray ideas and images worthy of contemplative study. Willa Cather's *Death Comes to the Archbishop* and Thomas Horgan's *Distant Trumpet* are about people and places in the West, conveying a sense of the region's history and beauty. The portfolios of painters George Catlin, Thomas Moran, and Edward Bierstadt, and photographers Carleton E. Watkins, Timothy H. O'Sullivan, Eadweard J. Muybridge, and William Henry Jackson, are magnificent revelations of several regions discussed in this book.

People interested in acquiring information about specific locations will find that some parks have National Park Service libraries and archives accessible to the public. There are also sales outlets in the parks, managed by the NPS, concessioners, or museum associations, which often have materials worth browsing, whether for general interest or research purposes. The National Park Service is continually publishing attractive and authoritative material. Not to be overlooked are the commercially published travel guides, usually well researched, well written, and illustrated with fine photographs and maps. *The Sierra Club Guides to the National Parks,* KC Publication's *Story Behind the Scenery* series, and Sunset Publishing Corporation's *National Parks of the West* are all recommended. Finally, the handsome series of folders designed and published by the National Park Service, available from the always helpful rangers at park entrances, will start visitors on their way to discovering the architectural landmarks in the western landscape.

General

Adams, Ansel. *This is the American Earth.* San Francisco: Sierra Club, 1959.

Adams, Ansel. *Ansel Adams: An Autobiography.* Boston: Little Brown & Co., 1985.

Albright, Horace M. *The Birth of the National Park Service: The Founding Years, 1913–1933.* Salt Lake City: Howe Brothers, 1985.

Appleton, William Sumner. *The Colonial Homes of New England, Shall They Be Preserved?* New York: Society for the Preservation of New England Antiquities, 1913.

Aslet, Clive. *The Last Country Houses.* New Haven: Yale University Press, 1982.

Bartell, Edmund, Jun. *Hints for Picturesque Improvements in Ornamental Cottages.* London: J. Taylor, 1804.

Bosselman, Fred P. *In the Wake of the Tourist.* Washington: The Conservation Foundation, 1978.

Brower, David, ed. *Wilderness, America's Living Heritage.* San Francisco: Club, 1961.

Butcher, Devereux. *Exploring Our National Parks and Monuments,* 5th ed. Boston: Houghton Mifflin Company, 1960.

Cameron, Jenks. *The National Park Service, Its History, Activities, and Organization.* New York: D. Appleton and Company, 1922.

Cather, Willa. *Death Comes to the Archbishop.* New York: Alfred A. Knopf, 1927.

Connally, Eugenia Horstman, ed. *National Parks in Crisis.* Washington: National Parks & Conservation Association, 1982.

Conservation Foundation. *National Parks for a New Generation: Visions, Reality, Prospects.* Washington: Conservation Foundation, 1985.

Cozzens, Samuel Woodworth. *Explorations and Adventures in Arizona and New Mexico.* Secaucus, N.J.: Castle, 1988.

Current, Karen, and William R. Current. *Photography in the Old West.* New York: Harry N. Abrams, Inc., 1978.

Delahanty, Randolph, and E. Edward McKinney. *Preserving the West.* New York: Pantheon Books, 1985.

DeVoto, Bernard. *Across the Wide Missouri.* Boston: Houghton Mifflin Company, 1947.

DeVoto, Bernard. *The Course of Empire.* Boston: Houghton Mifflin Company, 1952.

Downing, Andrew Jackson. *The Architecture of Country Houses.* New York: D. Appleton and Co., 1850.

Downing, Andrew Jackson. *A Treatise on the Theory and Practice of Landscape Gardening.* New York: Orange Judd Agricultural Book Publisher, 1865.

Elsam, R. *Essay on Rural Architecture.* London: Bernard Quariteh, 1842.

Everhart, William C. *The National Park Service.* Boulder, Col.: Western Press, 1983.

Fitch, James Marston. *Historic Preservation.* New York: McGraw-Hill Book Company, 1982.

Fletcher, Bannister. *A History of Architecture.* 18th ed. New York: Scribner's and Sons, 1975.

Flexner, James Thomas. *That Wilder Image.* Vol. 3 in *History of American Painting.* New York: Dover Publications, Inc., 1970.

Foresta, Ronald A. *America's National Parks and Their Keepers.* Washington: Resources for the Future, Inc., 1984.

Fox, Stephen M. *John Muir and His Legacy: The American Conservation Movement.* Boston: Little Brown and Company, 1981.

Fremont, J. C. *Narrative of the Exploring Expedition to the Rocky Mountains.* New York (n.p.), 1846.

Fuller, Harlin M., and LeRoy R. Hafen. *The Journal of Captain John R. Bell.* Glendale, Calif.: Arthur H. Clark Co., 1973.

Futagawa, Yukio. *Wooden Houses.* New York: Harry N. Abrams, Inc., 1979.

Gebhard, David. *A Guide to Architecture in San Francisco and Northern California.* San Francisco: Peregrine Smith, Inc., 1973.

Girouard, Mark. *Cities and People.* New Haven: Yale University Press, 1985.

Grattan, Virginia L. *Mary Colter: Builder Upon the Red Earth.* Flagstaff, Ariz.: Northland Press, 1980.

Grosvenor, Gilbert H. "The Land of the Best." *National Geographic Magazine,* April 1916.

Harmon, David, ed. *Mirror of America: Literary Encounters with the National Parks.* Boulder, Col.: Roberts Rinehart, Inc., 1989.

Harris, Thaddeus. *The Journal of a Tour into the Territory of the Allegheny Mountains.* Boston (n.p.), 1805.

Harrison, Laura Soullière. *Architecture in the Parks, National Historic Landmark Theme Study.* Washington: U.S. Department of the Interior, National Park Service, 1986.

Hawthorne, Hildegarde, and Esther Burnell Mills. *Enos Mills of the Rockies.* New York: Houghton Mifflin Company, 1935.

Hendricks, Gordon. *Albert Bierstadt, Painter of the American West.* New York: Harry N. Abrams, 1974.

Hosmer, Charles B., Jr. *Presence of the Past.* New York: G. P. Putnam's Sons, 1965.

Hosmer, Charles B., Jr. *Preservation Comes of Age: From Williamsburg to the National Trust, 1926–1949* (2 vols.). Charlottesville: University of Virginia Press, 1981.

Huth, Hans. *Nature and the American: Three Centuries of Changing Attitudes.* Berkeley and Los Angeles: University of California Press, 1957.

Huth, Hans. "Yosemite, the Story of an Idea." *Sierra Club Bulletin 33,* March 1948. In the *New York Times,* August 8, 1964.

Ise, John. *Our National Park Policy: A Critical History.* Baltimore: The Johns Hopkins University Press, 1961.

James, Harlean. *Romance of the National Parks.* New York: Macmillan Company, 1938.

Kaiser, Harvey H. *Great Camps of the Adirondacks.* Boston: David R. Godine, Publisher, 1982.

Kennedy, Richard S., and Paschal Reeves, eds. *The Notebooks of Thomas Wolfe,* vols. I and II. Chapel Hill: The North Carolina University Press, 1970.

Lane Publishing Company. *National Parks of the West.* Menlo Park, Calif., 1981.

Langford, Nathaniel. *Diary of the Washburn Expedition to the*

Yellowstone and Firehole Rivers in the Year 1870. St. Paul: F. J. Haynes, 1905.

Longstreth, Richard W. *On the Edge of the World.* Cambridge: MIT Press. 1983.

Maier, Herbert. "The Purpose of the Museum in the National Parks," *Yosemite Nature Notes,* May 1926.

Makinson, Randall L. *Greene and Greene: Architecture as a Fine Art.* Salt Lake City: Peregrine Smith, Inc., 1977.

McMillon, Bill. *The Lodges and Hotels of our National Parks.* South Bend, Ind.: Icarus Press, 1983.

Muir, John. "The World Parks and Forest Reservations of the West." *Atlantic Monthly,* January 1898.

Muir, John. *Our National Parks.* Boston: Houghton Mifflin Company, 1901.

Muir, John. *The Writings of John Muir.* Sierra edition. 10 vols. Boston: Houghton Mifflin Company, 1916–24.

Murray, William H. *Adventures in the Wilderness; or, Camp Life in the Adirondacks.* Boston: Fields, Osgood, and Company, 1869.

Myers, Phyllis. "The National Park Service as a Client: I." *Architecture,* December 1984.

Naef, Weston. *Era of Exploration: The Rise of Landscape Photography in the American West, 1860–1885.* Boston: New York Graphic Society, 1975.

Nash, Roderick. *Wilderness and the American Mind.* 3rd. ed. New Haven: Yale University Press, 1982.

National Trust for Historic Preservation. *America's Forgotten Architecture.* New York: Pantheon Books, 1976.

Newcomb, Rexford. *Spanish Colonial Architecture in the United States.* New York: J. J. Augustin, 1937.

Newhall, Nancy. *Ansel Adams, The Eloquent Light.* Vol. 1. San Francisco: Sierra Club, 1963.

Olmsted, Frederick Law. "The Yosemite Valley and the Mariposa Big Trees: A Preliminary Report (1865)," with an introductory note by Laura Wood Roper. In: *Landscape Architecture,* October 1952.

Paige, John C. *The Civilian Conservation Corps and the National Park Service, 1933–1942.* Washington: U.S. Department of the Interior, National Park Service, 1985.

Pierson, George Wilson. *Tocqueville in America.* New York: Doubleday and Co., Anchor Books, 1959.

Pinchot, Gifford. *The Fight for Conservation.* New York: Doubleday, Page and Co., 1910.

Pinkett, Harold J. *Gifford Pinchot: Public and Private Forester.* Urbana: University of Illinois Press, 1970.

Powell, John Wesley. *The Exploration of the Colorado River and Its Canyons.* New York: Dover Publications, Inc., 1961.

Roper, Laura Wood. *FLO, A Biography of Frederick Law Olmsted.* Baltimore: The Johns Hopkins University Press, 1973.

Runte, Alfred. *National Parks: The American Experience.* Lincoln: University of Nebraska Press, 1979.

Scully, Vincent J. *The Shingle Style and Stick Style.* Rev. ed. New Haven: Yale University Press, 1955.

Shankland, Robert. *Steve Mather of the National Parks.* 3rd ed. New York: Alfred A. Knopf, 1976.

Sharps, Grant W., ed. *Interpreting the Environment.* New York: John Wiley and Sons, 1976.

Shepard, Augustus D. *Camps in the Woods.* New York: Architectural Book Publishing Company, 1931.

Shoemaker, Florence Johnson. "The Story of Estes–Rocky Mountain National Park Region," M.A. thesis, Colorado State College, Greeley, 1940.

Sierra Club Guides to the National Parks: Desert Southwest. New York: Stewart, Tabori & Chang, Inc., 1984.

Sierra Club Guides to the National Parks: Pacific Northwest and Alaska. New York: Stewart, Tabori & Chang, Inc., 1984.

Sierra Club Guides to the National Parks: Pacific Southwest. New York: Stewart, Tabori & Chang, Inc., 1984.

Sierra Club Guides to the National Parks: Rocky Mountains and the Great Plains. New York: Stewart, Tabori & Chang, Inc., 1984.

Stegner, Wallace. *Beyond the Hundredth Meridian.* Boston: Houghton Mifflin Company, 1954.

Stegner, Wallace. *One Way to Spell Man.* Garden City: Doubleday & Company, Inc., 1982.

Stegner, Wallace. *American Places.* New York: Greenwich House, 1983.

Stegner, Wallace. "The Best Idea We Ever Had." *Wilderness,* Spring 1983.

Stephenson, Susan H. *Rustic Furniture.* New York: Van Nostrand Reinhold, 1979.

Stillman, Andrea G., and William A. Turnage, eds. *Ansel Adams, Our National Parks.* Boston: Little, Brown and Company, 1992.

Strong, Douglas H., *The Conservationists.* Menlo Park, Calif.: Addison-Wesley Publishing Co., 1971.

Sturgis, Russell. *A Dictionary of Architecture and Building,* vol. 3. New York: The Macmillan Co., 1905.

Swain, Donald C. *Wilderness Defender, Horace M. Albright.* Chicago: University of Chicago Press, 1970.

Taylor, Bayard. *Colorado: A Summer Trip.* New York: G. P. Putnam and Son, 1867.

Teale, Edwin Way, ed. *The Wilderness World of John Muir.* Boston: Houghton Mifflin Company, 1954.

Throop, Elizabeth Gail. "Utterly Visionary and Chimerical: A Federal Response to the Depression." M.A. thesis, Portland State University, 1979.

Throop, Elizabeth Gail. *A Characteristic Expression.* Contract Abstracts and CRM Archeology. U.S. Department of Agriculture. Vol. 3, no. 2, 1983.

Tilden, Freeman. *The Fifth Essence.* Washington: National Park Trust Fund Board, n.d.

Tilden, Freeman. *The National Parks.* New York: Alfred A Knopf, 1951.

Tilden, Freeman. *Interpreting Our Heritage.* Chapel Hill: University of North Carolina Press, 1957.

Torrey, Bradford, and Francis H. Allen, eds. *The Journals of Henry David Thoreau* (14 vols.). Boston, 1906.

Truettner, William H., and Robin Bolton-Smith. *National Parks and the American Landscape.* Washington: Smithsonian Institution Press, 1972.

Tweed, William E., Laura Soullière, and Henry G. Law. "National Park Service Rustic Architecture: 1916–1942." National Park Service, Western Regional Office Division of Cultural Resource Management, 1977. Unpublished manuscript.

Udall, Stewart L. *The National Parks of America.* New York: G. P. Putnam's Sons, 1966.

U.S. Department of Agriculture, Forest Service Division. *Acceptable Plans Forest Service Administrative Buildings.* 1938.

U.S. Department of the Interior, National Park Service. *Annual Report, 1918.*

U.S. Department of the Interior, National Park Service. *Park Structures and Facilities.* 1935.

U.S. Department of the Interior, National Park Service. *Park and Recreation Structures.* 1938.

U.S. *Public Law 235,* 6th Congress.

Vaux, Calvert. *Villas and Cottages.* New York: Harper & Brothers, Publishers, 1863.

Warren, Nancy Hunter. *New Mexico Style.* Santa Fe: Museum of New Mexico Press, 1986.

Weinberg, Nathan. *Preservation in American Towns and Cities.* Boulder, Colorado: Westview Press, 1979.

Weislager, Clinton A. *The Log Cabin in America.* New Brunswick: Rutgers University Press, 1969.

Whiffen, Marcus. *American Architecture Since 1780.* Cambridge: The MIT Press, 1969.

Wicks, William S. *Log Cabins: How to Build and Furnish Them.* New York: Forest and Stream Publishing Company, 1889.

Winks, Robin. "Conservation in America: National Character as Revealed by Preservation." *The Future of the Past.* New York: Watson-Guptill Publications, 1976.

Winks, Robin. "Upon Reading Sellars and Runte." *Journal of Forest History,* July 1983.

Wirth, Conrad. *Parks, Politics, and the People.* Norman: University of Oklahoma, 1980.

Zaitlin, Joyce. *Gilbert Stanley Underwood: His Rustic, Art Deco, and Federal Architecture.* Malibu, Calif.: Pangloss Press, 1989.

THE FAR WEST

Olympic National Park

Throop, Elizabeth Gail. "Utterly Visionary and Chimerical: A Federal Response to the Depression." M.A. thesis, Portland State University, 1979.

Throop, Elizabeth Gail. *A Characteristic Expression.* Contract Abstracts and CRM Archeology. U.S. Department of Agriculture. Vol. 3, no. 2, 1983.

U.S. Department of the Interior, National Park Service. *Historic Resource Study, Olympic National Park.* 1983.

U.S. Department of the Interior, National Park Service. *Historic Structures Report, Rosemary Inn.* August 1986.

Mount Rainier National Park

Toothman, Stephanie. "Mount Rainier: The National Park as a Cultural Landscape." Unpublished manuscript.

U.S. Department of the Interior, National Park Service. *Historic Resource Study, Mount Rainier.* 1981.

U.S. Department of the Interior, National Park Service. *Historic Building Inventory, Mount Rainier National Park.* 1983.

U.S. Department of the Interior, National Park Service. *Pacific National Park.* 1983.

Fort Vancouver National Historic Site

DeVoto, Bernard. *The Year of Decision: 1846.* Boston: Houghton Mifflin Company, 1942.

DeVoto, Bernard. *Across the Wide Missouri.* Boston: Houghton Mifflin Company, 1947.

Hussey, John A. *The History of Fort Vancouver and its Physical Structure.* Tacoma: Washington State Historical Society, 1957.

Hussey, John A. *Fort Vancouver National Historic Site, Historic Structures Report, Historical Data* (2 vols.). Washington: U.S. Department of the Interior, National Park Service, 1972.

Irving, Washington. *Astoria.* New York: The Hovendon Company (n.d.).

Lavender, David. *Land of the Giants: The Drive to the Pacific Northwest 1750–1950.* Garden City, N.Y.: Doubleday, 1957.

Meinig, Donald W. *The Great Columbia Pass: A Historical Geography.* Seattle: University of Washington Press, 1968.

Parkman, Francis. *The Oregon Trail.* New York: Charles E. Merrill Company, 1910.

U.S. Department of the Interior, National Park Service. *Fort Vancouver National Park Handbook 113.* 1981.

Timberline Lodge

Griffin, Rachel. *A Guided Tour of Timberline Lodge.* Portland, Oregon: Friends of Timberline, 1979.

Griffin, Rachel, and Sarah Munro, eds. *Timberline Lodge.* Portland, Oregon: Friends of Timberline, 1978.

Stanley, Susan. "Rescue on Mount Hood." *Historic Preservation,* March/April 1987.

Weir, Jean Burwell. "Timberline Lodge: A WPA Experiment in Architecture and Crafts" (2 vols.). Ph.D. dissertation, University of Michigan, 1977.

Zaitlin, Joyce. *Gilbert Stanley Underwood.* Malibu, California: Pangloss Press, 1989.

Crater Lake National Park

Greene, Linda. *Historic Resource Study: Crater Lake National Park, Oregon.* Denver: National Park Service, Denver Service Center, 1984.

Harrison, Laura Soullière. *Architecture in the Parks, National Historic Landmark Theme Study.* U.S. Department of the Interior, National Park Service, 1986.

Schiltgren, Lora, ed. "Munson Valley, Crater National Park: A Manual for Preservation, Redevelopment, Adaptive Use and Interpretation." A Project of the Department of Architecture and Department of Landscape Architecture, University of Oregon, 1984.

U.S. Department of the Interior, National Park Service. *Historic Structures Report, Crater Lake Lodge* (n.d.).

U.S. Department of the Interior, National Park Service. *General Management Plan, Crater Lake National Park,* 1977.

U.S. Department of the Interior, National Park Service. *Cultural Resources Management Plan, Crater Lake National Park,* 1984.

U.S. Department of the Interior, National Park Service. *Environmental Assessment, General Development Plan, Crater Lake National Park,* 1984.

Yosemite National Park

Adams, Ansel. *Yosemite Valley.* San Francisco: Five Associates, 1959.

Adams, Ansel. *Yosemite and the Range of Light.* Boston: New York Graphic Society, 1979.

Adams, Virginia, and Ansel Adams. *Illustrated Guide to Yosemite.* San Francisco: Sierra Club, 1963.

Hall, Ansel. *Handbook of Yosemite National Park: A Compendium of Articles on the Yosemite Region by the Leading Scientific Authorities.* New York: G. P. Putnam's Sons, 1921.

O'Neill, Elizabeth Stone. *Meadow in the Sky.* Fresno, Calif.: Panorama West Books, 1983.

Roper, Laura Wood. "The Yosemite Valley and the Mariposa Big Trees," *Landscape Architecture,* October 1952.

Sargent, Shirley. *Wawona's Yesterdays.* Yosemite National Park: Yosemite Natural History Association, 1961.

Sargent, Shirley. *Yosemite and its Innkeepers.* Yosemite, Calif.: Flying Spur Press, 1975.

Sargent, Shirley. *Yosemite's Historic Wawona.* Yosemite, Calif.: Flying Spur Press, 1979.

Sargent, Shirley. *Yosemite's Rustic Outpost: Foresta Big Meadow.* Yosemite, Calif.: Flying Spur Press, 1983.

Sargent, Shirley. *Yosemite: The First 100 Years, 1890–1990.* Yosemite, Calif.: Yosemite Park & Curry Co., 1988.

U.S. Department of the Interior, National Park Service. *Historic Resource Study, Yosemite: The Park and Its Resources* (3 vols.). 1987.

U.S. Department of the Interior, National Park Service. Yosemite: *A Guide to Yosemite National Park.* Handbook 138, 1990.

Sequoia and King Canyon National Parks

Tweed, William C. *Sequoia–Kings Canyon: The Story Behind the Scenery.* KC Publications, 1980.

Tweed, William C. *Exploring Mountain Highways.* Sequoia Natural History Association, 1984.

U.S. Department of the Interior, National Park Service. *Development Concept Plan: Cedar Grove, Sequoia/Kings Canyon National Parks,* 1976.

U.S. Department of the Interior, National Park Service. *Development Concept Plan: Giant Forest/Lodgepole, Sequoia/Kings Canyon,* 1978.

U.S. Department of the Interior, National Park Service. *Master Plan, Sequoia & Kings Canyon National Parks, California,* 1981.

U.S. Department of the Interior, National Park Service. *Sequoia & Kings Canyon National Parks: Architectural Character Guidelines, Inventory of Significant Structures* (2 vols.). 1989.

THE ROCKY MOUNTAINS AND THE PLATEAU COUNTRY

Glacier National Park

Beaumont, Greg. *Many-Storied Mountains: The Life of Glacier National Park.* U.S. Department of the Interior, National Park Service, 1978.

Ise, John. *Our National Park Policy: A Critical History.* Baltimore: The Johns Hopkins University Press, 1961.

Sheehan, Patricia. "Glacier Park's Rocky Mountain High." *Lodging Hospitality.* October, 1985.

Sheire, James W. *Glacier National Park Historic Resource Study.* National Park Service, Eastern Service Center, September 1970.

U.S. Department of the Interior, National Park Service. *Historic Resources Study, Historic Structures Survey; Glacier National Park,* 1980.

Yellowstone National Park

Campbell, Regita. "Grand Hotels in National Parks." *Arts and Architecture* 1:53–54.

Haines, Aubrey L. *The Yellowstone Story* (2 vols.). Boulder: Colorado Associated University Press, 1977.

Hampton, H. Duane. *How the Cavalry Saved Our National Parks.* Bloomington: Indiana University Press, 1971.

Ise, John. *Our National Park Policy: A Critical History.* Baltimore: The Johns Hopkins University Press, 1961.

Scofield, Susan, and Jeremy Schmidt. *The Inn at Old Faithful.* Crowsnest Associates, 1979.

Shankland, Robert. *Steve Mather of the National Parks.* New York: Alfred A. Knopf, 1954.

Grand Teton National Park

Adams, Ansel, and Nancy Newhall. *The Tetons and the Yellowstone.* Redwood City, California: 5 Associates, 1970.

Albright, Horace M. *The Birth of the National Park Service: The Founding Years.* Salt Lake City: Howe Brothers, 1985.

Betts, Robert B. *Along the Ramparts of the Tetons: The Saga of Jackson Hole, Wyoming.* Boulder, Col.: Colorado Associated University Press, 1978.

DeVoto, Bernard. *Across the Wide Missouri.* Boston: Houghton Mifflin Company, 1947.

Hough, Donald. *The Cocktail Hour in Jackson Hole.* New York: W. W. Norton & Company, 1956.

Irving, Washington. *Astoria, or Anecdotes of an Enterprise Beyond the Rocky Mountains.* Philadelphia (n.p.), 1836.

Lane Publishing Company. *National Parks of the West.* Menlo Park, California: 1980.

Righter, Robert W. *Crucible for Conservation: The Creation of Grand Teton National Park.* Boulder: Colorado Associated University Press, 1982.

Sierra Club Guides to the National Parks: The Rocky Mountains and the Great Plains. New York: Stewart, Tabori, & Chang, 1984.

U.S. Department of the Interior, National Park Service. *Grand Teton: Handbook 122. A Guide to Grand Teton National Park.* 1984.

Rocky Mountain National Park

Atkins, D. Ferrel. *The Old Fall River Road.* Denver: Rocky Mountain Nature Association, 1982.

Buchholtz, C. W. *Rocky Mountain National Park: A History.* Boulder: Colorado Associated University Press, 1983.

Bryce Canyon National Park

Ise, John. *Our National Park Policy.* Baltimore, Md.: The Johns Hopkins University Press, 1961.

Scrattish, Nick. *Historic Resource Study, Bryce Canyon National Park.* Denver: National Park Service, Denver Service Center, 1980.

Scrattish, Nick. "The Modern Discovery, Popularization, and Early Development of Bryce Canyon, Utah." *Utah Historical Quarterly* 1(1981): 348.

Woodbury, Angus M. "A History of Southern Utah and its National Parks." *Utah Historical Quarterly* 12(1944): 111–223.

Pipe Spring National Monument

Lavender, David. *Pipe Spring and the Arizona Strip.* Springdale, Utah: Zion Natural History Association, 1984.

Powell, John Wesley. *The Exploration of the Colorado River and Its Canyons.* New York: Dover Publications, 1961.

U.S. Department of the Interior, National Park Service. *National Register of Historic Places – Nomination Form: Pipe Spring National Monument.* 1976.

Woodbury, Angus M. "A History of Southern Utah and its National Parks." *Utah Historical Quarterly* 12(1944), reprinted 1950.

THE SOUTHWEST

Grand Canyon National Park

Grattan, Virginia. *Mary Colter, Builder Upon the Red Earth.* Flagstaff: Northland Press, 1980.

Tumacacori National Monument

Southwest Parks and Monuments Association. *Tumacacori* (n.d.).

Petrified Forest National Park

Harrison, Laura Soullière. *Architecture in the Parks, National Historic Landmark Theme Study.* U.S. Department of the Interior, National Park Service, 1986.

Petrified Forest Museum Association. *The Historic Painted Desert Inn* (n.d.).

Skidmore, Lorimer. "Report to the Chief of Planning on Construction of the Painted Desert Inn." Transmitted by Milton J. McColm, Acting Regional Director Region III. Santa Fe, New Mexico, January 4, 1939.

Hubbell Trading Post National Historic Site

Southwest Parks and Monument Association. *Hubbell Trading Post* (n.d.).

U.S. Department of the Interior, National Park Service. *Historic Structures Report, Hubbell Trading Post,* 1970.

Utley, Robert M. *Special Report on Hubbell Trading Post.* The National Survey of Historic Sites and Buildings. Santa Fe: U.S. Department of the Interior, National Park Service, 1959.

Mesa Verde National Park

Lister, Robert H., and Florence C. Lister. *Mesa Verde National Park: Preserving the Past.* Mancos, Col.: ARA Mesa Verde, Inc., 1987.

Newman, T. Stell, and Harold LaFleur. *Mesa Verde Historical and Administrative District: An Architectural and Historical Study.* Denver: National Park Service, 1974.

U.S. Department of the Interior, National Park Service. *Mesa Verde National Park,* 1956.

Bandelier National Monument

Bunting, Bainbridge. *Early Architecture in New Mexico.* Albuquerque: University of New Mexico Press, 1976.

Harrison, Laura, and Randy Copeland. *Historic Structures Report, CCC Buildings, Bandelier National Monument.* Denver: U.S. Department of the Interior, National Park Service, 1984.

Rothman, Hal. *Bandelier National Monument: An Administrative History.* Santa Fe, N.M.: U.S. Department of the Interior, National Park Service, Southwest Cultural Resources Center, Professional Papers No. 14, 1988.

Southwest Region Headquarters Building

Burke, Steven M., and Marlys Bush Thurber. *Historic Structures Report: Southwest Region Headquarters Building.* Santa Fe: U.S. Department of the Interior, National Park Service, 1985.

Index

Picture Credits
All photographs and illustrations are by the author or from the author's collection except those noted below, which are used by permission (page numbers indicated).

National Park Service: 1, 2, 3, 4, 5, 7, 10, 12, 16, 20, 21, 22, 30, 31, 33 below, 35 upper right, 36, 37 below, 38 above, 41 upper right, 44 above, 45 above, 48 center, 51 below, 53, 57, 60 lower right, 61 right, 65 right, 78 center and below, 83, 84, 87, 88, 93, 96, 104, 111 lower center, 113 upper left and lower left, 118 center, 121 upper right, 123 center, 134 left, 136, 138 upper left, 141 above, 153 above, 163 below, 164 above, 166 below, 172, 174 below, 177 below, 184, 195 right, 200 lower right, 206 below, 209 below, 214, 215, 222 center, 224 lower right, 230, 231 upper left and below, 233 upper left, 245 below, 248 above, 260 lower left and right, 272 below, 273 upper center, 275 below, 276 upper left, 280, and 282 below.

Laura Soullière Harrison: 48 below, 49 center left and right, and below, 52 lower left, 89, 100 center left, 105 below, 124, 125 upper left and upper right, 150 upper left, 217 left and center, 244 left and lower right, 253 left, and 277 above.

Yale Collection of Western Americana, Beinecke Rare Book and Manuscript Library, Yale University: 55.

Joyce Zaitlin, Gilbert Stanley Underwood: His Rustic, Art Deco, and Federal Architecture (Malibu, California: Pangloss Press, 1989): 99 plan.

Dial Corporation: 128.

Jeanne Falk Adams: 135 below.

Nebraska State Historical Society, Union Pacific Railroad Collection: 180.

Union Pacific Railroad Company: 186, and 196 above.

National Museum of American Art, Smithsonian Institution. Lent by the Department of the Interior, Office of the Secretary: 214.